SEX PISTOLS

SEX PISTOLS

POiSON in the MAChinE

John Scanlan

rEaktion BoOks

Published by REAKTION BOOKS Ltd
Unit 32, Waterside
44–48 Wharf Road
London N1 7UX, UK
www.reaktionbooks.co.uk

First published 2016
Copyright © JOHN SCANLAN 2016

Printed and bound in Great Britain
by TJ International, Padstow, Cornwall

A catalogue record for this book is available from the
British Library

ISBN 978 1 78023 754 1

CONTENTS

What counts is to jump
out of the twentieth
century as fast as you
possibly can in order
to create an environment
that you can truthfully
run wild in.

Malcolm McLaren,
Sex Pistols handbill,
December 1977

INTRODUCTION: Tales from the Near Future

Julien Temple, the earliest chronicler of the Sex Pistols, has described the first time he encountered them as being akin to witnessing an alien visitation: four figures, silhouetted against the light, making a racket of noise inside a darkened warehouse that was located amid the ruins of London's Docklands – a site, in fact, that had been deemed 'irrelevant and redundant' just a few years earlier.[1] Johnny Rotten, the singer of this group, with his unusual spiky hair – which might have been dyed green, perhaps orange – was clad in a fuzzy, striped mohair sweater and a pair of trousers that disobeyed the current fashion for denim flares that skirted the floor. He contorted himself into unnatural shapes. And with a pair of thick rubber-soled brothel creeper shoes seemingly sucking him to the ground, his arms held on to a microphone stand as his limbs moved, marionette-like. This was August 1975, and Rotten looked like he belonged on another planet.

It had been just a few weeks since the Sex Pistols had started to rehearse with Rotten, their newest member. As Temple watched, he might have had little sense that he was standing just a mile or so from the prime meridian at Greenwich, a spot that had, since the nineteenth century, assumed something like the status of the centre of the world. If it wasn't that exactly, it was at least the precise point at which the globe was definitively split into east and west: the earth's eastern hemisphere lying to one side of the line, its western hemisphere to the other. But there, at that moment, the sense of place – London, England – was recon-figured inside the peculiarities of that time: the 1970s, an era

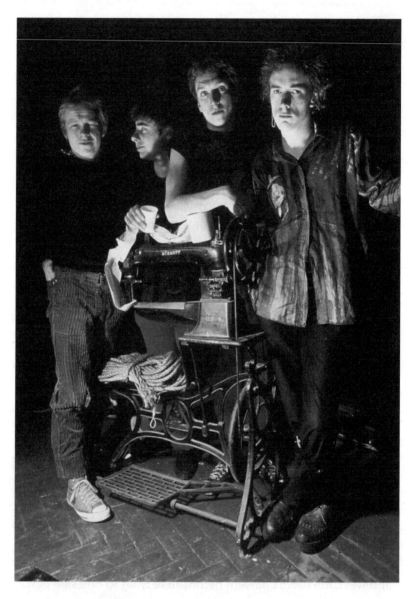

Paul Cook, Glen Matlock, Steve Jones and Johnny Rotten at
the Paradiso, Amsterdam, January 1977.

marked by an economic decline and existential unease, when the end of empire was symbolized by the wasteland that had replaced the once thriving docks. There was the past, and there was a future, the shape of which could never quite be known. But the near future, a quickening of the present, was always at hand, if only you could sense it, or catch a glimpse of it. This is where the Sex Pistols would exist for something like the next two years – until early January 1978 – always running ahead of, and out of, time.

Malcolm McLaren, who might be described as the originator or instigator of the Sex Pistols as an idea or event (it is misleading to describe him simply as 'their manager'), once renamed the shop that he owned Too Fast to Live, Too Young to Die. It was a slogan that was in part inspired by the legend of James Dean, who crashed to a premature death racing in a sports car, but perhaps also by the devil-may-care attitude of motorcycle rock 'n' roll enthusiasts, who wore it as an emblem on their black leather jackets as they hurtled at great speeds across the nearby Chelsea Bridge, where since the 1950s they had staged deadly illegal contests. It also signified something that the Sex Pistols embodied, and that McLaren had always wanted them to embody: all of the demented radicalism of youth as it leaped into a kind of nihilistic self-destruction. That is what history seems to suggest the Sex Pistols were always about. They were too fast to live. They were almost designed to fail, and their actions met with predictable consequences. But their recklessness accounts for why historians of twentieth-century popular culture say there is *before the Sex Pistols*, and there is *after the Sex Pistols*: they stepped out of their surroundings and signalled the future. However familiar the format of their music appears to us today, it said something greater than popular music typically does, something that was not just about them, and it did so in such a way that it marked not only a decisive break in the culture and history of popular music, but in twentieth-century Britain.

*

In many ways, the story of the Sex Pistols reveals that in the 1970s Britain seemed to be caught in some kind of temporal disorder – it seemed to be going backwards and forwards at the same time. The very perception of the future, as J. G. Ballard once remarked, seemed to have defined the twentieth century like no other before it:

> Every year planes were doubling their speed, and then after the war we had antibiotics, computers, motorways were being laid down. People were constantly predicting what the future was going to be like in ten or fifteen years, and all those vast futurama exhibitions were sources of enormous pride.[2]

However, after two or three decades of sustained acceleration into this near future after the interruption of the Second World War, the London of the early-to-mid-1970s, if viewed askance, could easily seem to belong to a world that was entering a phase of marked and perhaps irreversible decline. In 1974, as the British government pressed ahead with the development of the super-futuristic Concorde – designed for 'supersonic' passenger travel – the public had meanwhile grown used to gathering around candles for half the week as power outages brought the country to a near standstill. And not long after the country had emerged from the twilight of the three-day week, a consequence of those power shortages of 1974, it nevertheless often presented a shabby, grey exterior, bearing the traces of a heavy industrial past in the soot-covered facades of its great landmarks.

Present-day London tourist locations such as Covent Garden had been all but abandoned, and elsewhere pockets of the city still looked as if the Blitz had been a recent occurrence. For many in those days of relative media scarcity, leisurely hours were quite often confined to the kind of dilapidated street-corner pubs that could be found up and down the country, and which seemed to be closed more often than they were open. By the summer of 1976, when the Sex Pistols suddenly burst into public consciousness as the apparent leaders of some new phenomenon called punk rock, it was apt that it was during the 'equatorial' conditions of July and August, when the country seemed to be 'boiling up, partly with crisis, partly with rage', as Martin Amis wrote. 'Everything seemed ready for the terminal lurch.'[3]

If it is true to say that by 1976 Britain was practically bankrupt, it is equally true to say that economic woes alone do not account for the sense of boredom and anomie that seemed to propel into existence a band – and, in punk, a phenomenon unlike anything before or since – that came to be viewed in almost apocalyptic terms. The labelling of punk as 'dole queue' rock may have had some relevance as it related to the rash of new groups that sprung up after the Sex Pistols, and insofar as it referred to the fans all over the country and beyond who embraced those bands. But the Sex Pistols' origins lie elsewhere. As Jon Savage – author of *England's Dreaming: Sex Pistols and Punk Rock*, the definitive witness account of the entire phenomenon – has said, to see punk in terms of dole queues, or simply in terms of 'social realism and rock music', is a mistake: 'It was for a brief period very futuristic.'[4] As Malcolm McLaren put it, the point was to step out of the twentieth century and into the future.

*

The story of the Sex Pistols, or some version of it, has been told and retold so many times that whatever it was they expressed or represented has been obscured by the way we now look at, and engage with, the past. While the passage of time has, on the one hand, made the 1970s seem like an often strange and unusual period of recent history – like a distant 'other world' we have travelled far from – we also live, on the other hand, in an era of present pasts, which are the product of 'cultural memory'. Cultural memory, in a sense, changes how we understand the relationship between the past and the present, precisely because it aims to bring the past into the here and now. And it is through the apparatus of cultural memory – the panoply of media artefacts, material objects and memoirs that feed into various forms of reanimation (film documentaries, commemorative events, exhibitions and so on) – that the Sex Pistols seem close to us. Yet for those who lived through the events that marked the rise and fall of the Sex Pistols, there was no all-embracing perspective that could sum up what was happening, what the Sex Pistols were about or where they were heading. In their time the Sex Pistols scandalized the population of a country that had, most remarkably of all, probably never even seen or heard them, except through the outraged shock headlines of the tabloid press. Today, however, they are everywhere. Anyone can now see them, listen to them, read about them and follow their fates in the afterlife of their seminal moment.

While the media-saturated world we now live within seems, on the one hand, to bring the lives and times of those who created this phenomenon into view – the Internet, for instance, is awash with sounds, images and film footage of the Pistols, unseen and unheard at the time – and allows us to see them now, in some ways, more in context than ever before, it nonetheless also dampens the power of the Sex Pistols as an *event* unlike any other, and helps to obscure and neutralize what was an explosive cultural moment. Their headline-grabbing appearance in December 1976 on the *Today* programme – the so-called 'Grundy' show – during which Steve Jones, the Sex Pistols' guitarist, fell into one of the most memorable bouts of swearing ever seen on television – genuinely shocked a nation, and turned a run-of-the-mill TV promo into something whose cultural consequences are hard to comprehend today. In the words of someone who was there in the television studio, seeing it replayed over and over on television throughout the years has turned it into something 'like the moon landing or Kennedy being shot, not something you actually participated in'.[5]

The fact that the footage of the event exists on the Internet to be replayed at will today is a matter of chance. Julien Temple, engaged by Malcolm McLaren in 1976 to document the Pistols, managed to track down one of the then rare people who possessed the equipment to record television broadcasts. He then re-filmed the clip from a TV set playing the videotape of the show, and now it is an ever-present, free-floating fragment of a vast and seemingly infinite digital cultural archive. Out of its time and its place, however, the event is something different.

Today it might look quaint or tame, leaving us wondering what all the fuss was about. If it does, it is because it has so successfully come to exist outside of the context of 1970s Britain. What's probably even stranger to us today is that at the time most of the country never actually saw the show in the first place – Thames Television was only broadcast in Greater London and some other parts of the south of England. The news of the Pistols' exploits spread, like rumour of some alien invasion, through shock headlines, not replays of the television footage. By the beginning of 1977 the band was already taking on mythical proportions, a situation that continued to develop as it became

13

more difficult to hear and see them due to the combination of media blacklisting and performance bans that, in the end, led to only greater infamy. Like every good myth, by the time it reached those most distant from the actual events, the story had become something much larger than it originally was.

As a musical phenomenon, the Sex Pistols were remarkably short-lived. Throughout an existence that lasted little more than two years, the media perception of the band was shaped by the way that Malcolm McLaren – for a while – seemed able to deploy the notoriously scandal-hungry tabloid press like so many pieces in a game he actually had no control over, but was making up as he went along. From there, the Pistols faced repeated attempts by the forces of respectability to cast them back into a demi-monde of freaks, villains, rubber fetishists, junkies and prostitutes that the public believed they must have sprung from. It was a perception that was not entirely without foundation. The band's origins, after all, were in Malcolm McLaren and Vivienne Westwood's King's Road boutique, SEX – which was more an expression of a political-aesthetic idea than it was simply a shop – for which they were initially intended to be a vehicle. The Pistols' early followers were, in the words of one of them, 'the most bizarre carnival of subterranean people.'[6]

It is perhaps remarkable that the Sex Pistols managed to produce any records at all. In fact, their one and only official album released during their existence, *Never Mind the Bollocks, Here's the Sex Pistols*, emerged after more than a year of false starts, towards the end of 1977, and after a host of other bands whom they had inspired had released their own records. Following their sacking from two major record companies and the withdrawal and non-appearance of records due to factory workers refusing to handle Sex Pistols product in late 1976 and early 1977, not much had emerged to reach beyond the eyes and ears of the few who had actually witnessed the Pistols in person, although they had by then recorded more than a full album's worth of material. But what had been released in dribs and drabs was enough to cause the authors of 1978's *Illustrated 'New Musical Express' Encyclopaedia of Rock* – a book that went to press before the Pistols' album was released – to declare that their first three singles ('Anarchy in the UK', 'God Save the Queen' and 'Pretty Vacant') were 'arguably the most powerful sequence of debut releases rock has ever seen'. By the time that book was in the hands of most readers, however, the Pistols were no more. This gap between the reality and its representation – so at odds with the world we live in today, where the gap is non-existent – also added to the perception that the Sex Pistols had, by 1977, already entered the realms of myth. In fact, by the end of 1977 the punk phenomenon beyond the Pistols had arguably lapsed into self-parody as musicians and record companies, sensing their opportunity, joined the bandwagon. The Pistols themselves had also begun to come apart during the summer of 1977, and Rotten – having by then reverted to his real name, John Lydon – would extract himself from what had become an unbearable situation in January 1978, as the media frenzy surrounding the Sex Pistols' tour of America became uncontrollable.

This is a book about something more than a bunch of people who once made some music that we still listen to today. It is about the times, the ideas, the coincidences and the characters that led up to and played a part in a year of self-destruction that began in December 1976, and ended early in January 1978 when the Sex Pistols – beaten, bloody and overdosed – ceased to exist.

Grosvenor Square, 1968.

1 I Will Be So Bad

It was October 1964. Malcolm McLaren, then a few months shy of his nineteenth birthday and going by the name of Malcolm Edwards, found himself looking on in surprise as The Rolling Stones, laughing and puffing away on cigarettes, appeared in front of him. He was perched on Chelsea Bridge with an etching pad, looking over at Battersea Power Station, its four iconic chimneys pumping white smoke, and outlining its imposing presence on the south bank of the Thames.

He knew who The Rolling Stones were, of course; but it was only here, seeing them out on the street, in the daylight, that he was struck by the way they looked and how unlike pop stars they actually were. The way they were dressed they could have been Beat writers, or young French existentialist poets and philosophers. Bill Wyman, the least star-like of the group, was dressed in a knee-length black leather mac and standing in front of a wooden hut, plonked on the Battersea side of the bridge, that sold tea and hot dogs. He spoke to Charlie Watts as Keith Richards and Brian Jones ordered cups of tea. Mick Jagger was prancing around, posing for some photographers. Together, with their long hair and slightly unkempt appearance, they looked bad – they looked mean, dirty and possibly dangerous. It was an interesting look. But all that – pop music – was something that belonged in the past. McLaren had once had time for The Rolling Stones, and others, like The Pretty Things, but in the year or so since he had first started taking art classes at Saint Martin's School of Art, he had more or less lost interest in it all. When The Beatles and the rest of the upbeat pop music that swept through the 1960s had taken over, something had been lost. The action was to be found elsewhere – possibly in art, and living the life of an artist. Why bother being some kind of spectator of popular culture, he thought, when as an artist you could reshape the future through your own actions.

*

The 1960s were a time of upheaval in Britain's art schools and colleges, shaped both by events in the world outside and by the structures and relationships that then existed within the institutions, and which seemed to act as obstacles to the kind of freedom that young artists wanted. By 1966 Malcolm Edwards had made the first of many attempts to instigate events and situations that might ruffle the feathers of the authority figures he so despised. In July that year he appeared in the headlines of a national newspaper for the first time, when *The Times* reported that he and a friend named Henry Adler had been found guilty at Marlborough Street Magistrates Court in London of 'insulting behaviour contrary to the Public Order Act'. Adler, a few years older and more woven into the life of the counterculture, would be the 'conduit' that linked the then Malcolm Edwards to radical politics, and to King Mob, a London Situationist group that he was later loosely associated with. The twenty-year-old Edwards – described by *The Times* as 'a sculptor' – was caught with 23-year-old Adler trying to set light to the Stars and Stripes outside the US Embassy, in a 'symbolic act against American policy in Vietnam'. They were both fined and bound over to keep the peace for twelve months, as the magistrate explained, to ensure that there would be no more such incidents.[1]

There would be no more headline-grabbing incidents in those twelve months, although the one-time sculptor later wrote that in 1968 – the year when a revolutionary fervour gripped students across Europe – he could be found scrambling through the South African embassy as all around him Molotov cocktails flew into the air. And he remembered spilling bags of marbles on the ground at a charge from the oncoming mounted police at Grosvenor Square, scene of the most famous confrontations with the police in 1968:

> Suddenly it looked like these horses were on an ice skating rink, and then, like Agincourt, we ducked down and people behind us had catapults and started firing gobstopper marbles at the windows of the American embassy.[2]

Since 1966 Edwards had lived with Vivienne Westwood, sister of his best friend Gordon Swire. Gordon was connected to the capital's music scene, and had been booking bands on the burgeoning London rhythm and blues (R&B) scene in the early days of The Rolling Stones, when Malcolm would sometimes follow him around the circuit, often with more interest in the beer than the music – unless The Pretty Things or The Rolling Stones were playing. He was impressed that the Stones would get on-stage wearing dirty collars and cuffs, and – like many others at the time – loved the whiff of danger that these small details communicated.

Westwood had been around then, too, working with her brother Gordon, handing out tickets and checking coats and bags into the cloakrooms at the gigs he organized. By 1966 she had already been married. She was a few years older than Malcolm Edwards, who fascinated her, but who also seemed strangely resistant to her attempts to woo him – there was always something occupying his mind that he didn't want to be distracted from. At that time she was working as a primary school teacher, and she would come to realize that she saw the world through different eyes than the impish would-be artist. Malcolm, she later said, always hated the kind of authority figures who were representative of the adult world, including teachers. He always wanted to hold on to something of that adolescent outlook, to have a disregard for the rules, to be the leader of a gang.[3] He understood it as a way to get on the outside of things, and that is where he wanted to be.

At the age of five, he was thrown out of school for tearing up all of the classroom exercise books, and then educated at home by his grandmother until he was nine years old, when he reluctantly returned to school. 'I was never on time,' he admitted, 'and I always kicked everyone when I played soccer.'[4] At the age of nine, he formed his first gang – a 'box gang', as he called it:

> It was a gang that hid inside a box outside of the school, making sure they could not be seen ... I liked that. I adored people calling me bad because it felt good. I think it felt important because when things were good, I seemed to feel terrible.[5]

Years later, during the peak of the Sex Pistols' notoriety, not much had changed. Steve Jones, the Pistols' guitarist, remembered that McLaren wasn't happy until everybody absolutely hated what they were doing. Once, during a lull in the hostilities that had been directed towards the Sex Pistols with a ferocity that was unmatched, he thought it would be a good idea if Westwood went down to Madame Tussauds and set alight the wax statues of The Beatles that were on display; he reasoned that she would be less conspicuous than him, and it would cause a great outrage, so beloved were The Beatles.[6] So in school when the teacher rumbled his box gang, it was a defining moment; as Westwood wrote later, 'he never hated anyone more in his life than that teacher.'[7]

Malcolm Edwards's tendency to upend whatever the accepted order had prescribed can be traced back to his enforced attendance at school, but it was all grist for the mill; it just inspired him to mutilate the emblem of the school's authority that he had to wear every day on the pocket of his blazer:

> I would go to great effort, picking the badge off the blazer and sewing it back on upside down in perfect position. I spent an entire evening doing that, in front of my grandmother, who would only praise me for sewing so brilliantly![8]

Unlike Westwood, he could never have donned the cloak of respectability that being a teacher entailed. He had no interest in the kind of discipline and order that such a calling demanded, and that was then to be instilled in the young; but he could *show*, he could *reveal*, and he could get people to see things differently. Once, he took over Westwood's class of eight- and nine-year-olds, and talked to them about how the random debris that they might find lying around on the streets or on the patches of wasteland that had been left behind where bombs had fallen during the Blitz – a broken toy, a bird's feather, a tin can – could be the most fascinating materials for an artist. You could show these young kids a photograph of a Robert Rauschenberg junk sculpture, he thought, and they would think it was the greatest thing they had ever seen. What the child and the artist seemed to share was a fascination with the unformed and the deformed, with making and breaking and doing it over and over and over again. It was a way of seeking out the space where the imagination could be allowed to play out for hours, even days, in its slightly altered reality.

For those who had left childhood behind, yet had been captured by the romantic lure of the imagination – artists or writers for instance – and who felt, like Malcolm Edwards, increasingly marooned and out-of-time, the point was not to give in to the world, but to work in ways that would alter whatever unsatisfactory state of affairs had temporarily gripped the circumstances in which one had to live. As a student of art history, Edwards knew that the present had always extended backwards as well as forwards, and that artistic culture preserved 'the memory of things past', which meant that to be steeped in this culture would be to find the means of identifying the future's promise.[9] In so much of the rush towards the future following the Second World War, however, huge swathes of the past had been declared obsolete, and 1960s modernism – under the sway of what Britain's then prime minister Harold Wilson termed 'the white heat of technology' – sought to find new corners of social life that might be remade. But Edwards knew that the past that had been cast aside in this process was not just a storehouse of dead matter or discarded looks or styles; it retained, in the right hands, an abundance of potential for change.

Becoming an artist was an obvious choice for an upsetter of expectations, and the country's art schools were still accepting of activities that allowed their students a great deal of freedom. Edwards spent eight years, from 1963 to 1971, hopping from one art school to another on the back of the easily obtainable grants that London's numerous local authorities disbursed for the students attending colleges in their area – thus making it a possibility for one to move around and collect cheques with each new enrolment. During this time he became 'an art school dandy and aesthete' with an eye to becoming a great artist.[10] But the restlessness that saw him shifting between schools was matched by an inability to settle on a particular medium and work on it to the point where he might define an artistic vision. He pursued his objectives in painting and drawing, environmental and installation art and, eventually, film.[11]

His first work to be exhibited was a combination of installation and environmental art, which took place at the Artists' Own Gallery, located at 26 Kingly Street, just off Regent Street in London's West End. The gallery had opened in late 1964, offering 'painters and sculptors of standing and promise' a new outlet for their work.[12] It was a large, generous space that occupied a couple of floors and had a pool on the lower floor. For this show, mounted in 1965, the space was transformed into a maze designed to ensure that visitors got lost; it was filled with corrugated white cardboard, as his friend Fred Vermorel recalled:

> Malcolm had now decided he was an 'environmental artist', and persuaded this gallery owner to turn his premises over for transformation into an 'environment'... a kind of obstacle course made from rolls of corrugated cardboard, empty shoe boxes and other debris. You had to crawl through tunnels and negotiate false floors.[13]

As visitors clambered around, they caught occasional glimpses on the walls of the gallery of flickering outtakes from an old Audie Murphy western that Edwards had edited together from scraps found in the bin outside a nearby cinema he frequented. Everything was going well, Vermorel recalled, until two policemen turned up and started muttering about the display being a danger to the health and safety of visitors:

> Just then a drunken soldier, one of a group of squaddies, crashed through a false floor on to some people below. There

was cursing and pandemonium. The show was closed and everyone went home.[14]

It was like the box gang being rumbled all over again.

As far as his experiments with painting and drawing went, Edwards came to specialize in pieces that were heavily dominated by black – and with his desire to upend prevailing norms wherever he saw them, he found in black something strangely and unusually beautiful. His teachers instructed him that black was a colour that should be allowed to sink into the background, but for him it was the opposite: it was white that receded into the background, allowing black to give definite form to bold shapes and contours, or else it would form the basis of portrait drawings, which contained 'so much graphite that they just ended up big, lumpen, granite blocks'.[15]

The fact that he had become obsessed with black undoubtedly reflected something else. Unlike blue or red the associations that black has accumulated in Western cultural history are extensive and exceptionally powerful: black has been associated with negativity, evil, anarchy and a host of other traits that would be easy enough to pin on the future Malcolm McLaren through what has been said of his activities and his association with the Sex Pistols. By the time Malcolm had started painting his own black canvases, however, this turn towards black in painting was not new. For some time black had been accepted among artists as a colour that was available in the modern painter's palette, and was used in ways that had not been as obvious in the past. Some artists, indeed, had begun to use black exclusively, producing canvases that were entirely composed of and often sculpted from thick layers of paint, effectively producing surfaces rather than pictures.[16] McLaren began to see painting as

Malcolm Edwards (McLaren) with one of his black paintings, Croydon Art College, 1968.

a dead end. But, in the *idea* of black – in whatever black stood for – he recognized something that could be deployed for other purposes.

In the clothes he and Vivienne Westwood would make and sell during the early to mid-1970s, black would be ubiquitous – from the black T-shirts of their Let It Rock shop (1971–3), such as the famous 'Vive Le Rock' T-shirt, which he and Westwood produced at a time when virtually no one else was making or selling black T-shirts, to the black leather and rubber wear that was a feature of their boutique in a later guise, as SEX (1974–6). Indeed, the front half interior of Let It Rock was all black.[17] 'Black expressed the denunciation of the frill,' McLaren wrote thirty years later: 'Nihilism. Boredom. Emptiness.'[18] The colour of 'anarchy' – that watchword of the punk 1970s – was, after all, black. Even the interior of the Clapham flat that he and Westwood shared was almost entirely painted black.[19]

After attending a number of colleges and art schools across the capital – Saint Martin's School of Art (1963), South East Essex College of Art (1964), Chiswick Polytechnic (1966) and Croydon College of Art (1968) – Edwards spent his last three years at Goldsmiths College of Art (1968–71). In his last days there he was already becoming bored with trying to be an artist by conventional means. In 1969 he orchestrated an event to resemble those that would follow in the mid- to late 1970s, when a five-day 'Art Freak Out' that he was organizing at Goldsmiths was trailed in the pages of the *International Times*, London's main underground newspaper. The invitation to the event promised that everything was free (apart from the beer), including the entertainment of a 'galaxy of musicians' – elsewhere said to include The Pretty Things and King Crimson – as well as appearances by poets, film screenings and much else. The five-day 'happening' was to end with a discussion to which the names of a host of contemporary luminaries – among them, William S. Burroughs, Jim Dine, R. D. Laing and Alexander Trocchi – had been tagged on, giving the impression that they were all signed up for the event.[20] The plan was for everything to take place in an amphitheatre located behind the Goldsmiths art building that could accommodate 2,000 people, but word got out that everything was free and on the first day, recalled a fellow student, 'there must have been something like 20,000 people' wandering around.[21] Trouble started brewing when random and unknown bands began appearing in place of the advertised top groups of the day. Malcolm disappeared. The leader of the students' union, who was placed in the firing line by college bosses, was only one of many

The announcement for the Goldsmiths Arts Festival, 1969.

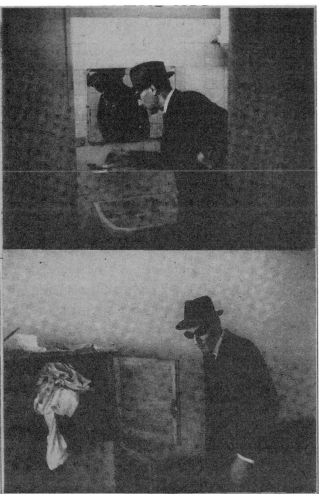

Two previously unreleased pictures of Inspector J Lee of the Nova Police, recently arrived to 'sort out this planet'.

GOLDSMITH'S 5—DAY ARTS FREAK PLAN

Goldsmith College's Arts Festival will run from 30 June to 4 July. Everything's free (including barbecue) except for beer. Apart from an incredible galaxy of musicians (see Music Supplement for details) there'll be all kinds of films from War Game to Magical Mystery Tour, including films of the Columbia Revolt, Chicago Convention, Black Panthers, and Paris May 68. Many poets, Bruce Lacey, Action Theatre, Turquoise Pantomime, Bread & Puppet Theatre, Burroughs & Trocchi films, ending with a discussion on Friday night to pick up the debris, to which are invited: R.D. Laing, Wm Burroughs, Alex Trocchi, Michael X, Jim Dine, Simon Vinkenoog and others. A mammoth event. Ring Niall Martin or Malcolm Edwards at 692-2082 for details and check our What's Happening columns.

who 'wanted Malcolm's head on a plate', although 'others wanted him to be glorified as a saint for bringing life to Goldsmiths.'[22]

In 1969 during his time at Goldsmiths Edwards also began working on a film about the history of Oxford Street for his degree show, and with the help of a number of friends who would later become involved in activities around the Sex Pistols – Jamie Reid, Fred Vermorel and Helen Wallington-Lloyd – much filming was done with the aim of exploring the street in its contemporary guise, which is to say, as symbolic of the kind of consumer culture that had managed to eradicate the street both as a place where it was possible to relax in bars or cafés and watch the world go by, and as the site of a forgotten bloody history.[23] In the film, this history was to be traced back to the Gordon Riots of the eighteenth century, and presented anew as a means to 'induce a violent uprising'. The film was also to include a segment that 'considered fan worship as a facet of spectacle,' which was centred around 'an interview with the head of the Billy Fury fan club'.[24]

The latter encounter with the lingering presence of '50s rock would, in time, offer a pointer to the direction that Edwards would take in late 1971 (and the Gordon Riots would feature as a prelude in his fable of the Sex Pistols, as told in *The Great Rock 'n' roll Swindle*). But, whatever footage was actually shot, there was never any finished film. Instead, Edwards submitted something else to meet the college degree requirements, haphazardly composed of discarded film found in a college dustbin, and supposedly featuring

8mm footage of one of the lecturers' summer holidays, all chewed up and mangled ... He stuck it all together, upside down or back to front, in the order it came out of the bin. The head of film, Malcolm LeGrice, an experimental film-maker, said it was a breakthrough and brilliant. But he still wanted to see the Oxford Street stuff, which the college had paid lots of money towards.[25]

It never materialized. At the end of the 1970–71 academic year Malcolm Edwards told one of his tutors that he was finished; he never wanted to paint again. Not long afterwards, he put his words into action by dumping the canvases he kept in the campus studio outdoors, where they were left to the wind and the rain.[26]

Some of the pieces he produced during his time at Goldsmiths – which today seem only to exist in photographs – were themed around the idea of school punishments. They were part of a series that took inspiration from the practice familiar to any naughty schoolboy, whereby the writing of lines on paper was prescribed as a form of corrective punishment. Edwards took this idea of writing lines to reinforce behaviour, and used it as the basis for a succession of pictures all bearing the same words, over and over, as if to communicate to himself the most important lesson that he had learned through his eight years of art school. One photograph, discovered decades later, featured one of the works: it showed a 'black silhouette . . . surrounded by an upside-down scrawl that read: I will be so bad.'[27] It was, perhaps, an announcement of the decade of devilish exploits to come.

*

Sometime in 1971, Malcolm Edwards – taking the name of the father he never knew – became Malcolm McLaren. It was a transformation that went hand-in-hand with a different approach to art. McLaren exchanged painting for a different kind of creative expression that would, in time, blend commerce, design and the use of ideas to instigate an interaction with the world around him

Portobello Road market, London, 1965.

– the stuff of art was the world and things and people. At the turn of the 1970s there was a craze for second-hand clothing and 1950s revivalism that had been gathering momentum for a while. It was arguably part of a much wider cultural trend in Britain towards preserving the past, and establishing 'theatres of memory', which embraced everything that seemed to be on the verge of disappearing as the post-war world hurtled ever onwards.[28] We see a glimpse of this changing attitude, Simon Reynolds suggests, in Michelangelo Antonioni's *Blowup*, where a 'bric-a-brac shop full of curiosities' piques the interest of the hip fashion photographer

Thomas, who is seen otherwise driving around a London where buildings are demolished and new modernist towers have been erected in concrete. By this time in 1966,

> there were London clothes boutiques that merged fashion and antiquarianism, the psychedelic and the passé. Opening on the King's Road in February 1966, Granny Takes a Trip was the pioneer. Catering to the new pop aristocracy – stars like Pink Floyd, The Small Faces, Jimi Hendrix, The Rolling Stones – the boutique sold antique garments along with new clothes inspired by late-nineteenth-century designs ... Granny Takes a Trip grew out of the emerging bohemian micro-economy based around Portobello Road and similar flea markets, which had benefitted from the early-sixties boom in antique collecting.[29]

McLaren's disillusionment with the idea of being an artist in any conventional sense was manifested in his rediscovery of the rock 'n' roll of his adolescence, which he had turned his back on after The Beatles appeared on the scene in 1963 (precisely the time that he had entered art school with the serious ambition of becoming a painter). During the art school years, according to Fred Vermorel, popular culture and music were fairly peripheral to the lives they were then living. Malcolm at that time was not 'the slightest bit interested in rock or any sort of popular music', and had more of an interest in 'the wilder shores of jazz', Bartók and atonality.[30]

But the implication that McLaren was merely an opportunist who saw popular music as a vehicle for his own non-musical artistic intentions ignores his real teenage engagement with popular culture. He had been one of the very few to see The Beatles at the Pigalle Club in Piccadilly in April 1963 (their first London club date), and had followed the progress of The Rolling

Stones and – in particular – The Pretty Things, in the days when they were still playing around London as the R&B boom got under way.[31] Sometime towards the end of his art school years, Malcolm started spending his student grant on old records he found in London's street markets. He would trudge around Portobello Road, and Brick Lane in the East End, with an old pram, filling it up with as many 45s and 78s as he could find, amassing large quantities of vinyl – numbering in the thousands by some accounts.[32] But it wasn't only records: in addition to the 'hundreds of original rock 'n' roll singles' he also obtained other 1950s artefacts and ephemera from 'flea-market stalls and the dusty shelves of old shops in far-flung suburbs' of the city.[33] After a while it became apparent that what he ought to do was trade in these items himself. These records might have cost only a shilling apiece, as Vivienne Westwood remembered, but they could be resold for higher prices to people who didn't go near the flea markets, if the proper location could be found. According to McLaren's later version of events, he took some film equipment he had managed to borrow from Goldsmiths College to make the aborted Oxford Street film, and sold it to fund his entry into the world of second-hand records and vintage clothing. The equipment was bought for 'an incredible price' by a friend who ran the student union at another college – using student union funds – which gave McLaren enough to lease out the rear part of a shop at 430 King's Road, soon to be called Let It Rock.[34]

While it was just over ten years since the emergence of rock 'n' roll in the 1950s, original records did not stay in print and in some cases almost vanished from existence, to be heard only on the off-chance that they were played on contemporary radio, or spun at some dance hall on the weekends. One reissue compilation album from 1972, titled *Rock Archive,* features a text on the rear sleeve that presents its contents as lost treasures of the golden

era of rock 'n' roll, 'rediscovered from amongst the dusty piles
of old 78rpm records':

> Imagine the amazement and unbelieving joy experienced by
> the archeologist as he prises open the sarcophagus hidden for
> centuries within the bowels of a pyramid. Or the incredulous
> gleam in the eye of the collector of fine antique furniture who
> discovers an excellent piece amidst the valueless bric-a-brac of
> the local junk shop. That's how you feel when you first hear the
> memorable tracks on this remarkable record.[35]

It was partly as a result of this interest in the past that the shop
at 430 King's Road ended up as a 'homage to the late fifties British
rock 'n' roll era of Teddy boys and British bikers – a land where Gene
Vincent was god and Billy Fury was something like the second
coming'.[36] Although the initial idea was just to sell these vintage
records out of the rear half of the shop that he had leased – the
rest of the shop was still used by someone else – in late 1971
McLaren and Westwood took over the premises completely, and
began to expand the stock of the shop to include a much wider
representation of the era. It now also sold 'second-hand clothes
and bits and pieces' sourced in markets and from suppliers who
had leftover 1950s stock locked up in warehouses. Westwood
was going to help McLaren make '50s clothes. They searched
for 'motifs of rebellion', she later wrote. 'We wanted action.'[37]

The most obvious motifs of rebellion relating to the era came
from the look and style of the Teddy boys – thick crepe-soled
shoes, drape suits and lace ties – that McLaren remembered as
promoting badness so successfully. The Teddy boys seemed like
an obvious antidote to the air of hippy mellowness that hung
over the early years of the 1970s. McLaren realized that as well
as simply being (or acting) bad, it was possible just to *look* bad

and convey a sense of menace through appearance. As he wrote later: 'I realized that fashion could provoke something that made you look completely out of step with everything else that people were terming good.'[38] It was another way – this idea of dressing to provoke – that could lead one to the outside of things, where it might be possible to attain a different perspective on the world.

The Teddy boys represented not only the first serious youth cult in Britain to essentially scare the hell out of an older generation – due to the way they were able to step out of their mundane social environment with a stylistic flourish and a hint of menace – but also, in the context of the end of the 1960s their reappearance offered an alternative, and more visceral, expression of youth culture than what was then on offer from the laid-back hippy culture of the time. But by the mid-1960s it seemed that the Teddy boy phenomenon was all but dead, aside from a few outposts in places that seemed far-detached from the heartbeat of youth fashion. At least that was how those who kept abreast of youth culture saw it, with Colin MacInnes – author of seminal books about London youth, such as 1959's *Absolute Beginners* – declaring that:

> though caricaturists still draw dated Ted stereotypes, the style, in its authentic pure absurdity, is now only to be found in outlying holes and corners (I last saw it in a caff at Goring-on-Thames).[39]

The Teddy boys had been supplanted in the public imagination as well, by the equally reviled mods and rockers, whose mobility – using motorcycles and scooters to bring their havoc to seaside towns such as Margate – made them seem like a more potent threat to public order than the Teds had once been. As George Melly put it in *Revolt into Style*, while the Teds were not against 'borrowing cars' they actually 'had no regular transport as part of their equipment, and so were unable to sally forth en masse'.[40] Unless, that is, they were parading down the local high street taking up the whole width of the pavement and jostling passers-by.

So, in 1971 it might have seemed somewhat strange to try and revive the formal elements – if not the attitude and spirit – that had once fired the now ailing cult. But Barry Martin, McLaren's ex-tutor at Goldsmiths who had been on the receiving end of the rant that signalled his abandonment of painting, recalled seeing his former student and some of his friends around this time dressed up in Teddy boy outfits, charging 'up the King's Road in a V-formation, knocking people as they went' – just like the Teddy boys in the old newsreel footage that used to frighten the wits out of law-abiding citizens – and with Malcolm notably 'hanging at the back'.[41]

Anachronistic a sight as that may have seemed, it was part of an attempt to apprehend an attitude from the past, to get back to something that had not had its sense of menace rubbed out by the successive waves of pop culture that had swept the 1960s in a mood of prolonged euphoria. The prevailing easy-going, doped-out hippy ideal, which McLaren hated, seemed to have mellowed out the youth of the day too much. The music that went along with it was safe and boring, and lacked the wild abandon that had been characteristic of so much '50s rock. The Teddy boy cult in its first wave had been symptomatic of a so-called 'generation gap' that had according to experts attracted a generation of post-war children to new forms of delinquency. Studies, in fact, had noted that many of the young people who landed in trouble had complained of 'being bored' with what life had to offer. The new modernist housing estates that they had often been brought up on were found to be factors in their sense of alienation.[42] The potentially delinquent act of dressing up to step out of such circumstances, when coupled with the energy of rock 'n' roll music, made for a potent antidote to boredom that was also a conduit for self-invention. As George Melly wrote, the appeal of rock 'n' roll to the Teddy boys was simple: it was 'an incitement to fucking and arbitrary vandalism'. It was, when you took it right down to its essentials, 'screw and smash music'.[43]

But it was also about a certain idea of style. McLaren, who came from a rag trade background – a family of tailors – had long been obsessed with clothes. Clothes, he once said, were the heartbeat of British popular culture; they possessed the power to serve as a vehicle for self-invention, and not least as a possible route out of the strictures of the British class structure, in which the way one dressed had always been related to social status.[44] The Teddy boys represented a certain ideal of style overcoming the mundane. The so-called drape suits they wore harked after the 'vividly bright-coloured jackets and zoot suits of American jazz bands' of the 1940s, which were combined with the elegance of the Edwardian period.[45] Drape jackets and bootlace ties gave the average youth who donned them the appearance of a saloon gunfighter from a Hollywood western. The drainpipe trousers and 'brothel creeper' shoes – with their strange thick crepe rubber soles – made for a menacing sight to the older generation.[46] In the 1950s, especially, the Teddy boys were feared, not merely for the spectre of violence that a hysterical media attached to their every appearance, but because they symbolized a new kind of youthful innovation that marked itself out from what sociologists termed the parent culture, with 'defiance, anger, [and] gestures of separation'.[47] There were, indeed, Teddy boy 'wars', with the press devoting 'acres of newsprint' to lurid descriptions of 'their violent exploits':

readers recoiled in horror as they read of the Teds arming themselves with axes, coshes, flick-knives, razors, knuckle-dusters, studded belts and bicycle chains. [Their] victims included not only other Teds but innocent members of the public.[48]

Some of McLaren and Westwood's early momentum as the capital's specialist retailers to this unique market had resulted from the press coverage the shop was receiving soon after they took it over in late 1971, with features appearing in the *Daily Mirror* and the *Evening Standard*, among others. A full-colour *Sunday Times Magazine* photo spread featuring Screaming Lord Sutch and his band wearing McLaren's clothes was published in summer 1972. Earlier that year, word about the shop had spread internationally, with a prominent feature on the front page of the main hippy countercultural bible, *Rolling Stone*. Ostensibly about the Teddy boy resurgence in London, it featured McLaren and a description of the customers who were attracted to Let It Rock. The author of this piece, the American writer Jerry Hopkins, viewed the strange phenomenon with a bemused gaze. There was no real equivalent to it in America. It almost seemed, he thought, as if he had fallen 'through a time-warp':

Today the Teds have their own boutique, Let It Rock, situated on fashionable Kings Road. The walls are papered with movie posters the owners bought from the Elvis Presley Fan Club of Paris when it folded and framed studio stills of James Dean. On the floor are boxes of 45s and stacks of old fan magazines. Two-tone Slim-Jim neckties, flashy combs, 3-D rings, jars of hair cream and sequined belts fill a sizable display case.[49]

The '70s revival of Teddy boy culture, although focused predominantly on 1950s American rock 'n' roll, was a peculiarly

Malcolm McLaren and a model outside Let It Rock, London, March 1972.

British phenomenon. The music of the 1950s, in fact, was making something of a comeback in the early '70s, perhaps driven by the feeling that rock music had been taken over by prematurely aged musicians who were often actually still in their twenties. As Max Décharné notes, at just around the time McLaren and Westwood were moving into 430 King's Road, one of the heroes of the Teddy boy scene, Gene Vincent, had recently been mobbed on arrival at Heathrow Airport by 'a posse of Teds'. There were '50s echoes elsewhere, too, in some of the glam rock bands who portrayed a 'strong fifties rock 'n' roll element, with bands such as Wizzard and Mud appearing on *Top of the Pops* in full Teddy boy gear'.[50] In America, where one of the following year's biggest movies – along with its rock 'n' roll soundtrack – was the 1950s-set film *American Graffiti* (1973), the resurgence of interest in the decade did not have quite the same stylistic bent; they had bikers wearing black leathers and denims, but not Teddy boys. The *Rolling Stone* feature focused not on the revival of the music, with which as a music writer Jerry Hopkins was more than familiar, but rather with this strange subculture that had found a focal point in Let It Rock. McLaren revealed the lengths that one busload of provincial Teddy boys went to in order to make the most of their day trip to the shop:

> They came boldering in 'ere, all dressed up in their gear, their drapes and everything, they spent three hours playing the records, buying glow-in-the-dark sox and pants and magazines. It was quite dynamic, really. All the way from Wakefield in Yorkshire, which is a bloody long way, it really is. It's about 150–200 miles nearly. They'd especially 'ired the coach for the day.[51]

As with everything else he became involved with, McLaren approached the venture at Let It Rock with great enthusiasm and a will to succeed, producing in the interior of the shop something that visitors said seemed as much like an art installation as a commercial venture. It was like 'a living [Ed] Keinholz sculpture', one profile suggested, 'designed to reflect the whole ambience of the working class Teddy boy's world':

> in the back room we devised a whole Willesden front-room set, where the Teddy boys would have been sitting watching TV with their old ladies. Brylcreem in the cocktail cabinet. Photographs of James Dean, Elvis Presley and Eddie Cochran, piles of old magazines.[52]

On Friday evenings, the night before their busiest trading day, Westwood would often be up all night 'studding or painting leather jackets', and McLaren would work late arranging the contents of the shop to ensure that the interior looked exactly as he had conceived it. It was because he was initially driven by a genuine affection for those signifiers of his own past – the clothes, the attitude and the music – that Let It Rock had worked.[53] Ultimately, however, McLaren became bored of the Teddy boys, who had turned out not to be the avatars of change that he imagined. They seemed to be motivated by a deeper and more conservative nostalgia than he was, too nostalgic to ever be truly subversive in the way he had hoped. Revisiting the past had been the beginning of something new for McLaren – but now he had to meet the present head-on.

2 Dolls, Crims and Rock 'n' Roll

Into the shabby, dirty heart of North London in 1972 – a cityscape scarred by disappearing buildings and the remnants of abandoned industry – arrived a bunch of glamorous-looking specimens. Streetwise hustlers, a riot of tousled hair, silk scarves and cheap jewellery, they could be seen precariously balanced atop platform shoes and ladies' high heels. The girls' blouses that stretched over their skinny, and mostly effeminate, male bodies exuded a new kind of enthusiasm for the back-to-basics rock 'n' roll music that they played. After all, how else could something this retro be made to seem new? Well, they could paint their faces in rouge and black. If you caught them as they strutted for effect, it would be with lips pouting or – in the case of the guitarist, who looked like a cross between the singer from The Ronettes and Keith Richards – an Elvis-style lip-sneer always at the ready for the cameras. For anyone who had seen them play over the last year or so, it was like witnessing mutant beings from another dimension.

Since late 1971, almost a year before they arrived in London, the New York Dolls had raised a stir in New York City, especially among the new, younger, rock 'n' roll aficionados who had grown bored with the way things were panning out at the turn of the decade. So far, it was looking like the 1970s could be the most sluggish and bloated decade in the history of pop culture. Where the '60s fizzed, the '70s were already engendering a new kind of indifference. No one seemed to be singing anymore about things that raised the pulse or chimed with the enthusiasms of urban teenagers all over the country. By the start of the 1970s, young people newly interested in popular culture had seemingly been forever cut adrift from the excitement of that decade that had just passed. Instead of the handful of trailblazing rock acts inventing themselves anew every few months – The Beatles, the Stones, The Kinks, The Byrds, Dylan – there had been an explosion in the number of rock bands and record companies promoting whatever they thought would latch on to the hippy mood of the Woodstock generation. But amid the deluge of product, something had been lost.

Outside the Top 40, which was colonized by records aimed at the teenybopper market, rock music had turned introspective and mature at alarming speed. This was evident in the multiplying ranks of singer-songwriters who seemed to appear in ever-greater numbers as 1971 faded into 1972, as if it were inevitable – rock music *growing up*. If it wasn't confessional and laid back, even soporific, it tried to carry the listener along into its sci-fi and fantasy obsessions, as the deluge of concept albums exposed the world to a new kind of rock indulgence. Forget the audience, it seemed to say: journey inwards, into the mind of the artist.

It was only a few that seemed to grasp the point of the New York Dolls – which was to poo-pah the wisdom of these grown-ups. Given that their visual appearance suggested they might be extras from some trashy sexploitation movie, maybe it wasn't surprising that they weren't popular. What might the casual observer make of the Dolls' guitarist and founder member Sylvain Sylvain, for instance, 'darting around the stage' as he chugged out a primitive R&B groove, clad in 'tights, a mini skirt, toy gun and holster.'[1] The Dolls embodied something beyond even the campy late-'60s incarnation of The Rolling Stones. Non-believers, appalled by these 'transvestite scum', quickly latched on to the group with as much enthusiasm as their new-found fans.[2] They were turning things around and inside-out in other ways, too: musically, they were pitching towards a destination that lay in the past. Whatever 'progressive rock' meant, the Dolls were its antithesis. From the day they started in 1971 until the day they collapsed in 1975 under the dubious guidance of their would-be saviour, Malcolm McLaren, the Dolls were a polarizing phenomenon.

Binky Philips, whose own band The Planets was just getting going at the same time that the Dolls began appearing in New York City, was invited to one of their gigs by a friend – 'the most amazing bullshit', his friend told him, but it would be fun anyway; 'This time I'm bringing tomatoes,' he added. But Philips was stunned when he encountered what immediately seemed to be 'the most outlandishly cool band' he'd ever seen. Their guitarist, the one with the Ronnie Spector/Keith Richards vibe (who had changed his name from John Genzale to Johnny Thunders), turned out to be an old friend. According to Philips:

> These guys were not changing into stage outfits. They were sauntering on stage in their street clothes. They were living it! Johnny counted off and they went into 'Bad Girl'. The song was dead simple, maybe four chord changes. And, incredibly, a masterpiece. The band's musical skills were rudimentary. The singer seemed to have maybe a four-note range . . . I hadn't heard music this crude in years, maybe ever.[3]

Philips didn't throw tomatoes. Instead, over the months that followed, he watched as the Dolls 'instigated TWO genres, glam and punk' during a residency at the crummy, semi-derelict building that housed the Mercer Arts Center in Manhattan. All the while, they were gathering new young followers – from Queens, the Bronx and Brooklyn, who would end up one way or another looking like offspring of the New York Dolls – as well as curious local luminaries connected to the 'art and drag crowd'.[4] These included, at various times, Lou Reed, John Cale, Andy Warhol and various others from the Factory scene, and the visiting (and then largely unknown in America) David Bowie.

When they arrived in England that autumn it was on a wave of enthusiasm generated by sections of the London music press, where they were being lauded as the saviours of rock. But in an age of media scarcity, it didn't count for much more than cult status. The lack of mainstream coverage meant that they remained an unknown quantity, even to those who gawped at the pictures – were they transvestites, or a bunch of Manhattan hookers? – and read the reports from New York. The weekly music press meant that London was a different prospect from New York. In theory, with three or four papers looking to capitalize on the next big thing, there was a possibility that the Dolls could meet their moment. As with their target readership, however, the music press seemed to have lost its ceaseless appetite for new flesh and new blood. The images that padded out the pages of the weeklies were dominated by men with beards and unkempt hair, wearing flared everything – denims, lapels, collars. The truth was that the New York Dolls arrived too early, ultimately falling victim to chronology and confined to history. Nevertheless, as originators of the next wave they signalled one way out of the stagnant early 1970s – and where they failed, many would later prosper.[5]

Playing at the Speakeasy in London, they were heckled from the wings by a rowdy white guy sporting an impressive afro and shades who was screaming obscenities about the band being unable to play; it was Mick Farren, front man of The Deviants and sometime writer for various organs of London's underground press.[6] Lou Reed, whose show in Liverpool they were supposed to open, seemed to have to come to England only to remember that he hated fellow New Yorkers, the Dolls, and wanted them off the bill. And, worst of all, their drummer, Billy Murcia, died of an overdose in a London flat, after drifting into the orbit of some rakish fans whose main purpose was to have the wrong kind of fun. Before that last disaster the band had been booked to play the biggest show of their career so far (and the biggest show they would ever play), opening for Rod Stewart and the Faces at a benefit concert at Wembley Empire Pool. As the band lounged around backstage, gripped with fear at the prospect of performing in front of the huge crowd, the Duchess of Kent – patron of the charity they were ostensibly there to raise funds for – entered their dressing room to present them each with a personalized bottle of champagne.[7] That would be the highlight of their day.

The New York Dolls backstage at Wembley Empire Pool, October 1972. From left: Billy Murcia, Johnny Thunders, David Johansen (seated), Arthur Kane and Sylvain Sylvain.

Unused to playing anywhere but tight, sweaty clubs, the band seemed lost and out of sorts in the hangar-like space of the arena. They were booed and heckled when Johnny Thunders twice had to stop the show to change broken strings, with his guitar still plugged in and at full volume – it made a sound that was akin to steel girders crashing together, and set the audience even more against them. Representatives of Mercury Records, whose A&R man had been in pursuit of the band in New York, were in the audience, including the label president, who thought that this was the worst show he had ever seen. In the following week's *Melody Maker*, the Dolls' performance was panned in a review that made note of the level of hostility that the New Yorkers had faced before they played a single note. Maybe, people began to think, this band was just the latest hype after all.

Yet out there among the crowd of 9,000 there were enough people who were impressed with what they saw, and who took something away from the Dolls' calamitous visit. Steve Jones and Paul Cook, two Faces fans and friends from west London, loved the fact that the audience were outraged at the band's display.[8] Elsewhere in the crowd was Glen Matlock, whom Jones and Cook would come to know when they were introduced to him the following year. But for now, inspired by the example of the New York Dolls, among others, Jones and Cook started their own band. Sometimes they were called The Swankers, and at other times The Strand. It didn't matter, really, because they weren't playing gigs yet.

The impression the Dolls made in those early days had as much to do with look and attitude as it did with the music. The Dolls were interested in looking around London, where the rock 'n' roll style and attitude was for sale on the King's Road, and whose fashion boutiques – such as Granny Takes a Trip, Mr Freedom, Alkasura – were frequented by the stars of the day. Eventually the Dolls found themselves in Let It Rock, purveyor of clothes for 1950s revivalists, where Malcolm McLaren was whiling away the afternoon looking out as the rain blew across an empty street, listening to the '50s rock 'n' roll that played on the jukebox. 'In burst a gang of girly-looking boys looking like girls dressed like boys.' They were dressed in

> Tiny lurex tops, bumfreezer leggings and high heels . . . They crawled all over the jukebox, destroying the neat racks of Teddy Boy drapes in their wake. Their tongues revealed they were not from the old country. The Uxbridge teddy boys were stunned into silence by this alien invasion.[9]

The Dolls were 'quite staggered' by what they found, McLaren later said, because it was unlike anything in New York – 'nobody in New York was selling rock and roll culture in the form of dress and music, in one particular place.'[10] It wasn't long before McLaren learned that two of the band, Sylvain and Thunders, used to have their own clothing line called Truth and Soul back in New York. They exchanged phone numbers, and McLaren – handing them some Let It Rock leaflets to give to their friends back home – promised to call them if he was ever in New York.

*

Westwood and McLaren would embark on the first of several redesigns of 430 King's Road in spring 1973, renaming the shop Too Fast to Live, Too Young to Die – a reference to James Dean. It was a short-lived attempt to move away from the Teddy boy crowd and attract a different kind of customer, by embracing the then popular American collegiate-style fashion of peg-bottomed pants and fraternity sweaters, and moving away from the idea of

1950s rock 'n' roll's delinquent potential that had inspired them to open the shop in the first place. It was a change that lasted a year or so, and which McLaren would describe in 1975 as a big mistake. 'I just got involved in style, line and cut,' he said. 'It was clothing to pose in, but not clothing to inspire action.'[11] And that, as it had been with Let It Rock, was his motivation: to be the source of action, to do something that could instigate trouble and inspire the youth of the day.

McLaren always took an interest in the people who frequented his shop; he wanted to know what enthused them, what made them interested in the clothes. The shop's location on the King's Road meant that it attracted a lot of passing trade who wound up there – in the part of Chelsea known as the World's End – after having had an eyeful of the wares on sale in the other trendy boutiques. Not long after Let It Rock had opened, Steve Jones and Paul Cook started hanging around the shop; it was a good place to kill time on a Saturday afternoon and indulge in a spot of people-watching without being hassled to buy something, or chased away for scaring off customers. Jones was a bored teenager attracted to mischief, whose mother had on many occasions been called out to local police stations to collect him after his latest exploits had drawn the attention of the law. He would steal anything – cars, electrical goods, clothes.[12] For well-educated Sex Pistols associates like Julien Temple, who came to know him well, Steve Jones was a fascinating character. He seemed to have stepped right out of some submerged London subculture, which was reinforced by the way he spoke: 'this underground 1940s argot that by that time had already half-disappeared'.[13] Paul Cook, by comparison, was a far more upstanding citizen. He was an apprentice electrician at the Watney's Brewery at Mortlake, in the London borough of Richmond upon Thames, where, he later claimed, he spent most of his time watching the old lags at the brewery helping themselves to the beer.[14]

Jones and Cook were both on the fringes of the then popular mod/skinhead culture in terms of the way they dressed, but even they experimented with the 1950s-style fashions that were on display at Let It Rock. Jones recalled that the first pair of trousers he bought from the shop were a pair of pink peg trousers, drawn in at the waist and the ankles and baggy through the hips and legs – probably an outrageous statement of crazed individuality at a time when it seemed like everyone else was wearing flared denims. 'I was getting a lot of clothes like that [and] Teddy boy shoes,' said Cook.[15] At the time, as he recounted later, they were just there for the clothes:

> We used to go in there round about 1971, every week like. We didn't talk about anything to do with music [with Malcolm] – we'd just go in there and talk to him. And we knew all the people who worked in the shop – we were friends with them, 'cos we used to hang about the King's Road a lot.[16]

Glen Matlock, who had been working in Let It Rock on Saturdays since the summer of 1972 to earn some extra spending money, had the job of spotting and ejecting people who looked like they were intent on stealing the one-off designs that could be found in the shop.[17] In 1974 he began attending art school as a foundation-year student, with the aim of going on to study for a fine arts degree. He first became acquainted with Jones and Cook as potential thieves, little knowing that Jones in particular had his sights on a different kind of booty, which, in time, would help to create the circumstances in which the Sex Pistols could take shape.

McLaren eventually formed a close bond with Steve Jones, whose prowess as a burglar he soon became aware of, and

49

which he much admired – here was someone who just went out and took what he wanted, who knew how to be bad and, for the most part, get away with it. In those years before he started to take getting a band together seriously, Jones was more of a fan of pop music, and aware that through the shop and the kind of customers who shopped there, he could probably gain access to some of the rock stars of the day. As time went on and Jones took an interest in making music himself, he would hang around the premises, badgering McLaren to help him with the band. Slightly older than Jones, Cook and Matlock was a young American woman, Chrissie Hynde, who worked for McLaren and Westwood at the shop in late 1973. She remembered Jones as a bit of a wayward teenager whom McLaren and Westwood seemed to have taken under their wing. Jones would help Hynde to put up the shutters and close up the shop, and although she too was already intent on forming a band – but would not become known for doing so until the Pretenders were formed in 1979 – the two never discussed their respective musical aspirations at the time.[18]

Glen Matlock, on the other hand, let it be known that he could play a bit of bass guitar, and McLaren informed him that Jones and Cook – whom he really only knew at the time as two guys who were always in the shop and looked like they were probably shoplifters – were trying to get a band going:

> Steve and Paul had all this equipment around and they didn't know what to do with it . . . So that's how they started. Then they started to get a little bit more serious. Then they had this bass player who was married and had a wife and kid, you know, never turned up for rehearsals and all that. About that time I met them.[19]

Back then, in 1973, the future Sex Pistol Jones and his pal Warwick 'Wally' Nightingale (who had been practising with Paul Cook since leaving school the previous summer) realized that as well as the possible fun to be had playing in a band, there was a little spending money to be made in stealing and selling guitars, and whatever other items of musical equipment they might be able to lay their hands on. They discovered that it was quite easy to get into the backstage area at local gigs at major venues like the Hammersmith Odeon, Hammersmith Palais and Wembley Empire Pool, which seemed to be on the itinerary of every rock band of the day. 'Hammersmith Palais', Jones told the New Musical Express writer Nick Kent, 'was a great place to get amps – mini-van round the back.'[20] When he decided at one point that he was going to play the drums, Jones dismantled and nabbed a complete drum kit from the Palais, straight off the venue's revolving stage – which conveniently wheeled around to facilitate easy access – into their minivan, also stolen (vehicles were Jones's other speciality as a thief), which was waiting outside in the loading bay. One way or another, Jones was intent on breaking into the music business; once he even staged a raid on the Faces' dressing room at Wembley, digging into the refreshments laid out backstage for the band and guests, as he chatted away to his hero, Ronnie Wood.[21]

It was the early 1970s and the country seemed always to be on the verge of either darkness (due to regular power cuts) or industrial strife and economic woes of one kind or another. With his patchy school education, a string of juvenile convictions and a primal attachment to the excitement of thieving, Jones was too enterprising a young man to settle for becoming a victim of the circumstances that had beset 1970s England, as he told Fred and Judy Vermorel:

I couldn't be bothered going on the dole. I was really lazy . . .
I was just interested in music and all, you know, pop stars and
that. I used to go to try and get into the Speakeasy, just to see
the pop stars.[22]

It was around this time that Jones and Nightingale staged
one of their most audacious heists, after the final performance of
David Bowie and his band as Ziggy Stardust and the Spiders from
Mars at Hammersmith Odeon on 3 July 1973. It had been a strange
show in front of a hysterical audience that seemed at times to
fulfil a vision of 'bacchanalian excess'.[23] D. A. Pennebaker's film of
the event showed 'row after row of delirious teenagers, mostly
female, writhing to the music, hands outstretched, enchanted'.[24]
The newspapers later reported that teenagers were engaged in
sexual acts at the back of the stalls, as if anticipating that this was
the end of something – as indeed it was. To the shock of all those
present, David Bowie announced from the stage that not only
was this 'the last show of the tour . . . it's the last show we'll ever
do. Bye bye.'[25] The stunned crowd slowly left the theatre, and it
was some time before the place had been cleared. As the other
fans slowly filed out, Jones and Nightingale lay down on the floor,
hiding between the rows of seats.[26] On the spur of the moment,
they thought that if the band were really finished, it would be a
shame to let all that fabulous equipment sitting up on the stage
go to waste. After a while, when it seemed that the theatre had
been cleared of people, they quietly climbed on-stage. None of
the sound equipment had been broken down, and – as the music
press reported later – Bowie and the band had gone straight off
to a post-tour party, with Mick Jagger and other illustrious guests.
It soon became apparent that the one obstacle to the ruse was
a sleeping roadie, slouching in a chair off in the wings, probably
left there to keep guard over the stage. Jones and Nightingale

David Bowie in concert at the Hammersmith Odeon, the last gig he performed in the guise of his spacerocker alter ego Ziggy Stardust, 3 July 1973.

went to work, moving quietly across the famous wooden boards of the Odeon stage, looking for anything they could carry that could be easily separated from the place it had been left using garden clippers. 'All you could hear was the snip, snip,' Jones told Nick Kent in 1979.[27] Their haul included microphones and Mick Ronson's Sunn amplifier. Because the show was being filmed that night by Pennebaker and his crew, the stage had a number of expensive Neumann microphones dotted around it for audio recording; these were also snatched by the curious Jones, who wasn't sure what they were: 'they looked like a bleedin' gorilla's dildo.'[28]

By the time that Glen Matlock had hooked up with the band, Jones and Nightingale were already acting like habitual thieves, and making little secret of it. After his first rehearsal with them in Covent Garden, Matlock was dropped off by the others, who were on their way to pinch some new cymbals for the band.[29] They told him that the cheap replica bass guitar he had brought along wasn't going to be good enough, because they were aiming for the top. They gave him an almost new Fender Precision Bass, which Steve Jones had seemingly conjured out of nowhere.[30]

Jones's persistence was also felt by McLaren, whose shop, Jones believed, was his way to access the world of popular music. He kept on hanging around 430 King's Road, talking to McLaren in the hope that he could at least help get him into the Speakeasy, and maybe do more to help out with the band. McLaren did eventually go to see the band, but was unimpressed by them. They didn't have it, there was nothing distinctive about them – yet. What was worthy of his admiration, on the other hand, were Jones's street smarts, and most of all the kind of enterprise he had shown in kitting out his band with only the best equipment.

McLaren, whether or not he was aware of what was coming, seemed to be gearing up for a change in direction, and perhaps going back in search of something that might be able to recapture that long sought-after buccaneering spirit of 1950s rock 'n' roll. As it turned out, he didn't have far to look. On one November evening in 1973 he and Vivienne, along with then shop assistants Chrissie Hynde and Glen Matlock, went to see a special performance by the New York Dolls in the lush Art Deco surroundings of Biba's Rainbow Room on the King's Road. It had been almost a year since their last performances in the UK. As with their appearance the year before – when they had been feted by everyone from Kit Lambert, manager of The Who, to Mick Jagger (scouting for his own label, Rolling Stones Records), Richard Branson and the heads of a variety of record companies – they were treated as the stars that they would, in reality, never be. The Biba show was nonetheless, as Hynde later recalled, 'a pivotal night for us all, each in our different ways'.[31] It was apparent that the Dolls were not only the embodiment of everything McLaren had loved about rock 'n' roll, but they were in many ways doing what he had been trying to do himself. They appropriated elements of a seemingly dormant cultural attitude (in the Dolls' case, producing a mode of rock 'n' roll and R&B that was redolent of the 1950s), but revitalized it through the melding of new and more unusual influences that were as much Hollywood Babylon as hit parade. It all culminated in the production of a seemingly 'mutant offspring of the Rolling Stones', in the words of one admirer, who wondered how it had come to pass:

the unholy marriage of traditional R&B as interpreted by British effete snobs, fops and cuckolds; the gay glam of Marc Bolan and David Bowie; the subtlety of Russ Meyer; the balls of Bette Davis and Marlene Dietrich; the romantic sensitivity of Charles Bukowski; and the girl-group naughty innocence of the Shangri-Las would end up with the somehow heterosexual-transvestite street hookers of the Dolls.[32]

Whatever the sources of what at the time seemed like a bizarre combination of street hustler attitude, louche glamour and lust, communicated through their short, catchy tunes and ramshackle appearance, it made McLaren believe that perhaps it was still possible to make something – music, even – that celebrated being bad, and which was itself both bad (insofar as it displayed relative musical naivety) and, at the same time, brilliant.

Little did the New York Dolls' newest fan know that they were just as much fans of what he had been doing in his shop. As the band were laying down tracks in the Record Plant studio in New York City earlier that year, there was a little bit of McLaren in there with them, to add a little bit of bad to the occasion. As Ben Edmonds recounted in a report for *Creem* magazine, from the studio where the Dolls were recording their debut album, they seemed to be spending much of their time testing the patience of their producer, Todd Rundgren. Maybe they felt it helped to liven up proceedings if they could annoy the one guy in the studio who could play everyone's parts, and probably play them better, while keeping everyone on their mettle. If the relationship between the band and the record company's man in their camp (Rundgren) was difficult, well, so much the better. Edmonds, with a journalistic eye for the defining moment, was looking on as the producer on the other side of the studio console – now facing a gaggle of laughing, sneering and uncooperative Dolls – barked out his orders to the band: 'Get the glitter out of your asses and play.'[33] It was just then that the band's singer, David Johansen, a look of contempt contorting his face,

> strolled over to the plate glass partition which separates the studio from the control room, and scotch-tapes an advertising flyer he's just picked up to the window so that it faces the booth. 'Too fast to live, too young to die,' it reads, 'LET IT ROCK.' He spins around and the band launches full-throttle into 'Trash,' an electric explosion that seconds his gesture with a vengeance, and without which his action would have been empty and melodramatic.[34]

It was one of McLaren's flyers, which the Dolls had brought back from London when they had stumbled into Let It Rock around the time of their Wembley gig. Their mutual admiration was further sealed in August 1973, when members of the band met McLaren and Westwood at the annual fashion trade fair – known as the Boutique Show – that was held at the McAlpin Hotel in New York. It was a showcase for independent designers to seek out buyers and distributors for their goods. In the past, New York

Dolls members Syl Sylvain and Johnny Thunders had sold their own 'multi-coloured homemade sweaters' under their own label 'Truth & Soul', but on this occasion were just looking around when they unexpectedly ran into the Let It Rock stall located in one of the hotel rooms that had been repurposed for the show. They were surprised that it was actually the same Let It Rock that they had visited in London, 'but there, in a tiny chamber blasting [out] Bill Haley and plastered with pics of Little Richard, Jerry Lee Lewis, and old nudie pinups, was the strange sparrow-headed fashion maverick', Malcolm McLaren.[35]

A handbill for the 1973 National Boutique Show in New York.

For the three weeks that McLaren and Westwood were in New York, they made a point of introducing themselves to anyone they could in the downtown scene and, at the suggestion of Sylvain, moved to the bohemian Chelsea Hotel in order to take full advantage of Sylvain and Thunders as guides to what was happening in the city.[36] During these weeks, McLaren, it was said, 'began to study the band in their natural habitat at Max's [Kansas City]', a bar and restaurant that was the epicentre of the seedier, more rock 'n' roll end of the city's artistic cultural nightlife.[37] Max's featured an exclusive back room where the Warhol crowd and assorted luminaries on the music scene, as well as visiting musicians and artists, would gather. It was here, too, during 1975, that elements of the emerging New York punk scene would begin to take shape, with McLaren around to witness it.

Soon after the Dolls arrived in Britain on their second visit in late 1973, McLaren was so overjoyed at their reappearance that he and Westwood briefly abandoned the shop and took to the road with them:

They were like the worst strip-tease rock act you can imagine. I loved their awkward trashy vibe. We became part of their entourage and like groupies we followed them to Paris.[38]

The New York Dolls' trip to London in 1973 would also be remembered for their appearance on the UK's only TV show devoted to rock music as a 'serious' endeavour, *The Old Grey Whistle Test*. A key feature of the flared and sagging seventies, the *Whistle Test* took rock very seriously. While popular music had its most recognizable TV outlet on the main channel – BBC One's *Top of the Pops* – it was purely for the Top 40 hit makers; the *Whistle Test* was broadcast on the less popular BBC Two and focused on album rock. In order for a group to appear on the show, they had to have an album out or one about to be released. Fortunately, the Dolls' debut album had arrived in Britain on import a few months before, making it excellent timing for an appearance on this particular show. It might have been just the boost the band needed, after a glowing review in the *New Musical Express* late that summer. The review opened with the unambiguous declaration of the devotee – author Nick Kent – who wrote:

> The New York Dolls are trash, they play rock 'n' roll like sluts and they've just released an album that can proudly stand beside Iggy and The Stooges' stupendous *Raw Power* as the only album so far to fully define just exactly where 1970s rock should be coming from.[39]

McLaren and Kent, as it turned out, shared a liking for both acts and recognized in each other someone who could possibly help to foster the conditions that would push rock music forward into its next mutation. But while McLaren couldn't help being struck by the sheer force of Iggy Pop – for a while in 1972 Iggy was a visitor to the shop while then living just off the King's Road – and adored *Raw Power*, he didn't fall for him the way he fell for the New York Dolls. He sensed that that they were doing something that could make a greater impact. Iggy came across as a guy, he said, 'with a lion's head full of drugs and pills, shouting and screaming "RAW POWER" at me'.[40] There was something that set the two trailblazers, Iggy and the Dolls, apart – not only in looks and style, but in lyrical approach and attitude, and what these could communicate. Iggy, McLaren thought, was a continuation of Jim Morrison and The Doors, with songs that were, on the whole, 'far more insular and emotionally-orientated'. This was in contrast to the Dolls' tendency to set their songs in the kind of urban settings that kids on the street would be able to identify with; their attitude was more outward-looking, less about personal neuroses.[41]

The future Sex Pistols drummer Paul Cook, who had already seen the New Yorkers at Wembley Empire Pool the previous October, was one of many who immediately got what the Dolls were about, and he was bowled over as he watched them tottering on their platform shoes as they lit up the *Old Grey Whistle Test* studio with two songs from their new album, 'Jet Boy' and 'Personality Crisis', only to suffer the taunts of the snickering presenter Bob Harris, who was conveniently several feet away from the stage, addressing the camera. 'I was fucking really knocked out by them,' Cook said:

> all falling about all over the place, all their hair down, all knocking into each other. And they just didn't give a shit, you know. And Bob Harris at the end of it went: 'Tut, tut, tut, mock rock,' or something. Just cast it off in two words. I thought it was great though.[42]

Nick Kent, who had become quite well acquainted with McLaren by this time, and would have long discussions with him about the state of youth culture and pop music, penned an article in 1974 on the relationship between pop music and fashion in the 1970s. The article prominently featured McLaren, and described his shop as 'probably the most notorious of all King's Road's more esoteric clothes-dives'.[43] That notoriety in part derived from the fact that the Teds who frequented the shop were often out in force and – true to their long-standing media-influenced reputation as a violent cult – seen as trouble in waiting. 'Very heavy', was how McLaren described to Kent the reputation the shop had gained as a result of the Teddy boy crowd. But it prompted him to adapt to the circumstances:

No one'd dare come in the place unless they were Teds. Mick Jagger stood outside the shop for half an hour once and never came in. Ringo Starr was the only one who actually dared come in on a Saturday. [So] I had to do deliveries. I thought it was the customary thing for the King's Road shops to do until I realised everyone was too scared to come inside the shop.[44]

As it happened, Kent's article contained some additional commentary on this meeting with McLaren, revealing that just as the article was going to press in April 1974 the shop had been attacked by '52 surly Teds', presumably unhappy that their Teddy boy emporium seemed to be disappearing before their eyes, as it entered yet another phase of transition. How, wondered Kent, could McLaren possibly have known so precisely in the midst of such a melee, during which there had been a lot of smashing and ransacking, that there were 52 of them? 'Oh, after they'd ransacked the shop,' McLaren said, in an early example of off-the-cuff inventiveness he became known for later, 'they went to the restaurant over the road and ordered 52 cups of tea.'[45]

The timing of Kent's article coincided with the beginning of the rebranding of the boutique from Too Fast to Live, Too Young to Die to, eventually, the far more direct SEX (which would involve much more than a simple change of name). But before the shop had been reopened with the huge new SEX sign, in fluorescent plastic pink, it temporarily acquired the far stranger legend of 'Craft must have clothes, but truth loves to go naked' on the sign above the door, written graffiti-style in spray paint (in fact the slogan would later be still visible beneath the 'SEX' sign). Some of those who spoke to Nick Kent for his report on the state of pop fashions were only too aware of the decline that had gripped their industry, which remained 'shrouded by this spectre of the swinging 60s', as Bryan Ferry's outfitter Anthony Price told him:

Jordan (Pamela Rooke), who often appeared as the public face
of SEX, pictured in 1975.

'There's no such thing as futuristic fashion in England. It's all dead and there aren't even any decent clubs for [the clothes-obsessed pop stars] to show off the extent of their decay.'[46] Price was then a man who wanted nothing to do with pop stars of the day, aside from Bryan Ferry, whose increasingly suave and straight male film-star look stood in contrast to Roxy Music's early, more futuristic image. Ferry's smooth and natural look, Price thought, was what set him apart from the hackneyed parade of glitter and leather that had conquered the pop charts and marked the pop fashions of the early 1970s.

Not for long, though, because 430 King's Road would reopen later that summer with an eye very much on the future; as Nick Kent signalled in his piece, the 'clothes will get more transexual [sic]', more driven by ideas, with McLaren 'trying to get renowned philosopher R. D. Laing interested in designing suits for him.'[47] SEX was the indication of a more determined move into what McLaren thought was slightly more artistic territory, engaging with 'complicated ideas' pushed by Westwood, in particular, to help combine 'sexual taboos with Situationist slogans.'[48] To achieve this goal, McLaren and Westwood had to draw on the help of others, such as McLaren's old friend Bernard Rhodes, who became involved in the exchange of ideas and, more practically, with T-shirt printing.[49] Without knowing or revealing a great deal about McLaren's art school background, Nick Kent's *New Musical Express* article of April 1974 made several allusions to the influence of artistic movements like Dada on McLaren – and mentioned that the shop owner had stumbled into rock 'n' roll clothes and memorabilia after attempting to make a film about Billy Fury at art school. McLaren didn't reveal anything about the influence of his years as an art student, although he admitted that he and the others he was working with were basically all artists. He thought that now was the right time, with the new revamp of the shop that would be happening later that year, to 'get a more personal angle, in the way of design, on what the spirit of the '50s represented'.[50]

It was around this time that Kent was introduced to the ways of the wannabe pop stars – future members of the Sex Pistols, then known variously as The Swankers or The Strand – who seemed to be fixtures at McLaren and Westwood's shop. In fact, soon after meeting them his attention was drawn to the streetwise ingenuity of Steve Jones, who in short order sold Nick Kent a stolen Fender Telecaster Deluxe guitar. According to the journalist, it was one of a haul of 'thirteen expensive electric guitars [stolen] one by one from various instrument shops situated on London's Denmark Street'.[51] From that point on, the teenage louts were on his radar as aspirant music industry gatecrashers who seemed to go to any lengths to get what they wanted. The next time he saw them was when they literally broke in to a special press performance for Ronnie Wood's recent solo album, 1974's *I've Got My Own Album to Do*, at the Kilburn Gaumont, where Wood, Keith Richards and a band entertained a select audience of music business types. Yet 'Jones, Cook and Matlock got in', Kent recalled, 'by literally dismantling and then climbing through a trapdoor on the building's extremely high roof'.[52] Little did Richards and Wood know that the budding Sex Pistols' love for the Faces kept them working pretty hard on how to get close to their heroes. They knew, for instance, that Ronnie Wood lived at a big house known as the Wick, located on Richmond Hill, which he had bought from the actor John Mills a couple of years earlier. Moreover, Keith Richards was, at the time, staying in a little cottage at the bottom of the garden, during the sessions for *I've Got My Own Album to Do*, which had been recorded in a studio in the basement of the house. Jones and his fellow Faces freaks managed to find a way into Richards's den whenever the place was empty, as Glen Matlock recalled:

> Steve and the others would get in there, rifle around it, have a go on one of Keith's guitars, nick a shirt, and leave a note saying, 'Steve was here.' That was their fun of a Saturday night.[53]

The early fruits of the soon-to-be Sex Pistols' attempts to gatecrash their way into the music business could be found in all their glory near their home base in Hammersmith, at an old and recently vacated BBC property known as Riverside Studios that contained abandoned auditoria and sound stages. It was a matter of luck that Wally Nightingale's father, who was involved in the work to decommission and strip out the electrics from the studios, controlled access to the property, and had given Wally and his pals permission to set up and rehearse on what was rumoured to be one of the best sound stages in the country. It was there, set up on the stage, that the band kept much of the equipment they had stolen – a proper 'little Aladdin's Cave', as Matlock recalled.[54]

One of the reasons that McLaren was so taken by these youngsters, despite their initially limited appeal in the badness stakes, was that he believed in the importance of the criminal element in pop culture, and they at least had that as a starting point. This connection between youth culture, pop music and crime was something that had, one way or another – whether through mafia money-laundering, payola scandals or the actions of rip-off record companies – always defined an important relationship between popular culture and the wider culture. In this diffuse way, McLaren thought, those delinquent values seeped into the minds of young people, who were drawn immediately to rock 'n' roll's wild and disruptive potential.

McLaren, for instance, harboured a lifelong romantic fascination with the (often) mythical tales of the record industry's gangsterism, and of unlucky victims supposedly strapped to great lumbering Rock-Ola jukeboxes and thrown off bridges by the Mafia in strange ritual sacrifices. McLaren would tell anyone who would listen that Bobby Fuller, who was best known for the great 1960s hit 'I Fought the Law', had been one such casualty: tied to a jukebox and dumped into the East River in New York City for complaining too much about not being paid his royalties – killed with the aid of the very machine that helped send his music out into the world to make him a star.[55] It wasn't true, of course, but imagining that *this* was the world that spawned rock 'n' roll – with its shady record company hustlers, gangster enforcers and badness everywhere – certainly made it seem more exciting than what it had become by the early 1970s.

By summer 1975 it was obvious that the band's set-up at their Aladdin's cave was not destined to last, as the availability of Riverside was dependent on Wally Nightingale, and McLaren had persuaded them that Wally had to go because he would never be cool enough. After Nightingale was told he was out, Jones switched from lead vocals to guitar, and McLaren brought Nick Kent into the picture, to spend some time rehearsing with the band in the hope that some of his decadent cool would rub off on them.[56] So, with Kent on occasional guitar, they rehearsed during July and August 1975 in their Aladdin's Cave while they still had access to it, and at other times Jones would visit Kent at his flat where he was supposedly picking up guitar-playing tips, appearing, true to form, as if he had come to rob the place. 'I'd know when he'd arrived', Kent wrote,

> when I heard the window to my first-storey garret creak open and saw him climb through. Being an inveterate cat burglar,

Malcolm McLaren's flyer for the Sex Pistols Christmas Day
1977 show in Huddersfield.

Steve rarely entered any building through the front door – it was against his religion.[57]

Kent later recollected the first time that McLaren took him to visit the band in the abandoned Riverside Studios. He was very impressed by the professional set-up that lay within the otherwise dormant complex: 'I complimented them on their choice of equipment – it was all very state-of-the-art – and they told me that it had all been stolen, every last stick of it.'[58] By now McLaren had seen enough in Jones to understand that his desire to pilfer anything he could lay his hands on showed a certain kind of enterprise that was not to be ignored. 'He saw Jones in particular as a seventies update of the Artful Dodger from Charles Dickens's *Oliver Twist*,' Kent later wrote, 'and in time would start fantasizing that he could invent a role for himself as their very own Fagin.'[59] It was an image McLaren played up to until the end began to close in on the Sex Pistols; he even produced a flyer for a Christmas Day 1977 Huddersfield gig that featured an illustration from Dickens onto which he had appended a text in his favoured heavy, black scrawl: 'They are Dickensian – like urchins who with ragged clothes and pock marked faces roam the streets of foggy gas-lit London. Pillaging.' In fact, it wouldn't be long before McLaren and Jones were in cahoots, with the erstwhile guitarist pilfering musical equipment that even McLaren himself would fence.

3 London and New York

SEX, McLaren and Westwood's renamed and re-conceptualized boutique, opened in autumn 1974 after the interior had been remodelled to live up to the new, more direct identity it had been given. It was around this time – possibly inspired by the fact that Tommy Roberts, who owned the King's Road's Mr Freedom, was managing a band named Kilburn and the High Roads – that McLaren and an old friend, Bernard Rhodes, became interested in finding a group or a singer to enable them to break into the pop world. An early target for their attention was Robin Scott, the co-instigator of sit-ins and protests with McLaren at Croydon Art College, who had helped out in Let It Rock during the early days of the shop. It was on the back of the notoriety he attained through a Croydon sit-in in 1968 that Scott had made appearances on BBC television and radio as a singer, and had been able to make an album – a 1969 release titled *Woman from the Warm Grass*. By 1974, however, he was languishing in obscurity as a singer-songwriter, playing low-key gigs in a hamburger restaurant in North London, where by chance one evening McLaren, Rhodes and Tommy Roberts were dining.[1] They offered to manage Scott, but he didn't think he was the right person for what they wanted to do: to use music to promote the ideas and clothes that they were developing, hand-in-hand. Robin Scott eventually found fame in 1979 under the name M, when his multimillion-selling single 'Pop Muzik' topped the charts all around the world.

One of the first lines of clothing that SEX became known for was its custom-made T-shirts, the most notable of these being designed in 1974–5 by combinations of McLaren, Westwood and Bernard Rhodes.[2] Rhodes and McLaren had known each other since the 1960s, and the former was already adept at producing screen-printed shirts. Like McLaren, Rhodes had some connections to the London music scene, had been a sixties mod and was friends with some well-known figures (he shared a flat for a time with Led Zeppelin's road manager, Richard Cole, and knew people in Marc Bolan's band T. Rex). But, also like McLaren, he was a small-time entrepreneur who had a stake in the DIY and second-hand rag trade that had risen with the proliferation of street markets and stall-holding in the early 1970s – the same culture that had provided the impetus for McLaren and Westwood establishing Let It Rock.

More important was the fact that Rhodes was, like McLaren and Westwood, buzzing with ideas and a sense of purpose that had yet to be suitably channelled. These ideas, as Neil Spencer wrote in a profile a few years later, 'were formed on the fringes of the rock culture, from the things the culture brushes [up against] in its giddy spin: art, style, bohemia, literature, protest, even folk music.'[3]

When Rhodes began collaborating on the T-shirts with McLaren and Westwood, he was operating a stall in Antiquarius, the

Bernard Rhodes in 1977, from the film *Punk in London*.

well-known and popular antiques market on the King's Road, selling leather jackets and custom-made shirts, and where he would 'play reggae on a little Dansette' record player as he tended his stall.[4] He even had 'a sideline doing repairs on Renault cars in the Railway Yard in Chalk Farm', and it was there under the railway arches in 1976 that he would find space for the band he had begun looking after, The Clash, to rehearse.[5] Reports have it that he even worked in Granny Takes a Trip, the King's Road's main outfitter to the rock stars of the late '60s, which catered to Keith Richards, the Faces and almost all the popular rock bands of the time. While Rhodes was later more well known as the manager of The Clash – who would turn out to be the Pistols' rivals – he played a crucial role in the development and formation of the Sex Pistols in 1974 and '75.

What was key to the relationship between Rhodes and McLaren, and to the emergence of the Sex Pistols, was that like McLaren and Westwood, Rhodes seemed to be on the lookout for a way of making an impact on culture in some way, a route into the popular arts, as he saw it, and rock music seemed to offer a way to do so. He wasn't necessarily a fan of the pop and rock music of the time, but he was fascinated with the idea of popular culture as a medium for transmitting ideas. He thought that the audience for this music – which had always been mainly young people – were smart enough to sense that something new was on the horizon, and the clothes, whether they were explicit or otherwise in conveying ideas, were one way to achieve his aims.

As they worked together on the clothing side of things, Rhodes and McLaren would have discussions about establishing a teenage pop group, like the Bay City Rollers (the country had recently been in the grip of 'Rollermania'), a vehicle for something more than just music, something maybe even revolutionary, that could be communicated through the immediacy of popular music. The power of popular music was precisely in its immediacy, because, McLaren and Rhodes thought, teenagers would just know when something was real or authentic without having to stop and analyse it. This ability to grasp pop in its immediacy was the reason successive generations of teenagers had been able to use clothes as the outward expression of a style and attitude. That fact alone was enough to convince McLaren and Rhodes that clothes could be a vehicle for something else. It wasn't that McLaren and Rhodes had a manifesto – they just wanted to shake things loose, to unleash a new wave of creativity among the young:

> We didn't have a rule book, and we were hoping that . . . I was thinking of what I got from Jackie Wilson's 'Reet Petite', which was the first record I bought. I didn't need anyone to describe what it was all about, I knew it; but I thought we were a little bit more articulate than that.[6]

In fact, Rhodes's first T-shirt to be sold in SEX in late 1974 might be said to have stood in lieu of a manifesto. Conceived with Vivienne Westwood – and true to the cottage industry-style origins of Let It Rock and SEX originals – it was seemingly screen-printed by Rhodes in his kitchen. As a conceptual gambit, this new T-shirt was executed, Jon Savage wrote, in a 'polarizing style that echoed the heated rhetoric of 1968, in which fathers are killed, contemporaries despatched, lone heroes rewarded in an incantation that, transcending nostalgia, brought the new age into being through an act of will'.[7]

Under the handwritten slogan, 'You're gonna wake up one morning and KNOW what side of the bed you've been lying on', it featured two dense lists that looked like they had been transferred from a typewriter. These ranged across art, culture, popular music and politics, and separated the field into those who were 'in' and those who were 'out' – over one hundred of them on each side of the divide. Somewhere nestling in the middle of the closely typed small print on the list of likes, among the familiar avatars of cool, appeared the strange name 'Kutie Jones and his SEX PISTOLS'. Jones, Cook and Matlock's group were taking shape as something that might be useful to the new purposes of the revamped shop. Chrissie Hynde, who was working at SEX at the time, remembered walking home with McLaren over the Albert Bridge to Clapham, with their discussions revolving more and more around popular music, and where things might be going.[8]

But whatever might be about to happen in London, it had to wait. In late 1974 McLaren moved to New York to help out the New York Dolls – whose early momentum had begun to fizzle out under the influence of various problems – and asked Bernard Rhodes to look after Kutie Jones and the Sex Pistols, to keep working with them and encouraging them to write their own songs. His experience in America contained many valuable lessons for what would follow with the Sex Pistols in a few years' time.

McLaren may or may not have been the New York Dolls' manager – they never signed any contracts with him, but he was certainly managing their affairs and finding them work – but whatever his role, it was carried out in the guise of a kindly benefactor looking out for their best interests. Sensing that their bad habits were going to spell the end for them, he began by sending members to rehab to tackle their various drug and booze problems. That the Dolls had failed to take off in the way that most people had expected following the buzz around them in 1972 was baffling – but then again, they had always divided opinion. So much so, in fact, that in one year they were voted both the best *and* the worst band in *Creem* magazine's annual reader's poll.[9] If being good at being bad was what it was all about, then the Dolls were still the best.

McLaren's recent reinventions of the shop back in London made him more aware than the members of the New York Dolls of the dangers of standing still: there had now been two incarnations of his shop since he had first met the Dolls in 1972, but the band was still on the same shtick. He thought it was time that they underwent their own transformation, overhauled their look and came up with some new material. So using his own money – and by some (probably mythical) accounts, cleaning windows to earn cash to support them – McLaren found the Dolls somewhere to rehearse, and set about booking dates for the band. As Dolls biographer Nina Antonia puts it: much 'like Professor Higgins in *My Fair Lady*, McLaren set about rehabilitating the Dolls.'[10]

His main contribution might well have been to save the lives of a couple of band members. David Johansen, who was much more willing to listen to McLaren's ideas than some other members of the group, once said that Malcolm had been their 'haberdasher' – a reference not only to the fact that McLaren was in the clothes business, but to the drastic image makeover that he had prescribed as a way to erase the Dolls' existing look. Being dubbed 'fag rock' and 'transsexual scum' – and described in other, less kindly terms – had not helped them to reach the masses in the way that their botched rescue mission to save rock 'n' roll had deserved. McLaren's idea was to establish an entirely new image, and an idea, that he hoped would finally get the attention of an American public who had so far refused to take notice of the Dolls. Unfortunately – or, perhaps, precisely in line with McLaren's gift for being bad – his choice to drape the band in red leathers and adorn their stage with hammer-and-sickle Communist flags struck too many as simply baffling. It made them look like 'the rent boy division of the Chinese Red Guard', but it was a look that was in tune with a new song, titled 'Red Patent Leather', which had been written by David

WHAT ARE THE POLITICS OF BOREDOM?   BETTER RED THAN DEAD.

Contrary to the vicious lies from the offices of Leber, Krebs and Thau, our former "paper tiger" management, the New York Dolls have not disbanded, and after having completed the first Red, 3-D Rock N' Roll movie entitled "Trash" have, in fact, assumed the role of the "Peoples' Information Collective" in direct association with the Red Guard.

This incarnation entitled "Red Patent Leather" will commence on Friday, February 28th at 10 P.M. continuing on Saturday at 9 and 11 P.M. followed by a Sunday matinee at 5 P.M. for our high school friends at The Little Hippodrome--227 E. 56th St. between 2nd and 3rd.

This show is in coordination with The Dolls' very special "entente cordiale" with the Peoples Republic of China.

                         NEW YORK DOLLS
              produced by Sex originals of London
                      c/o Malcolm McLaren
                       New York--212-675-0855
                        all rights reserved

An early 1975 press release for the New York Dolls by Malcolm McLaren.

Johansen and Syl Sylvain before McLaren had even shown up in New York.[11] He had simply taken an idea that they didn't know they had and, through the filter of his seditious imagination, had brought it to life in a way that never would have occurred to the Dolls. The change was publicly announced in a press release that appeared under the heading 'What Are the Politics of Boredom? Better Red Than Dead', and signed 'The New York Dolls, produced by Sex originals of London, c/o Malcolm McLaren'.

In an attempt to further enhance the communist ambience, the tables in the Little Hippodrome were 'draped in red fabric' and Malcolm had requested that 'every drink that was sold while the Dolls were appearing should have an injection of red dye.'[12] Thinking that McLaren and the Dolls had totally lost the plot, the New York music cognoscenti, led by influential rock columnist Lisa Robinson, shunned the new Dolls – this despite the band putting on what some witnesses regarded as their best shows in these early appearances under the red flag. 'The red leather stuff that Malcolm presided over', said Blondie's Chris Stein, 'was the best they ever were.'[13] Others, like Richard Hell, who was fronting a new band called Television that opened for the Dolls at those Little Hippodrome shows, appreciated McLaren's style and the humour of the communist scam, but was only too aware of the double misfortune that would likely, in all truth, strike the hapless Dolls. With all the rhetoric, the red patent leather outfits and the communist paraphernalia, it was likely to signal to the public that the Dolls 'were not only fags but Commies' as well:

> I was deeply impressed, but not many other people were. I mean it was obvious that the guy'd misread American psychology, but it was a fantastic gesture anyway, like a perfect suicide note or famous last words. The Dolls went down defiant, and leaving a good-looking corpse.[14]

While he was trying to keep the New York Dolls alive, McLaren was quick to notice what was going on around them in New York. By early 1975 a new scene, partly inspired by the opening made by the Dolls' trash-rock – but also distinctly removed from it, in its looks and posture – was beginning to emerge. New bands like Television, Blondie and the Ramones, as well as Patti Smith, had made their debuts in 1974 at a number of New York clubs. During the Dolls' 1975 shows at the Little Hippodrome, McLaren, according to one observer, seemed to 'spend most of his time backstage in earnest conversation with the bass player of the support act, Richard Hell of Television.'[15]

McLaren first spotted Hell performing on-stage at CBGB, the dive club in the city's Bowery district that hosted most of the New York punk bands that began appearing in 1975. The singer/bassist was dressed in a way that immediately connected with McLaren's understanding of how the visual side of rock 'n' roll, as much as the music, defined a position. The right look could catapult the one who was bold enough to be different into a new space with new possibilities. The clothes Richard Hell wore were not only reminiscent of some of the ripped shirts and holed clothing that McLaren and Westwood had been making, but his entire presence ensured that he came across as an instant icon. He had become known for wearing a T-shirt emblazoned with the words 'Please Kill Me'. And, for McLaren, his attitude was deeply artistic, expressing in its own way a deeper aesthetic awareness of the possibilities of rock 'n' roll. He arrived at his hairstyle, which was the first recognizable example of what would later be understood as the punk look, after a great deal of consideration over what it was about rock 'n' roll haircuts – those of The Beatles, for instance – that made them work, what gave them an effect that was almost as powerful as the music. 'My conclusion,' Hell said:

Richard Hell, pictured c. 1974.

was that it is grown men more or less wearing haircuts that five year olds of their generation wore. What kind of haircut, I thought, did I have when I was five or six? All the kids I grew up with had a kind of crew cut called burrs. It was a ship-to-shore crew cut that grew out because you didn't go to the barber that often and it all became ragged. That's the way I remember coming up with it.[16]

This was an idea of an almost ungraspable attachment to some remnant of youth. In those dog days, when rock 'n' roll had drifted far from its outlaw origins, it was something that was exceptionally potent. 'He had on this perfectly groomed, torn, holed T-shirt,' McLaren remembered, much like the shirts and blouses he had ripped and defaced back in London and tried to sell in New York at the National Boutique Show in August 1973:

> His head was down, he never looked up. He sang this song, 'Blank Generation', his hair was spiked, he had a kind of nihilistic air. He looked contemporary to me, he looked everything that rock 'n' roll wasn't. He had a poetry about him. He, for me, was very creative, he really was art and I thought, that's exactly who I want to sell in my store, that icon.[17]

Richard Hell, McLaren recognized – and Hell himself knew it – represented something different; something that had taken inspiration from the New York Dolls, but moved it in a new direction.

Despite the challenge that the Dolls' 'quasi-effeminate glam' had posed for audiences, they still represented the continuation – even if it was ironically – of the idea of the rock 'n' roll star. For all their street-level subject matter, they looked glamorous, something that Richard Hell, in songs like 'Blank Generation', had decisively moved away from.[18] His songs were cut through with 'alienation and disgust and anger', qualities that were expressed as much in looks and demeanour as in words and actions.[19] His band, Television, like the Sex Pistols to come – and punk in Britain more generally later on – rejected anything that smacked of glamour or that could be construed as encouraging star worship. When the Pistols' Steve Jones appeared on-stage with his speaker cabinet bearing the scratched and ironic legend 'Guitar Hero', and Johnny Rotten appeared on-stage with a shirt that declaimed with equal irony 'True Star', it was echoing the same contempt for audience expectations that Hell had already expressed – whether or not the audience was aware of the New York antecedents is beside the point.

McLaren made a play for Richard Hell, and told him that if he left Television he would help him in any way he could. He wanted to take Richard Hell back to London and build a band around him in surroundings that were more conducive to projecting the look and attitude he had perfected in New York, and where his songs and their explorations of boredom and apathy might have a real impact on popular music, and on young people across the country. The New York scene was really going nowhere – a landlocked island in the vast United States whose rumblings of a musical revolution had no real way of reaching beyond a small audience and, as a result, could gain little traction with the record companies. London, McLaren knew, was altogether different, and things could happen much more quickly due to how small it was. The British weekly music press also exerted considerable influence in charting what was up and coming, and communicating it to a national audience in a way that was entirely absent in the United States. Richard Hell opted to leave Television but stay in New York, where a year or so later he would form The Heartbreakers with ex-New York Dolls members (and, by then, fellow junkies) Johnny Thunders and Jerry Nolan. In late 1976 The Heartbreakers, minus Richard Hell, who had started his Voidoids by then, would meet with McLaren again, when they joined the Sex Pistols on the chaotic 'Anarchy' tour in late 1976.

That was all still some way off in the future, however, when McLaren returned from New York in May 1975. He landed back in London with renewed purpose, and put up posters and newspaper clippings about Television and Richard Hell on the walls of SEX. This, McLaren thought, transformed the shop into 'a sort of information centre' for visiting teenagers, lending it 'a kind of magic because it was different from all these other shops'.[20] Richard Hell was a perfect embodiment of the kind of romantic, destructive, rule-breaking attitude that McLaren had been so taken with when he had first fallen in love with rock 'n' roll, but which by the mid-1970s seemed to have vanished as a real force. Richard Hell, like McLaren, knew you had to hurtle into the future without thinking too much about it – to keep it simple and direct. 'One thing I wanted to bring back to rock 'n' roll', he said, 'was the knowledge that you invent yourself. That's why I changed my name, [it's] why I did all the clothing style things, haircut, everything.'[21]

Aside from a few exceptions, popular music in the early 1970s remained wedded to the 1960s generation, insofar as most of the performers who were still around and elevated to positions of respect in the rock world had been of that decade. But by the mid-1970s they were, McLaren thought, pretty ludicrous; like the 'aristocracy in armchairs', existing as part of some elite club that had gone unchallenged in its determination to stick it out for the long run.[22] Even The Rolling Stones, scourge of the establishment less than a decade before, had, in virtue of their wealth and exile abroad, become jet-setting figures who seemed remote from the concerns of the youth of the '70s. The triumph of what McLaren regarded as hippy culture – which was taken over by the music business once it saw the profitability of the emerging lifestyle – negated the influence of small-time operators and entrepreneurs, spivs even, who had been the pioneers that helped find the key to unlock the anger and passion of the buttoned-up English in the 1950s. Since the days of Andrew Loog Oldham (manager and producer of The Rolling Stones) and Kit Lambert (manager of The Who), there had been no one involved in promoting popular music who held to the view that 'chaos and disruption' were good things in an industry that was now obviously 'too self-satisfied'.[23]

It wasn't simply a matter of setting up four guys in a band and standing them up on-stage – it had to be the right people, with a demeanour and purpose that would catapult them out of the present and into the future.

*

The New York Dolls, for McLaren, came to an end in Florida after a run of dates out in the sticks, living a life on the road for most of March 1975 that was far from the kind of routine the New Yorkers were used to. On top of the problem of being away from their usual haunts and the buzz of urban nightlife, the fact was that 'outside New York, the band was anathema.' That was the summation of their de facto obituary in the New York Times, which added that, 'Out-of-towners found their music primitive and un-original and the image disgusting and irrelevant.'[24]

McLaren and Sylvain took a long and leisurely route back to New York, buying a car and driving via New Orleans (despite the fact that neither of them held a driving licence). As much as he wanted to stay and hang around the New York CBGB scene, McLaren knew he was going to have to go back to London and the shop; he was running out of money, and was finally forced into selling clothes out of the back of his car to raise funds for the plane ticket home. Johnny Thunders's girlfriend had told McLaren to pull up at a place on 13th Street and that he would find some buyers there. Debbie Harry, later to find fame with Blondie, went to look at what was happening, and there was McLaren, 'pulling out these rubber dresses and platform shoes and selling them on the street. And everybody was running down to the street to buy this stuff.'[25]

When Malcolm McLaren returned to London in May 1975, Steve Jones and Paul Cook met him at Heathrow. After trying, and failing, to pull the New York Dolls out of their death spiral, he was determined to try and make something of the opportunity the group of Jones, Cook and Matlock presented, and he was curious as to how they had been faring under the influence of Bernard Rhodes. Sylvain, McLaren thought, should come back to London and front the group who had been hanging around his shop. So McLaren headed back to London with Sylvain's guitar and a Fender Rhodes keyboard, with the intention of sending him a ticket to come to London once he was able to raise some cash. In the end, though, fearing that he would have to teach these London kids everything, Sylvain decided instead to go to Japan with a partially reconstituted New York Dolls.[26]

By 1975 Steve Jones had been hanging around 430 King's Road so much that he was soon acting as an ad hoc assistant and driver for McLaren.[27] Using Vivienne Westwood's Mini car, Jones and McLaren would drive around London making deliveries and sourcing fabrics for the clothes they were beginning to make more determinedly, and now with a renewed sense of political purpose.[28] These would supplement the stock that they had been selling to Teddy boys and King's Road boutique shoppers, although the shop continued to have Let It Rock items for sale, either in their original form or adapted to the shop's new theme. (Black 'Vive Le Rock' or Jerry Lee Lewis knickers, for example, were made of material that was recycled from unsold T-shirts from the Let It Rock days.)[29]

As Jon Savage has put it, the changes made to 430 King's Road were also part of a desire to 'get rid of an unwanted clientele by changing [the] shop's name, design and attitude'.[30] But in turning away from what they had established, there were more specific goals involved in the change from Too Fast to Live, Too Young to Die to SEX, reflecting a renewed understanding of what the role and purpose of their shop ought to be. In fact, these were expounded upon publicly by both McLaren and Westwood in interviews that they gave to softcore adult magazines soon after SEX opened.

While they would always rely on the commercial appeal of the clothes and accessories they sold to provide a regular flow of customers, the revamped shop was now more than ever conceptualized for definite cultural and political ends. In one illustration of how they reached beyond conventional sources for ideas, McLaren and Rhodes tried to persuade the anti-psychiatrist R. D. Laing, who had latterly written about the role of the family in repressing playful instincts and creating a 'one-dimensional conformity', to design some clothes for them.[31]

But the stress was firmly on the idea of the liberating possibilities of sex, and on quality and attention to detail in materials not usually associated with everyday wear, in order to create a new kind of person, from the outside in, through the clothes they wore. Clothing styles and habits, of course, are forms of what the British social anthropologist Paul Connerton termed 'incorporated memory': they are woven into everyday life in ways that may be all but imperceptible to us. What people wear has always reflected deeply held cultural attitudes and, often, the outward appearance of social hierarchies. Following the French Revolution of 1789, for example, new fashions gave rise to the feeling of a 'heady release' from previous social constraints and entrenched positions as people tried to 'mark out the boundaries of a radical beginning'.[32] In the 1970s, as in the aftermath of the French Revolution, the sign that some deeper sociocultural tectonic shift was taking place would be manifested in new ways of dressing, new styles and new materials, all of which would be identified as elements of a punk style and aesthetic.

Some of the rubber goods sold in SEX were 'made from fine and dainty shades of a thin, thin rubber' that looked as alluring as silk.[33] Sometimes these clothes were modelled by the already spectacular-looking Westwood, who sometimes dressed up for customers to demonstrate a particular look – 'I thought I looked like a princess from another planet . . . intergalactic,' she said years later.[34] In a series of very rare photographs from early 1975 she is pictured in a full-body diaphanous 'Rubber Johnny' bodysuit, made from exceptionally thin material that both reveals the body beneath and gives Westwood the appearance of an otherworldly being, an effect that is only heightened by her shock of blond hair – later recognizably 'punk' in style.[35] 'Her hair [was] dyed white blonde, with an inch of dark roots showing and clumpy spikes sticking out in all directions,' recalled Viv Albertine, the Slits guitarist. 'I have no idea where she got the look from, it doesn't reference anything I'm aware of, no films or art.'[36]

The hair, Westwood intimates in her autobiography, was styled by McLaren: 'the rubber short skirts, and the haircut by Malcolm, not hairsprayed or gelled. It was astonishing to look at.'[37] Almost everyone who encountered Westwood in those days was struck by how unique she looked, and she was aware of her ability to stop the traffic on the King's Road. Chrissie Hynde, too, remembered arriving in England in 1974 and meeting McLaren and Westwood, two people unlike anyone else she had ever met, and recalled how Vivienne looked like nobody else: 'Walking down the street with her, I knew what Colonel Tom Parker must have felt like walking next to Elvis.'[38] McLaren was perhaps less unique looking, but still unlike the other men around at the time:

Malcolm, too, had his own look, totally original and subtle – but you noticed: curly ginger hair, pale and sensitive looking, with an inquisitive, almost pervy expression of wonder. You knew this guy didn't play sports. It was all about the clothes; the clothes did the talking. If you saw Malcolm in any police lineup in the world you would say, 'Nope, I'd definitely remember him!'[39]

As far as the search for a singer for the group was concerned, a memorable face or look was all-important. What was required was a look that could stop people in their tracks. Everyone around the nascent Sex Pistols was on the lookout for a young man with a certain style and attitude that marked him out from the flop-haired, bell-bottom-wearing youth of the day. The faces of customers in the shop at 430 King's Road and out on the streets were eyed-up for potential. In Glasgow, on a trip looking for old clothing materials, Rhodes and McLaren had been persuaded to take along some of the group's stolen musical equipment to offload far from the scene of the crime. It was as they pulled up to a music store on Bath Street that they spotted a young man with a James Dean-style haircut and straight-leg trousers – a look they thought probably indicative of someone willing to buck convention. Rhodes shouted him over from the car and asked him if he was a musician, and McLaren 'started wittering on about the New York Dolls'. The young guy with the James Dean hair was Midge Ure, later vocalist for Ultravox. He already had a group in Glasgow at the time named Slik, soon-to-be one-hit-wonder teenyboppers in the Bay City Rollers mould, who topped the British charts in January 1976.

If he was not the singer they were looking for it was no great loss; they had travelled to Glasgow to sell some guitars and amps anyway. The back of the car contained a stash of equipment whose prices were so low Ure knew right away they must have been stolen; he took the plunge for a Fender amp, probably worth £200, but which McLaren and Rhodes sportingly sold him for a mere £40.[40]

Back in London the group had trialled a couple of singers, but nothing was working out. Then one day Rhodes spotted a badly dressed street urchin with a style all of his own, improvised from clothes that seemed to have been attacked with a razor blade, defaced with slogans, and put back together with safety pins. He wore a Pink Floyd T-shirt that had the words 'I HATE' carefully inscribed above the band's name. His hair was wild and unusual, and reminiscent of the kind of spiky crop Richard Hell wore. The guy was John Lydon. Some accounts say that Steve Jones had spotted Lydon around the shop some time before Rhodes finally caught him on the King's Road, and that Jones had told McLaren to look out for a guy with green hair who looked exactly right for the group.[41] Now that he had found Lydon, Rhodes arranged to meet him later that night in the Roebuck pub on King's Road with McLaren and the members of the group. When he got to the pub, Lydon later recalled, McLaren asked him if he wanted to be in a band with the three other guys – Jones, Cook and Matlock – who were sitting around a table having a drink. He thought it was some kind of joke, a set-up, but he sat there for a while trading insults with the others, until Rhodes eventually asked him to come back to the shop to sing along or mime to a song on the jukebox. Lydon chose Alice Cooper's 'Eighteen', the only song on the jukebox he knew. 'He stood there, shouting and flapping his arms around,' Glen Matlock remembered. 'He was Johnny Rotten from that very first moment.'[42]

McLaren, struck by the stylistic similarity between Lydon and Richard Hell, was convinced that he had what they were looking for. He made the decision, announced, 'He's the one,' and informed the other three that they had to try him out as the singer. Lydon remembers the others being a bit bemused by the situation:

Paul thought it was a joke and couldn't have cared less. Steve was really annoyed because he instantly hated me. 'I can't work with that fucking cunt! All he does is take the piss and moan!'[43]

Vivienne Westwood, Johnny Rotten and Jordan, 1976.

Since they had got rid of Nightingale they had to find somewhere new to rehearse, settling temporarily on an old warehouse that was serving as a community centre in Rotherhithe, right in the midst of London's near-abandoned docks. One sunny afternoon in September a film student named Julien Temple was wandering around the Docklands when the sound of a band mauling the Small Faces number 'Whatcha Gonna Do About It', carried on the wind, roused his curiosity. As he started walking towards the sound, he realized that instead of the declaration of love that he was familiar with, this singer was yowling the opposite – 'massacring the song':

> I wantcha to know that I HATE you baby
> I wantcha to know I don't care

Temple reached an old warehouse and walked in through the open doors, and there they were:

> silhouetted against this huge window as they were playing, and it was like seeing some weird mutant insect-men from outer space. They had tiny skinny legs, with these crepe-soled shoes and black-and-red-striped mohair sweaters on, and this weird cropped, spiky hair. I knew at that moment that I was looking at something truly extraordinary.[44]

Thinking that he'd 'seen the future' right there and then, he asked the band if he could film them. 'Fuck off, you middle-class cunt,' was their initial response, before letting on that they were playing their first show soon, and if he wanted to come along it was his choice.[45] Despite missing that gig, Temple would, in due time, become an archivist of sorts, documenting not only the Pistols but much of what was going on in London and the music scene

Sex Pistols: Steve Jones, Paul Cook, Johnny Rotten and Glen Matlock, Leicester Square, 1976.

during that time. The group, whose name had been shortened to the Sex Pistols with the arrival of John Lydon, were rapidly getting better and developing a live set consisting of a mixture of new material and carefully chosen cover songs. One of Lydon's first songs – later recorded as 'Seventeen' – was confirmation for McLaren that the Sex Pistols had found their voice, and he told anyone he could find that the boy was a genius. 'He came in the other day with the lyrics to a song he'd just written,' he said to a bemused Nick Kent on Charing Cross Road one day in October 1975. 'The title's "You're Only Twenty-Nine, You've Got a Lot to Learn". Absolutely bloody brilliant.'[46]

*

McLaren and Westwood's shop at 430 King's Road became an important influence on the style and attitudes of numerous young people who would become key figures in the London punk scene. Vivienne Westwood and Jordan, an iconic presence in SEX, were inspirational figures for young women who were looking for a new kind of role model. In a recent memoir, Viv Albertine of The Slits recalled the impact that the fearless Jordan made on her:

> Sometimes Jordan doesn't wear a skirt, just fishnet tights or stockings, high-waisted satin knickers, a leather or rubber bodice and bondage shoes. She paints two black slashes across her eyelids, looks like a robber's mask, a cross between Zorro and Catwoman, her face is dusted with white face powder and her lips are pillar-box red. Her hair is piled high, ash blonde and sculpted into a huge wave dipping down over one eye. Jordan

Jordan in Derek Jarman's *Sebastiane* (1976).

travels on the train from Sussex all the way into London dressed like this. Every day. She doesn't go into the loos at Charing Cross Station and change her clothes once she's arrived. Her attitude filters through to all of us. You have to live it.[47]

Jordan was one of the many important elements that went into establishing the identity of SEX, and she appeared in the contemporary photo spreads accompanying the interviews that McLaren and Westwood gave. If her example was to show how to carry off the transformation into a new kind of person, it made her the living embodiment of what McLaren and Westwood were aiming for when they refashioned the shop. As Westwood – the one-time teacher, now with little silver penises often dangling from her ears – would say, 'we're not here merely to sell sex toys and fetish clothing, but to convert, educate, and liberate.'[48] In the words of one contemporary profile, SEX took form not merely as a commercial enterprise, but as 'an apparently heterogeneous collection of images that . . . form in McLaren's mind a definite artistic statement.'[49] These were the words of David May, a writer for the soft porn magazine *Gallery International*. He introduced Malcolm McLaren to his readers as:

> a mixture of entrepreneurial cultist, sexual evangelist, business-man, artist, fetishist and political philosopher; a psychotic visionary in the ephemeral sub-culture of the fashion world.[50]

The kind of items that McLaren and Westwood were now selling – rubber and leather clothes, fetish wear, and their own line of T-shirt designs and bondage outfits that later became associated with punk – had previously only been found in the sex shops of Soho. But they wanted to make wearing the sort of clothes that sexual fetishists donned in private much more commonplace, and to liberate society from its antiquated and repressive attitude towards sexuality – rubber wear for the street and the office, as detailed in a feature that ran in another soft porn magazine, *Forum*, in June 1976:

> SEX now displays an amazing variety of 'hip' sex gear including rubber and leather fetish clothing: high-heeled boots, rubber panties, leather bras, leather wrist and ankle restraints ('Bound to please'), rubber mini-skirts (for £12). T-shirts with a page from a porno novel written across the front (for £4), a genuine 'dirty old man' raincoat (£25), and six different styles of rubber masks and hoods (£20–£50).[51]

We might wonder how McLaren and Westwood made the leap from selling Teddy boy clothes and 1950s revivalist styles into this milieu. The key was the idea of making what had been private fetish clothing into something that might be worn in day-to-day life (although they did also cater for those specifically interested in clothes for sexual purposes – only a fool, it seems, would walk down the street wearing an inflatable rubber mask designed to simulate asphyxiation). It has been suggested that SEX turned 'S&M gear into deviant fashion, removing it from the privacy of the bedroom and flaunting it in a juvenile "Up yours!" manner in the streets.'[52]

They were influenced, as McLaren acknowledged in interviews at the time, by the ideas of Wilhelm Reich, which dated from the 1930s and were found in books such as *The Function of the Orgasm* and *The Mass Psychology of Fascism*. Reich, who coined the term 'sexual revolution', believed that there could be no social and political freedom without sexual liberation.[53] Reich's ideas had undergone a revival of sorts through the work of authors such as Herbert Marcuse, popular in the 1960s and '70s, who sought to fuse the insights of Freud with Marxist revolutionary analyses.[54]

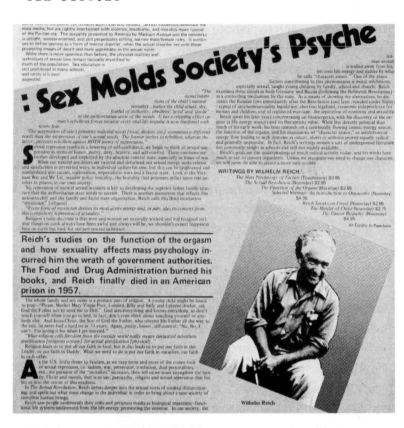

: **Sex Molds Society's Psyche**

Reich's studies on the function of the orgasm and how sexuality affects mass psychology incurred him the wrath of government authorities. The Food and Drug Administration burned his books, and Reich finally died in an American prison in 1957.

Wilhelm Reich

'Sex Molds Society's Psyche': Wilhelm Reich's influence reached a peak in the late 1960s and early '70s.

The political temper of the times made Reich's essential idea – 'better living through orgasms' – hugely appealing to the post-sexual revolution generation.[55] When the American *Rolling Stone* journalist Charles M. Young visited McLaren and Westwood in summer 1977 for a story on the Sex Pistols – a quest on his part to try and understand this seemingly alien phenomenon that was erupting in London, spearheaded by the Pistols – he was partly trying to get inside McLaren's head to find out what made him tick. In passing, he noted that alongside the rock 'n' roll albums that were visible in the McLaren-Westwood home sat books by de Sade and Wilhelm Reich.[56]

It is not unusual, given the nature of their business – and the early 1970s transformation of the '60s idea of sexual revolution into something more politically charged – that Reich, in particular, would exercise an influence. His 'advocacy of a revolutionary approach to sexuality, and his early politicization of sex, struck a chord with the developing counter-culture'.[57] From the events of Paris in May 1968, where the Reich-influenced slogan 'A revolution that expects you to sacrifice yourself for it is one of daddy's revolutions' circulated alongside the kind of Situationist slogans later employed by McLaren and Westwood ('Under the paving stones, the beach' was daubed on the wall inside SEX), to the rise in radical and alternative ways of escaping patriarchal morality, Reich's ideas became part of the consciousness of revolutionary thinking. This included many of the communal living experiments then springing up in London – most of which, of course, were symbolic of the rejection of bourgeois family values.[58] Figures like Reich and Marcuse (who drew on Reich's linking of sexual and social issues) advocated a new kind of political freedom that was rooted in the liberation of desire, and were briefly very prominent and influential.[59]

Reich's orgone accumulator, a device for allowing people to absorb the vital life energy he termed 'orgone', was parodied as an Orgasmatron in Woody Allen's futuristic comedy *Sleeper* (1973), due to its known sexual effects and probably Reich's ideas about the importance of orgasm. It also preoccupied writers such as William Burroughs in the 1940s and '50s, whose interest in it was described in Kerouac's *On the Road* (the character of Bull Lee was based on Burroughs). Burroughs built his own orgone accumulator based on Reich's plans and writings (which were later destroyed by the US Federal authorities).[60] The space rockers Hawkwind, who were practically the house band of the North London hippy communes and squats of the early to mid-1970s, even celebrated Reich's most notorious idea, of the revolutionary potential of the orgasm, in the fantastically sprawling 'Orgone Accumulator' (1975), a song that throbs and pulses ecstatically for ten minutes like a soundtrack to one of J. G. Ballard's near-future dystopias.

It was no accident that the ideas of Wilhelm Reich were enjoying a revival at the same time that the ideas of the French Situationists were attracting interest in light of the publication of two books in 1967: Guy Debord's *The Society of the Spectacle* and Raoul Vaneigem's *The Revolution of Everyday Life*. Reich was, in fact, one of a few thinkers whose ideas were considered acceptable by the Situationists. His work was discussed approvingly in Vaneigem's *The Revolution of Everyday Life*, particularly in recognition of the Reichian view that 'oppression' rules everyday life in modern societies because we have internalized the patriarchal structure – which he thought to be particularly oppressive – through the promotion of family values. Reich's work, Vaneigem thought, suggested that 'humans are divided not among themselves but also within themselves' insofar as patriarchal attitudes had to be overcome to arrive at a condition of social and personal freedom.[61] Aside from the brief discussions in *The Revolution of Everyday Life*, and the echoes of Reichian theories of the necessity of anger in Vaneigem's slogan 'Scream, Steal, Ejaculate Your Desires', there is little direct reference to Reich in the work of the Situationists, although as one recent observer notes, there are 'numerous parallels between their political philosophies'.[62]

Reich advocated anger as a remedy for repression: for circum-venting, or breaking down, the rigid structure of the internalized authoritarian character, thus 'provoking explosions of anger in neurotics' who had been constrained by 'emotional blocks and muscular arming.[63] The latter term was sometimes translated as 'body armour', which was Reich's idea of how one might conceptualize the neurotic equilibrium that has to be maintained in order to inhibit the orgasmic reflex.[64] It is interesting to speculate as to the influence of the 1971 Dušan Makavejev film *W.R.: Mysteries of the Organism* – an exploration of the revolutionary political potential of Reich's ideas – which chimed with the radical political experiments in living at the time.[65] In it, we see the figure of Tuli Kupferberg, an American countercultural devotee of Reich and founder of the band The Fugs, who wanders around the streets of Manhattan brandishing a toy gun at passers-by, but with which he simulates masturbation rather than gunfire – making him, perhaps, the original 'sex pistol'.

McLaren thought that if the ideas expounded upon by Reich were taken more seriously, then what he and Westwood were doing with SEX 'would appear to be very ordinary'.[66] The fact that it was not ordinary merely demonstrated that Reich's ideas, like those of the Situationists, were mostly confined to the fringe elements in society. Other advocates of similar ideas, such as the publishers of a magazine named *Libertine* who described themselves as sexual anarchists, were repeatedly raided by police who confiscated copies of the publication, yet still thought that defeating this kind of censorship could only go so far. 'In England', they wrote in a 1976 issue of *International Times*:

> Self-censorship is the strongest and commonest form of control. It is made possible by the maintenance of repressive attitudes and upbringing by fearful parents . . . schoolkids have no means of self-expression other than violence.[67]

The challenge for the McLaren-Westwood idea was to make the confrontation, the explosion of anger, something that impacted directly on the popular consciousness, without political manifestos, and engaging young people in the way that only popular culture could – at the level of pure instinct. One of the young teenagers who did feel it was Poly Styrene, whose band X-Ray Spex would in 1977 release one of the few songs – 'Oh Bondage! Up Yours!' – that embraced the liberating potential of what she saw in the King's Road shop. The bondage clothing 'sparked a flow of images: of Suffragettes chained to the railings of Buckingham Palace, and of David Bowie's "Suffragette City"; scenes from the film *Moses*; pictures of African slaves, chained and shackled; the arguments in Wilhelm Reich's *Sexual Revolution*', all of which 'combined to create her punk anthem'.[68]

In 1976, though, it seemed that there were many older customers who viewed SEX as merely a kinky boutique for fetish clothing; they saw Westwood parading around among the fetish wear in one of the shop's shirts featuring a Situationist slogan across the breast – 'Be Reasonable, Demand the Impossible' – and would usually misunderstand the sentiment. They read the slogan instead as a signal hinting at some further unknown sadomasochistic region they had yet to discover – they thought that 'the impossible', whatever it referred to, 'must be the ultimate kink, and they're missing out', Westwood told *Forum* magazine.[69] SEX, however, was just McLaren's latest attempt to find a way into the popular consciousness through youth culture, and he appropriated the slogans of the Situationists according to his belief that to make anything was to plagiarize – and what he did was selectively plagiarize ideas and materials, like a Dadaist artist who had turned to scandal-mongering.

During those days when SEX was establishing itself as a specialist outlet for kinky S&M wear among an older group of customers, it was also attracting new, younger, visitors, who could be seen walking up and down the King's Road dressed in

these odd-looking new clothes. The rock writer Nik Cohn, who
lived in an upstairs flat next door to the shop, recalled that his
young daughter would sit for hours at the window, captivated by
the sight of these alien-looking life forms as they sauntered up
and down the road with their shabby clothes and coloured hair,
parading in and out of the shop – 'There's another one! There's
another one!' she would say.[70]

*

From around September 1975, soon after Rotten had joined
the group, the Sex Pistols had enjoyed the luxury of their own
studio, a neglected and rundown property hidden behind a
Greek bookshop in the centre of London's Tin Pan Alley. This, in
many respects, was the heart of London's music world. The Pistols
entered it as a gang of raw, determined teenagers (Jones, the
oldest by a year, had just turned twenty), but it didn't take long
for them to become an irritant to their new neighbours.

Along the short and narrow thoroughfare of Denmark Street,
which lay just across Charing Cross Road from the streets of Soho,
the British music industry had established its home over the
course of the twentieth century. At street level, cafés and musical
instrument suppliers competed for the attention of visitors and
local music industry denizens alike. The alluring window displays
of desirable guitars and other musical instruments had been eye-
candy for generations of aspiring stars – people like Ray Davies,
David Bowie and Bryan Ferry – who had been drawn to Tin Pan
Alley to find publishers for their songs, or to try and catch the
eye of record company people passing time in the Giaconda (a
local café that was one of the main music business hangouts for
people who worked in the area) or the Tin Pan Alley Club next
door. If the Pistols knew anything about music history, they might

have been aware that nearby at number 4 Denmark Street, The Rolling Stones had recorded their first album in Regent Sounds Studio in 1964. A few yards down the street above a shop was another studio, Central Sound, where David Bowie had cut demos with his band The Lower Third ten years earlier.

The music stores of Denmark Street had been well known to Steve Jones in the past, as he had set about accumulating expensive musical instruments without paying for them. He had scouted these shop windows for their potential bounty on numerous occasions. Many years later, revisiting the street with a film crew, Jones explained a sure-fire method of acquiring new instruments from the generous Tin Pan Alley window displays as he outlined his smash-and-grab philosophy: 'You just get a brick and go WALLOP.'[71]

While the teenage Jones had gone, in the words of Nick Kent, 'from strength to strength as a thief, cat-burgling his way around London' and had developed the ability to make himself invisible once he assumed the guise of burglar, he had nonetheless still managed to acquire a long list of convictions, long before he turned his attention to making music.[72] In fact, he had been caught red-handed during one window display smash-and-grab raid around 1972. This time the target was a hi-fi store. Jones

WHIZZ KID
GUITARIST
Not older than 20
Not worse looking than Johnny
Thunders
Auditioning:
TIN PAN ALLEY
Ring 351 0764, 673 0855

'Whizz Kid Guitarist'. Advert for a second Sex Pistols guitarist, *Melody Maker*, 27 September 1975.

had casually tossed a brick through a shop window, drunkenly shedding his seeming ability to thieve with relative impunity, and walked off with a radio; unfortunately, the police had just happened to be lurking nearby.[73]

While enterprising musicians and songwriters of a straighter cast had found an outlet for their talents and obsessions on Tin Pan Alley since the early twentieth century, it was really in the post-war years, with the rise of rock 'n' roll and the new pop industry, that Soho became a hub of the British pop music industry. This was the area where music publishers, instrument dealers, specialist record shops, the music press and other players in the industry all found a home. In many ways the concentration of expertise and opportunity in the area was all out of proportion to its size – so much was housed on this one tiny street – and while Denmark Street was part of the same milieu as Soho, it was probably just one side street too far off the beaten track for most visitors to London.

In the popular imagination – largely oblivious to what was going on in the cavernous courtyards behind the likes of 6 Denmark Street, home of the Sex Pistols – Soho was probably better known as London's red-light district, home to prostitutes, bohemians, artists and writers, along with that most English of entrepreneurs, the 'spiv' ('a man,' the Oxford English Dictionary tells us, 'typically characterized by flashy dress, who makes his living from disreputable dealings'). The spivs had established themselves in Soho's promising streets, cafés and bars, as 'small-time profiteers on the wartime black-market who found the neon blink of primitive coffee bars, Caribbean drinking dens and experimental jazz joints an agreeable sequel to the Blitz', which had itself seen a boom in opportunities for the kind of chancers who made their living as part of London's subterranean economy.[74]

Given the recent history of this part of London, as well as its importance as a bohemian enclave, a magnet for the music industry and for entrepreneurs who operated on the fringes of respectable society, there is probably no other place that would have provided a similar stimulus to the developing Sex Pistols, given McLaren's own view of how interwoven delinquency, crime and popular music were. According to several accounts, once he had decided to take more of an interest in the band, McLaren purchased both the lease on the Pistols' rehearsal studio in Denmark Street for a sum of around £1,000 and the Fender Rhodes electric keyboard that had belonged to the New York Dolls' Syl Sylvain, and which McLaren brought back from New York with him in May 1975 after his stint managing the Dolls came to an end.[75] The combination of cash and valuable musical instrument helped to seal a deal to give the band somewhere to continue developing a live set, working on original songs and the occasional cover version, so that they might have enough material to start gigging. At the same time, they were also still considering recruiting a second guitarist – 'not worse looking than Johnny Thunders' – and placed an advert in the music press late in September, not long after moving into Denmark Street. The studio had already been used for the same purposes by the band Badfinger – best known for their early 1970s Top Ten hit 'No Matter What' – but by summer 1975 their manager was keen to vacate the premises after the band folded.[76] The studio was in a state of disarray, as Glen Matlock wrote:

Inside there were two rooms, one on each floor, both the same size, about 20 feet by 15. It was small and poky, the carpet stank of sweat from all the bands that had rehearsed there over the years, the floor was rotten and covered with fungus. More unpleasant smells came from the toilet that didn't work and the leaking skylight which let in so much rain that the place was always damp.[77]

Some work was required to make it a space that the band would want to spend time in. McLaren asked Ben Kelly, a young interior designer who was just making a name for himself and who had been one of the shop's customers since the Let It Rock days, if he could refurbish the place just enough to make it liveable for a new group that he was looking after. The Pistols had yet to play any gigs, so this was the first time that Kelly had heard of something new stirring among the ranks of teenagers who were always hanging around the shop. 'When he told me that he had this group and they were called the Sex Pistols, I reeled back in horror,' he said. 'I couldn't believe what I had just heard.' It was a good sign for McLaren: even people who seemed beyond shock found that the name of the group was one that would not easily be forgotten – wait until they heard them play. Kelly was sent down to Denmark Street where a few of the band were already in residence, and his first sight of the location didn't make him feel any easier about what he was getting himself into:

> I walked through the narrow corridor to the back, where the premises were a complete mess, and the first thing I saw was some graffiti – 'Throbbing Gristle'. I thought, holy shit. I've heard about the Sex Pistols, and now there's something called Throbbing Gristle.[78]

Kelly did the most basic of refurbishments to the downstairs space using some fibreboard, which Rotten used as a canvas on which to display the seemingly bottomless reservoir of boredom that sustained his sarcastic enmity towards the world at large, etching on it caricatures of McLaren, Steve Jones and others.

Most of the doorways on Denmark Street led through to cavernous back courts, with further properties located out of sight of the public who frequented the bars and shops out

The Courtyard at 6 Denmark Street, London, pictured in 2016. The Sex Pistols studio occupied the two floors of this building.

Detail of the walls inside the Sex Pistols studio at 6 Denmark Street, 2016. The drawings on the wall, now protected by English Heritage, were made by Johnny Rotten in 1975-7.

front. Sharing a common point of entry at 6 Denmark Street meant that the Pistols rubbed up against representatives of the old music establishment – the passageway that led to their studio opened on to a space whose walls were plastered with 'musician wanted' ads, and entrances to a number of other studios engaged in various types of business. One of the other studios located at number 6 belonged to the much in-demand designers Hipgnosis, whose artwork had visually defined a certain kind of rock art conceptualism since the late 1960s. Their clients included some of the most successful performers of the era, including Pink Floyd, Paul McCartney and Led Zeppelin, and they designed some of the most recognizable album covers of the 1970s (not usually adorned with any identifying text). It wasn't long before the Hipgnosis designers and a few of their clients began to feel the presence of

the new disruptive element, whose behaviour seemed to
be strangely of a piece with the later graphical style that came
to represent them. The Pistols and some of their hangers-on,
a gaggle of irritating youths, managed to be noisy and uncouth
enough that they conveyed a sense of menace to the older and
more conservative occupants of the close. Aubrey Powell, one of
the men behind Hipgnosis, wrote later that it wasn't long before
he 'sensed a malignant attitude in McLaren's mission' to install
his band, the Sex Pistols, in the middle of Tin Pan Alley. Indeed,
it wasn't long before it began to feel like the Pistols, and what
they represented, 'were in, and we were out'.[79]

Even before they had achieved their initial media notoriety,
the Pistols were rubbing Hipgnosis staff and clients up the wrong
way. Hank Marvin of the Shadows – among the oldest and most
respectable of the original stars of British pop, then in his forties
– couldn't hide his irritation on one visit to the Hipgnosis studio
to consult on some album artwork, when the air of easy calm
that he associated with the place was broken by the sound of
continual gobbing coming from across the back court. It was
Sid Vicious, then unknown, but the Pistols' number-one fan,
hanging out of a window and spitting loudly towards the ground
a couple of floors below, and clearly marvelling at how this little
performance echoed in the space of the vaulted courtyard. 'I was
never to complain,' Powell said of his encounters with the Pistols,
'they looked too un-cool and dangerous.'[80]

4 The Bizarro Cabaret Begins

Denmark Street would turn out to be within the immediate proximity of the first official Sex Pistols gig. The show took place on Thursday 6 November 1975 at Saint Martin's School of Art on Charing Cross Road, right at the end of Denmark Street. Glen Matlock, who had completed an art foundation course at Saint Martin's that summer, was due to begin full-time study for a degree in fine art in Autumn 1975, but after some consideration of what the future might hold – would it be painting, or music? – he had withdrawn from the course. The band looked like it might go somewhere, so he had reasoned that full-time education would probably be a waste of time and effort. As it happened, however, he had been elected social secretary of the student union for the coming year before he had left, and so using his connections he managed to wangle a gig for the Pistols, opening for another London band who had been around a little longer – Bazooka Joe.[1] They were a rock 'n' roll revival band of sorts, with Roxy Music aspirations in the visual department, but still coming across to some as 'sub-Teddy Boys'.[2]

The Pistols hauled their equipment across the Charing Cross Road at rush hour, into Saint Martin's and up the stairs into a top-floor room, where the gig was taking place. They set up right in front of the crowd – there was no stage, which meant that the bands and audience were all on the same level. The student crowd were few in number, but were warmed thanks to the student union refreshments, with cheap wine being served at twenty pence a cup.[3] Malcolm McLaren, clad in peg-leg trousers

– outlandishly incongruous in those 1970s days of bell-bottom denims – was rushing around reminding the band to be bad. At this point they were all still young enough to be pushed and cajoled. While the audience wondered who this weirdo with the funny trousers was, he made sure to ply the band with vodka to loosen them up.[4]

The Pistols, though, were so wound up before the gig that some of them resorted to additional chemical assistance to try to still the tide of anxiety that threatened to render them unable to play. Steve Jones dropped a Mandrax to calm his nerves, but the drug's hypnotic qualities seemed to have overcome the relaxation that he had been looking for. 'I cranked the amp up,' he said. 'Everyone was looking at us. It seemed like millions of people at the time.' In truth, there were only a few dozen people there.[5]

McLaren, Westwood and Jordan were there from SEX, along with Andy Czezowski (later to open the punk club The Roxy, but back then a friend who also helped Vivienne balance the books at the shop), Sid Vicious and other friends of the band. They played their usual early set of cover tunes, slightly altered. Through Rotten's almost gritted-teeth, chin out delivery, the Small Faces' 1965 hit 'Whatcha Gonna Do About It', became, as ever, a test for the audience: 'I want you to know that I HATE you, baby!' It seemed to be directed at the gathered students, rather than any hypothetical love interest.

If the audience had any ideas about the singer not respecting them, these were probably confirmed when Rotten started eating sweets in the middle of the set and spitting them out. This was no crowd-pleasing gambit – who on earth would do that, deliberately antagonize the audience? Stuart Goddard of the headliners Bazooka Joe remembered that 'they did five [songs] and that was it: goodnight. The rest of my band hated them because they thought they couldn't play.'[6] The Pistols'

short debut ended with Rotten attacking the PA equipment.
It had been borrowed from the headliners – as always, in those
early days – which in turn provoked the first of many scuffles
that would erupt during their early appearances. Too loud. Too
shambolic. Too insulting. They were a 'feral marauding group' that
November night, who 'hijacked the stage and hammered out a
cacophonous set' that sent people looking for the exits.[7] And so
it was that after a fast twenty minutes the plugs were pulled on
the noisy debutants and the gig was brought to an end. Rotten's
last words, mid-shutdown, were directed at Bazooka Joe: 'What
a bunch of fucking cunts.'[8]

In the first of many such occurrences that would take place
over the coming months, and despite, or maybe because of, the
chaos, one witness would have a transformative experience as
a result of what he saw. Stuart Goddard, bass player with the
headline act Bazooka Joe, changed his outlook from that moment
on. And, in time, he changed his name, too. He would soon
transform himself into Adam Ant, take on Jordan from McLaren's
shop as his manager, and adopt a new slogan – 'Antmusic for
Sex People' – that seemed to be referring to the shop SEX and
its customers. 'I thought fuck it, this is it, you know?' said Adam.
'I came out of that gig thinking, I'm tired of Bazooka Joe, I'm tired
of teddy boys.'[9]

The singer of the Sex Pistols was also tired, his first public
appearance having ended in chaos. Into the litter-strewn tunnels
of the London Underground went the homebound Rotten, no
doubt with one of those foul subterranean tunnel draughts
gathering pace on its way up from the depths, just in time to
blast into his face – a reminder that nothing had changed, yet.
There was no post-gig revelry, no back-slapping camaraderie,
no sudden transformation in material circumstances; he was
still as broke as ever. As an ending to this most momentous

day in his life, Rotten later said, it was all rather like 'a very dull muff-dive'.[10]

The following night the Pistols played once again in another London college, at the Central School of Art in Holborn. The opportunistic Matlock had already organized the gig before the Saint Martin's appearance. He had used his knowledge of how the art schools booked entertainment, and gone straight to the social secretary to ask if they would allow the band to play; as soon as they heard that the name of the band was the Sex Pistols, they said that they had to have them. 'On stage, the Pistols blazed,' wrote the journalist Caroline Coon. Rotten was wearing his unique anti-Pink Floyd T-shirt – defaced with his declaration of hate – beneath a jacket, which he would draw back like a flasher to taunt the audience, knowing that it probably included a fair few Floyd fans.

In these early days as a working band, McLaren's plan was to avoid taking the group down the favoured route for new bands at the time. This would have been to start playing the many pubs around London that formed part of a vibrant network of venues that since 1973/4 had been behind the emergence of a rash of exciting new bands who were taking rock music back to basics, back down to street level. Those back-to-basics bands, playing hard and fast R&B-inflected rock, injected a sense of purpose into a pretty dormant music scene that saw most of its superstar performers – the Stones, Bowie and Led Zeppelin, to name a few – go into exile in order to escape the punitive penalties of the taxman. The most successful of the new bands who embodied the sound and ethos of this 'pub rock' was Dr Feelgood. The band members were four dangerous-looking characters from Canvey Island in Essex, who projected a villainous aura, and who hit their peak of popularity in September 1976 with the number-one album *Stupidity* (a live album that was recorded in 1975).

The bands who came out of this pub rock scene were breaking through, and just around the time that the Pistols were getting ready to play their first shows, the *New Musical Express* was declaring another, newer, pub rock band, Eddie and the Hot Rods, to be the saviours of rock 'n' roll. They were younger and more energetic than Dr Feelgood, most of whom looked like they spent the majority of their time propping up bars.

The state of rock music in those days is fairly accurately indicated by the frequency with which new rock 'n' roll saviours were being hailed – the critical mood was that something had to change. In America it was Bruce Springsteen's (relatively) back-to-basics distillation of rock 'n' roll, R&B and Spector-inspired pop that was declared the future – most famously, or notoriously, by the critic (and Springsteen's future manager) Jon Landau. True, his records, and especially his on-stage commitment to energetic performances that brought himself and the audience together in an almost religious, revivalist celebration of rock 'n' roll, ran counter to the prevailing direction of much rock music at the time. But in truth Springsteen was too American to resonate with younger audiences in the UK; he was a favourite of older rock writers and critics and only received popular recognition in the UK in the 1980s. Despite Springsteen's first appearance taking place in London in 1975, it would be a decade before he received any real recognition in the UK.

Nonetheless, the pared-back approach of the bands on the mid-1970s pub rock scene was taken by some to be the first sign of a change that had been brewing since the early years of the decade, and which would finally come to a head with the punk explosion instigated by the Pistols in 1976–7. But despite a good deal of on-the-surface similarities, McLaren did not see these bands as trailblazers for the Pistols. In fact, he didn't like the idea of pub rock at all. The problem with it

was that the bands who took to the circuit would then end
up merely playing what they knew the punters would fall for:
familiar American-style R&B and rock 'n' roll, often performed
with an American accent to lend it a strange *non-authentic*
authenticity. It was a circuit that kept musicians in work, and it
made the pubs a lot of money as they split the takings with the
bands, but for McLaren it just wouldn't do as far as making his
group stand out as something genuinely new. If the Pistols were
going to make any kind of impact, they had to instigate the
circumstances of their own emergence. And that meant that no
one was going to be getting in free because they were buying
a few pints of beer. Quite the opposite: if people paid to see the
Sex Pistols, McLaren thought, they would be making a choice,
and they would pay attention to and get involved in what they
were witnessing. Jonh Ingham, a writer for the weekly music
paper *Sounds* and one of the Sex Pistols' earliest and staunchest
champions, thought that McLaren's approach was impressive
and likely to work, precisely because it went against what
everyone else was doing:

> What he was doing was creating an audience that was specifically
> for the band. And the shop, and the clothes. Even at that early
> stage it was about the clothes.[11]

Over the remainder of 1975 the Pistols played a handful of local
colleges and art schools around the city and in Greater London,
picking up new fans along the way. At Chelsea School of Art in
early December they played to a small audience that McLaren
had helped to drum up by calling everyone in his address book
and asking them to bring along anyone they knew who could
make it. At Chelsea the band played in the main school hall,
which, Viv Albertine wrote, was reminiscent of all the other school

halls she had ever known, and just as unremarkable, judging by her description:

> A bare wooden floor, stage at one end with tattered green silk curtains pulled to one side, vaulted ceiling with metal struts and grey plastic chairs stacked high along the walls. Smells like floor polish. Not many people in the audience, just a few clusters, clumped and dotted around the edge of the room.[12]

The Sex Pistols at Hertfordshire College of Art, St Albans, on 19 February 1976, one of their earliest performances.

As Albertine waited for the band, she started looking at what people were wearing. Everyone but her seemed to be dressed in black – apart from McLaren, that is: 'an impish-looking guy dressed in a powder-blue drape jacket' who introduced himself to people, saying how pleased he was that they could come out on a cold evening.[13] The Pistols eventually emerged, 'loud and raucous'. First-time viewer Albertine saw Rotten as a strange and compelling presence, who seemed to make a virtue out of being everything that a pop star was not supposed to be; there was no finesse about his act, no showing off in the conventional way that budding lead singers – always the stars – went about their business. There was nothing flashy or musically accomplished about the front man that would lead anyone in the audience to think that they could never do that, never be up there on-stage:

> Johnny Rotten slouches at the front of the stage, propped up on the mike stand. He's leaning so far forward he looks as if he might topple into the empty space in front of the audience. His face is pale and his body is twisted into such an awkward ugly shape he looks deformed. He looks ordinary, about the same age as us, the kind of boy I was at comprehensive school with . . . I think he's brave. A revolutionary. He's sending a very powerful message, the most powerful message anyone can ever transmit. Be yourself.[14]

For the music-obsessed Albertine, this was a moment of recognition that overturned every preconceived idea she had held about what she might do with her life. The Pistols, in particular the example of the 'twisting and yowling' Rotten, suddenly made it clear that she had to be in a band too.[15]

Most notable of the Pistols' early followers were a group of friends from the London suburbs, one of whom, Simon Barker, first caught the band purely by chance at one of those late 1975 shows, at Ravensbourne College on 9 December. The Pistols, he recalled, were met with abuse from the student audience, a fact that only added to their allure.[16] Some of these early followers – Siouxsie Sioux, Simon Barker and Bertie Marshall – already knew about McLaren and Westwood's shop on the King's Road. They had actually met the pair in the shop, and had bought their clothes, but knew nothing about the Sex Pistols' association with the shop until they were given a flyer for an early show.[17] These followers would be named the 'Bromley Contingent' by journalist Caroline Coon, who – sensing that something was happening that was bigger than just the music – started documenting the fans, as much as the bands, on the emerging punk scene, in her *Melody Maker* articles.[18] Only a few of the Bromley Contingent were actually from Bromley, but the name stuck. In the words of Jon Savage, they would become lodged in the public imagination as the 'teenage stylists who became a central part of the Sex Pistols' impact as they spread from the music press to the nationals'.[19] In the coming year the Bromley Contingent would be photographed for magazines and newspapers, and would crop up at most of the Pistols' London shows, dressed up for the occasion. Through their looks and attitude, they provided the first evidence that there was a new crop of teenage freaks and non-conformists emerging: young people who found something that resonated with them not only in the often chaotic performances of the Sex Pistols, but in the clothes and ideas that McLaren and Westwood had modelled SEX around in 1974. Pete Shelley, the singer in the Manchester band Buzzcocks, remembered that when they played a show with the Pistols in 1976 the sight of these fans was enough to freak out his drummer, who thought they looked like an alien species, something out of the sci-fi time-travelling adventures of the TV series *Doctor Who*.[20]

Some of the Bromley Contingent were among the crowd on Valentine's Day 1976, at one of the most notorious early Sex Pistols gigs, where Derek Jarman shot some of the earliest known footage of the band performing. The show took place at a party hosted by the artist and well-connected socialite Andrew Logan in his warehouse studio at Butler's Wharf, a building located on the south side of the Thames at Bankside.[21] Logan, known for hosting an Alternative Miss World contest since the mid-'70s – as well as other extravagant gatherings that were sure to bring out London's arty if 'frayed-at-the-edges beautiful people' – decided on this occasion to allow McLaren to bring along the new group, whom he claimed were going to be bigger than The Beatles.[22] For McLaren it was a significant opportunity to gain exposure for the Pistols in front of an arty bohemian crowd, and with probably enough media people present to give the band the opportunity of securing some mainstream exposure. Without asking Logan, 'McLaren phoned up the whole of London and invited them.'[23] When everyone in McLaren's address book turned up, it ensured that the Pistols and the SEX crowd looked as if they had gatecrashed the invitation-only party. 'There were hundreds of people, falling over my sculptures and smashing them,' Logan complained.[24] As the Pistols started playing there was a horrendous din caused by the sound reverberating off the studio's huge metal ceiling; scores of Logan's crowd scrambled for shelter.

It was a strange evening, where the gathering sense of violence that often seemed to accompany the Pistols began to take shape. Vivienne Westwood recalled being pulled away from some kind of swimwear competition that was taking place, during which Jarman ditched himself in the small swimming pool that contestants were parading around:

it was chock-a-block, you couldn't get in . . . I got a message sent to me that Johnny Rotten couldn't get in. So I went to the door and Rotten was so angry he punched me in the face. Everyone held me back – I was quite drunk – from hitting him.[25]

Although the Logan crowd contained many customers of McLaren and Westwood's shop, there was a sense of confrontation in the air, of a new scene coming to take over the old – and all set against the strange wasteland backdrop of the derelict riverside docks where the Pistols had been rehearsing six months before. As Nick Kent wrote in the *New Musical Express*, there was a kind of camp outrage, a scene of 'aesthetic warfare':

On one side was the by now long established Logan Set – a sprawling array of stagnating lounge-lizard males and predatory-looking females . . . And then there was the 'Sex' shop faction. They were quite easy to tell because of their chosen uniform: all tarty jet-black dyed hair plus an abundance of leather, ripped T-shirts and . . . a sort of insular 'don't mess with me' sense of tough.[26]

Steve Severin, then one of the so-called Bromley Contingent, thought that Logan's crowd represented the last hangover from the sixties: a kind of well-to-do, borderline upper-class Chelsea art scene crowd composed of effete intellectuals that he and his friends were desperate to usurp, and this was the event most symbolic of the shift that was beginning to take place:

They were pushed aside, starting when the Pistols played Andrew Logan's party, which actually seemed boring for the band. They played the same set twice. Nothing really happened until Jordan from the shop jumped up on stage. By the end of the evening I think the art crowd got the message that they were being pissed upon from a great height.[27]

Some of Logan's arty crowd of ageing – compared to most of the Pistols' crowd – bohemians would appear in the opening sequence of Derek Jarman's film *Sebastiane* (released towards the end of 1976). And it was the iconic figure of Jordan from SEX, who had also appeared in *Sebastiane*, who persuaded Jarman to shoot the Pistols against the backdrop of props and scenery from his film that he had lying around in his studio. His flickering and grainy silent footage, shot on Super 8 film at eighteen frames per second, brilliantly captured the band as if they were performing in the gaze of strobe lights (possibly an effect of the film's transfer to video), with Jarman twisting and rotating the hand-held camera, always in motion. The footage is, as a result, only loosely focused on the action on-stage, and instead catches the blur of indistinct bodies – Rotten, briefly, seems to be fighting with Vivienne Westwood – and fleeting close-ups of feet and squashed beer cans. The film captures the excitement that was reported by witnesses after first seeing the Pistols, but something spectral of the moment is also preserved. It is as if the Pistols' blast into the future was, on this occasion, the echo of some ancient pagan celebration during which they were both being born *and* catapulted towards the self-destruction that would soon begin to overtake them.

The chaos that took hold as Rotten flailed around in what Nick Kent described as a hallucinogenic rage was something that Pistols audiences up and down the country would see flashes of soon enough. Rotten would instigate trouble by abusing the audience, getting in the faces of people at the front, or trashing equipment that belonged to other bands. He was

The Sex Pistols in Derek Jarman's Super 8 footage,
14 February 1976.

everything that Malcolm McLaren wanted in the Sex Pistols: he
was exceptionally good at being bad.

The Pistols continued playing wherever they could through
the spring and into the summer of 1976, gathering new converts
along the way, some of whom picked up on the buzz from the
London music press and set out from other parts of the country
to see what it was all about. Some of the future members of
Buzzcocks, for example, had been intrigued by the first review

119

of a Pistols show to appear in the *New Musical Express* in February. The Pistols were only the openers at the Marquee for Eddie and the Hot Rods, the band most recently touted as 'saviours of rock 'n' roll', but they garnered all the attention in Neil Spencer's *New Musical Express* review: 'Don't Look Over Your Shoulder, but the Sex Pistols are Coming', ran the headline.[28] The review described the Pistols as 'spiky teenage misfits from the wrong end of various London roads, playing '60s-styled white punk rock' that shredded the competition, including that other much-touted, American, 'saviour' of rock, Bruce Springsteen. Spencer's piece famously ended with Steve Jones's after-show declaration that the Pistols were 'not really into music' – no, what they were into was 'chaos'. It was a sentiment perhaps influenced by the moment, and a result of the fact that the people in the audience that night at the Marquee had been shouting the usual abuse at them about not being able to play.[29] Others were more struck by the way the Pistols engaged with the audience. McLaren invited Alan Merrill, a member of chart band The Arrows and friend of one of the SEX shop assistants, Cheryl Newton, to a show to see if he had any pointers for the band. What Merrill witnessed struck him as some sort of 'negative masochistic bizarre cabaret':

> I didn't think it was a serious project, just a dark joke. You know the concept, bad is good. Garbage is valuable. An antiworld. Just like in the Superman comics that I read as a child, where it was called the Bizarro World.[30]

The soon-to-be Buzzcocks, Pete Shelley and Howard Devoto, drove south from Manchester to see the show for themselves, catching the Pistols in High Wycombe on 20 February. It was clear to them that whether or not you could play was utterly meaningless, that accepted standards of musicianship no longer mattered. This was something new: you got up, and you did it yourself. Within weeks, they had formed their own band and begun work on arranging a Manchester show for the Sex Pistols.

The principal effect of these early months in the development of the Pistols, was to convey the idea that there was no real distance between the stage and the audience. This began to have an immediate effect, with countless numbers of those who attended the early shows going on to form their own bands – bands that would later, in 1976 and 1977, comprise the punk explosion. In April of 1976 McLaren composed the first official band press statement. It began, 'Sex Pistols. Teenagers from London's Shepherd's Bush and Finsbury Park: "We hate everything".'

*

On Tuesday 30 March the Sex Pistols made the first of many appearances at London's 100 Club, a tiny basement venue located on busy Oxford Street, just a few minutes' walk from their Denmark Street rehearsal studio. After seeing the band in High Wycombe, the 100 Club's owner, Ron Watts, had become quite excited by the Pistols' performance, and the confrontational attitude that had shaken up the hippy types in the audience.[31] Watts was fed up with the sub-hippy, laid-back temper of live music; he saw something new and dangerous about the Pistols that he thought might bring in a crowd, but he had no idea how to contact them.

By chance, McLaren happened to turn up at the 100 Club not long afterwards touting for a gig for the band. Watts agreed immediately and offered the Pistols a regular Tuesday-night slot. Having been caught up in the early-'60s R&B boom, and

Johnny Rotten and Steve Jones at the 100 Club, 1976.

following his favourites, The Pretty Things and The Rolling Stones, around London, McLaren knew that the Stones' residency at the Richmond Hotel in Surrey during early 1963 was the cause of their initial rise to fame in the capital.[32] A residency offered the chance to build an audience, even when there was little else around in the way of gigs. In addition to the first show at the end of March, there were further dates on the 11, 18 and 25 May (then two in June, two in August and one in September). 'Sex Pistols: Tuesdays in May at the 100 Club', ran the posters for the May shows. Turn up any Tuesday and you'd know who would be playing.

The symbolism of the Pistols appearing here, at one of London's most iconic and long-established clubs (it was opened in 1942), was evident to observers who were aware of the venue's role in showcasing the hippest artists of the British jazz, blues and rock scenes of the 1950s and early '60s – from Humphrey Littleton to Muddy Waters and The Who, among others. In spring 1976 the drags out on Oxford Street that pulled in the punters were still advertising forthcoming attractions under the tagline 'London's Home of Dixieland and Traditional Jazz'. The Sex Pistols name gradually became a fixture on the boards, followed by other unfamiliar entities that were equally as distant from the sounds of Dixieland: The Clash and The Damned. 'One of the bizarre things about the 100 Club', recalled one member of the audience, 'is that there was a Chinese take-away in it. So in addition to the usual smells of beer and sweat, it smelled of egg fried rice, too.'[33]

The first 100 Club gig attracted few beyond the band's friends, including Sid Vicious, SEX shop acolytes such as John Paul Getty (heir to the Getty fortune) and the increasingly visible Bromley Contingent, who witnessed an aggressive, almost violent and probably sulphate-fuelled set by the Pistols.[34] Rotten had been drinking heavily before the show, and things were getting a bit loose and chaotic on-stage. One of the so-called Bromleys, Billy Idol, later recalled the sight that greeted him as the band took to the stage that night:

> Johnny Rotten, with orange, razor-cropped hair, was hunched over holding a beer and staring bug-eyed out at the crowd through tiny, tinted, square glasses. He was wearing a ripped sweater, striped baggy pants, and big flat rounded shoes with thick rubber soles dubbed 'brothel creepers'. He was constantly bantering back and forth with the band's manager, Malcolm McLaren, who stood in the wings of the stage.[35]

The performance was also notable because it publicly laid bare the tensions within the ranks, as Rotten – after trying to start a fight with Matlock during a number – walked off stage, straight through the audience and up the stairs out onto the street to look for a bus to take him home.[36] Turning back to the stage, Chrissie Hynde watched as Steve Jones wrenched all six strings off his guitar, in one swift, violent gesture.[37] It might have been part of the act, for all the onlookers knew, but the frustration was real; Rotten had been wound up by the band threatening to play a tune he didn't want to do at the gig, and turned up drunk and deliberately singing the wrong parts to the songs they were playing. Matlock responded by replacing his backing vocals with a chant aimed at Rotten: 'You're a cunt.' Just as it was about to explode into a fight, Rotten stormed off.[38] After about fifteen minutes, McLaren managed to drag Rotten back into the club and pushed him back on-stage. 'The whole show', Chrissie Hynde recalled, 'was chaos.'[39]

> When Rotten, after sneaking back in, realized that Steve was rendered unable to play, he jumped back on stage, grabbed

Glen Matlock, Johnny Rotten and Steve Jones at the El
Paradise club, Soho, London, April 1976.

the mic and announced the next song, fixing Steve with his
inimitable evil stare.[40]

The next time they met for rehearsal, Matlock recalled that
Rotten 'was standing there waiting for me, with a four-pound
hammer, swinging it in his hand. "Call me a cunt, will you?" he
said.'[41] Despite the rows, they continued to plough on with more
appearances across the capital during April and May.

When the unknown Pistols entered The Nashville, a grubby
North London pub favoured by 'Earl's Court low-life' that regularly
hosted bands, they trooped past the singer and guitarist – then
going by the name of Woody Mellor – in the headline band, The

101ers, as they made their way to the dressing room.[42] He was
stunned at what he overheard:

> in came these Sex Pistols people, I remember looking at them
> as they went past: Rotten, Matlock, Cook, Jones, McLaren, and
> coming up the rear was Sidney [Vicious], wearing a gold lamé . . .
> jacket . . . I heard Malcolm going to John, 'Do you want those kind
> of shoes that Steve's got, or the kind that Paul's got? What sort
> of a sweater do you want?', and I thought, blimey, they've got a
> manager, and he's offering them clothes! To me it was incredible.[43]

The Pistols eventually appeared on-stage, and apparently, despite
their concern with what they were going to be wearing, had no
intention of making any effort to please the audience – quite the
opposite. Rotten appeared on-stage and, after loudly blowing
his nose into a handkerchief that he'd pulled from his baggy
trousers, announced: 'If you haven't guessed already, we're the
Sex Pistols.'[44] While The 101ers played familiar old R&B tunes to
the crowd in the hope that they would be met with approval,
the Sex Pistols 'were standing there going, we don't give a toss
what you think, you pricks, and this is the way we're gonna play
it.'[45] The strange thing was that this attitude, combined with the
way they looked and the way that they attacked their songs,
changed everything. The difference was both blindingly obvious
in the way it cleared the mind, and yet subtle. In many respects
the Sex Pistols weren't a million miles away from The 101ers; they
both did versions of 'Steppin' Stone', for instance, an old Monkees
song from the 1960s. But the perception was that 'they were on
another planet, in another century,' said The 101ers singer. 'It took
my head off.'[46]

The 101ers' singer quit his band the next day. Within a matter
of weeks he would rename himself Joe Strummer and join forces

Sid Vicious and Vivienne Westwood in the audience
at the second of the Pistols' April 1976 shows at
The Nashville, London.

with a couple of teenagers, Paul Simonon and Mick Jones, who were being mentored by Malcolm McLaren's old friend and SEX collaborator Bernard Rhodes. Together they formed The Clash. The choice was simple, as he told Caroline Coon: 'Yesterday I was a crud. Then I saw the Sex Pistols and I became a king and I decided to move into the future.'[47]

The Pistols returned to The Nashville later in April and on that occasion attracted much more media attention courtesy of a ruckus that broke out midway through the performance, when Vivienne Westwood appeared to start a fight with a girl in the front row. As Sounds magazine's reporter Jonh Ingham told Jon Savage, this was just the start. Suddenly a man leaped into the fray, grabbing Westwood, before McLaren – with 'fists flying' too – joined the action, followed by Rotten, who, with a 'look of glee', jumped off the stage to join in:

> Vivienne said afterwards to Caroline Coon that she was bored and decided to liven things up. She just slapped this girl for no reason at all. It was completely electrifying, I'll say that.[48]

In her autobiography many years later, Westwood accepted that it was her fault that things had got out of hand that night, but denied that she had deliberately picked a fight to liven things up.[49] Whatever the cause of the fracas, the consequences were clear: the Pistols were not going to go quietly into the rest of their career; on the contrary, they were intent on being noticed. For Ingham, who became one of the Pistols' most ardent advocates over the coming months, this was the moment when a decision was forced upon him: the Sex Pistols, and the scene that was gathering around them, had to be supported, because it was the only thing that carried the kind of excitement that might act as a counter to the boredom of the times. The best way to do it, he felt, was not to try and describe the music to his readers or over-analyse what seemed to be going on in London, but rather to communicate to people all over the country what they couldn't see with their own eyes: the Sex Pistols as a performance spectacle unlike anything else out there. Ingham's attitude was that describing something like the chaotic scene of a band piling into a melee in front of the stage – rather than going on about the music – was a way to get that excitement across.[50] Thus the notoriety of the Sex Pistols began to be established, and the impression to onlookers, such as future Clash members Paul Simonon and Mick Jones, was that 'the Pistols were glamorous, dangerous street-trash.'[51]

The Sex Pistols' shows at the 100 Club allowed the band to establish their presence on the London music scene, and helped to create and galvanize a new punk scene, with audiences increasing in number with each appearance. It was because of those shows that the Pistols landed their first demo sessions with the guitarist and session musician Chris Spedding, who had been dragged along to their first 100 Club gig by Chrissie Hynde. Spedding had never seen anything like what he saw in that tiny basement, and he watched, stunned, the antics of the Pistols and the behaviour of their fans, who seemed to be spitting at the band.[52] At a later show Mark Perry, founder of the fanzine *Sniffin' Glue*, turned up still dressed like it was 1975, with long hair and a suit, which was promptly ripped off in the ruckus that erupted around him. 'It was almost symbolic,' he said: '"Right, let's get rid of that." Within a week, the hair had come off, just cut it all off myself. It was a life-changing experience. Within a month, I completely changed my life.'[53]

*

The sound of crashing drums and thunderous guitars emanating from the Pistols' rehearsal space 'clashed horribly with the delicate harmonies of Crosby, Stills and Nash' that played in the Hipgnosis studio.[54] It was there that in July 1976 the Pistols recorded their second set of demos on a small 4-track machine operated by their concert sound engineer, Dave Goodman, over two weeks in the second half of July. 'They'd play live, maybe four or five takes of each song,' Goodman told Jon Savage.[55] The tapes, including two new songs written in June of that year, 'Anarchy in the UK' and 'I Wanna Be Me', were later polished up at Riverside Studios in Chiswick, where Rotten also added his vocals to the backing tracks.

Between the two sessions, the Pistols had played the second of their early and influential Manchester gigs, the success of which arguably inspired Rotten's subsequent performance of the weeks'

Mark Perry, pictured fourth from the right, after the suit and hair removal, looks on as punks pogo at The Roxy, London, 1977.

old 'Anarchy in the UK'.[56] These early sessions also produced versions of 'Pretty Vacant', 'Anarchy in the UK', 'Seventeen' (then known as 'Lazy Sod'), 'Satellite', 'Submission' (featuring Steve Jones blowing into a half-full kettle to attain the sound of a vessel submerging) and two songs considered good enough in their original state for release as the first two single B-sides. 'I Wanna Be Me' (the most assured and full-throttle performance captured in these weeks) was coupled with the band's first single for EMI, a re-recorded 'Anarchy in the UK', and 'No Feeling' was on the flip side of the A&M release of 'God Save the Queen' (all of which, give or take 100 copies, were melted down after A&M sacked the Pistols in March 1977).

Inside Jones and Matlock's ad hoc living quarters the walls were adorned with messages stuck all over the place on pieces of paper – arrangements for meetings and gigs, with Rotten's handiwork in the form of pen-drawn cartoons of 'Fatty Jones' himself, 'Nanny Spunger' and her boyfriend, a sticklike Sid Vicious. Looming larger than most of the figures was a likeness of McLaren, holding a fistful of banknotes.[57]

Members of the band and their early Bromley Contingent followers, suburban teenagers who were around the same age as the Pistols, discovered new possibilities in Soho, among the company of those whom McLaren would characterize as 'the dispossessed'. Members of the band, and its associates and followers, were drawn to late-night Soho clubs such as Louise's, a lesbian bar where they were unlikely to outrage any of the patrons with the way they looked or behaved. There, according to Billy Idol, one of the regulars of the Bromley bunch, they 'devised our plans and consolidated a movement. By being like-minded, we ruled the night . . . we, the new aristocracy of the poor, knighted with fire, sallied forth and followed Johnny Rotten into the unknown.'[58]

McLaren knew enough about Soho, its lures and opportunities, from his own experience of hanging around its streets as a teenager 'gazing in awe at sights like the 2i's coffee bar in Old Compton Street', and later 'graduating to the exotic dives of the day – La Bastille Coffee bar, La Discotheque in Wardour Street, the Saint German Des Pres' (which many years later became the aforementioned Louise's).[59] Later in the 1960s, McLaren was reputed to have lived in a Soho brothel for a time, and later shared a flat in Berwick Street with his friend (and future Sex Pistols graphic artist) Jamie Reid.[60] But as well as encouraging the idea that the boys in the band should avail themselves of the freedom to explore the possibilities for enjoyment that Soho offered, he was also keen to make sure the band used the studio in Denmark Street to rehearse so that they could start to make things happen. He made sure to visit them almost daily, every morning, to see that Jones and Matlock were not languishing in bed all day.[61]

Throughout the summer and early autumn of 1976, the Pistols ventured out of London more frequently, with shows in the North, the Midlands, Wales and London's outer suburbs. The audiences outside of the capital tended to be disconnected from the buzz surrounding the Pistols and the fashion-conscious elements that had first created a following for the group in London. These audiences 'wanted a hippy group with long hair', something familiar and easy to accept.[62] What was often most provocative about the Pistols was the combination of the way they looked coupled with their unwillingness to court the audience, which came out in their flagrant lack of professionalism. Out in the provinces they would usually be opening for more established and more traditional – yet middling and aimless – bands who had been on the circuit for years.

It was in London, home to the UK music press, that events really accelerated, eventually drawing the attention of the

A flyer for a Sex Pistols show at the Screen on the Green in Islington, London, 1976.

London-based record companies. As far as the spate of new bands that had emerged in the wake of the Pistols were concerned, the journalists writing for the main music weeklies – *New Musical Express*, *Sounds* and *Melody Maker* – who ventured into London's clubs and pubs were in a better position and more open to seeing that something new was taking over. Charles Shaar Murray's report from the Sex Pistols all-nighter at Islington's Screen on the Green on Saturday and Sunday 28 and 29 August captured the sense of an arrival, a coming-out of sorts for some of these new bands – including the Buzzcocks and The Clash, both inspired by the Pistols – as well as, more notably, a curious new audience of freaks who were themselves the focus of reports in the music weeklies, and eventually Fleet Street stories.

Before the bands took to the stage, some of the Bromley Contingent members in the audience, dressed in their 'bizarre costumes', were on-stage, dancing to the sounds of Bowie and Bryan Ferry. Most conspicuously among them, and pictured in the *New Musical Express* report, was an unidentified 'chick in SM drag with her tits out' who would soon reveal herself publicly as Siouxsie Sioux.[63] The show, which was staged in an old cinema, was McLaren's way of demonstrating how to create an audience at a time when the pub rock ethos still held sway; when bands paying their dues (or going nowhere) had become caught in a rut. Many were only able to get gigs if they played familiar tunes to beer-swilling punters, which meant that they tailored their sets towards pleasing pubs full of people who had mostly come out for the beer.

Some aspects of the Screen on the Green happening, though, were a bit too pretentious for Charles Shaar Murray: the imposition of artsy films like Kenneth Anger's *Scorpio Rising*, in between the dancing and the bands, came across as an attempt to latch on to what might have been avant-garde a decade before. The real meat was the music. The Clash, Murray averred, were unimpressive; 'the kind of garage band who should be speedily returned to their garage, preferably with the motor [still] running'.[64] When the Pistols did finally appear it was as a welcome relief after the prolonged build-up, but also with an air of imminent chaos about them. 'The first thirty seconds of their set blew out all the boring, amateurish, artsy-fartsy mock decadence that preceded it,' Murray wrote:

watching them gives that same clenched-gut feeling that you get walking through Shepherds Bush just after the pubs shut and you see The Lads hanging out on the corner looking for some action and you wonder whether the action might be you.[65]

Journalists such as Murray at *New Musical Express*, Jonh Ingham at *Sounds* and Caroline Coon at *Melody Maker* – among others – ventured where the record company A&R people often didn't want to go. Another observer who witnessed the Sex Pistols was the (relatively) veteran rock writer Nik Cohn, author of the celebrated *Awopbopaloobop Alopbamboom* (1969), who had spied the developing punk scene from his window next to McLaren and Westwood's shop and felt drawn to what he was sure would be enemy territory for someone of his age. He ventured to a Pistols show as soon as he got a chance, and once there found himself 'circled, stared at, spat on' by the young punks in the audience:

> Then the Pistols started, incredibly bad, incredibly good, and the crowd forgot me in favour of beating up on each other. Punches, kicks, total chaos. One little bastard in particular seemed determined to start a riot. He was ugly and drunk, completely filthy, and every time the Pistols started a new number he half-turned to his left and punched whoever was next to him.
>
> Seeing this, I made sure to keep to his right. But I was soon tired of his act. The next time he turned and wound himself up to throw a punch, I beat him to it. I didn't hit him hard. Just a tap. But he wasn't expecting it, I caught him off balance and he was very fragile, so he went flying. Crashed into the guy next to him, and that guy also went flying. And the next one, and maybe even the next one, down they all went, skittles in a bowling alley. And that . . . was how I met Sid Vicious.[66]

The milieu that had formed around the Pistols and given them momentum was totally alien to the world in which record company promotion people normally did their business – where new bands were hyped to the music press through expensive parties and the laying on of various perks. Chrissie Hynde, who worked at the *New Musical Express* in the mid-1970s, recalled being drawn close enough to the culture of misdirected and excessive record company promotions to see through it. In a time when the A&R departments were digging up their own musical finds and trying to sell them as the next big thing to the music press, they were essentially 'burning money' without much in the way of tangible success. It was an era marked by:

> an endless succession of album launches – early afternooners, with plates of smoked salmon, sarnies, and lots of booze. The NME staff would hover over and hog the drinks table, get pissed, then stagger back up Long Acre to write an insulting profile of the artist whose launch it had been.[67]

The record companies seemed out of touch, and the seemingly spontaneous appearance of the Sex Pistols and the scene that was developing around them hinted at their own irrelevance. There was enough of a buzz around the Pistols that it was apparent something was going on outside their sphere of influence, but it scared many in the London music business at the time. Record company A&R people, said Al Clark of Virgin Records, were made to feel deeply 'insecure' about what this meant for the music business they had come to know:

> It was as if the lazy aristocracy was having to contend with a peasant's revolt on its own doorstep. They were having to go out on missions into a rather dangerous universe, and often at such gigs you would see A&R men standing together at the back, as

if holding on to a life raft, and what was going on at the front alarmed them.[68]

Yet while all this was going on, the UK record companies were still operating in their normal, if increasingly lifeless mode. The best-sellers on the album charts that autumn of 1976 were a spate of television-advertised compilation albums, golden oldies. In the same week as Murray's review appeared in the *New Musical Express*, the UK album chart was topped by *20 Golden Greats* by The Beach Boys, enjoying the seventh of a ten-week run at number one. A suitable soundtrack – the marketing men may have calculated – for that sweltering summer when Britain basked in Southern Californian conditions.

But it was perhaps not just the fact that it had been a long hot summer that had made The Beach Boys popular all over again. Other similar albums reached the top spot in the charts in the same period, providing just one indication of how stagnant popular music had become; they included Bert Weedon's *22 Golden Guitar Greats* (November 1976), Glen Campbell's *20 Golden Greats* (November 1976) and The Shadows' *20 Golden Greats* (January 1977). For quite a while even the old guard writers of the music press and the few music writers for the Fleet Street broadsheets didn't know what to make of the Pistols and their ilk, but seemed hopeful that they would soon recede into the distance, and that these years – 1976, 1977 – would belong to more recognizably refined and professional performers, such as Jackson Browne, Joan Armatrading or Bruce Springsteen. Some new homegrown bands, such as Eddie and the Hot Rods from Essex, seemed to be caught up in the wave of interest in this so-called punk phenomenon, as people cast around to try and identify where this had all started. The Pistols may have stolen the headlines from them at their February Marquee gig, but the Rods were still more palatable to many as flag-bearers for rock's future; with their short, fast and punchy songs focused on urban themes, they offered a similar kind of street-level energy but without the latent violence and the gathering of bizarre followers that attended the Pistols' appearances across London. The Hot Rods were, however, unhappy at being associated with punk, and sent their record company PR man to *Melody Maker* to tell the magazine to stop lumping them in with bands like The Clash and the Buzzcocks 'who really can't cut it'. They especially didn't want to be associated with the Pistols, 'because it's just more press for THEM'.[69]

The press attention did begin to work in the Pistols' favour. It led some music industry people, those who didn't mind stepping out among the punks, to see if they could find something new. Terry Slater of EMI Music's publishing division was captivated by the 'pure raw energy' he saw in the Pistols' performances during some of the 100 Club gigs, and was the first to take the plunge and sign the band up to a publishing deal.[70] EMI Publishing and EMI Records were two separate entities, housed in different buildings at opposite ends of Oxford Street, but they did communicate with each other, and word of Slater's deal soon reached the Records arm of the company.

On 20 September Mike Thorne, an EMI Records talent scout, and Graham Fletcher, a press officer at EMI International (another distinct entity), attended the punk festival at the 100 Club, which the Sex Pistols were headlining; 'unfazed by the gobbing and pogoing', they emerged as converts and quickly became 'ambassadors for punk and the Pistols' within the company.[71] Thorne's immediate boss, and EMI's A&R chief, Nick Mobbs, followed this up by travelling to see the band the next week at the Outlook Club in Doncaster, where they played – as was so often the case outside of London – to a very small audience of thirty or forty people.

The Pistols perform at the 100 Club punk festival, September 1976.

Many at the company – Brian Southall and Eric Hall in the Press division, as well as Bob Mercer, head of EMI Records in the UK – were unmoved by the Pistols and did not really want EMI to sign them. The one time that Mercer had seen the band perform he thought they were awful; on that occasion he had been caught up in a crowd that were gobbing, so when it came to the Pistols 'his gut reaction was to put a halt to proceedings there and then,' before they were signed. In the end, however, the will of the A&R department – all solidly for the Pistols – prevailed, and on 8 October 1976 the Sex Pistols signed a two-year recording contract with EMI. McLaren moved quickly to finalize the details of the deal and have it signed before anyone could change their minds, resulting in 'one of the fastest deals ever set by the company', according to the stories in the trade papers. McLaren

The Pistols celebrate after signing to EMI, London, October 1976.

had accepted Nick Mobbs's contract offer on the morning of 8 October, and the agreement was 'drawn up, checked and signed by the evening of the same day'.[72] There was a sense of 'indecent haste' about it all, said the EMI insider Brian Southall; a feeling only compounded later when the Pistols and McLaren met EMI's Managing Director, Leslie Hill, for the first time, over a celebratory drink. There it soon became evident that McLaren was a 'tricky customer, who knew exactly what he was doing' in rushing the deal through, and was possibly up to no good:

> Without ever being particularly offensive he gave Hill the impression that he had gleefully infiltrated a conservative behemoth and was going to make it work to his advantage, one way or another.[73]

As the Pistols prepared for the release of their first EMI single, 'Anarchy in the UK' (due out in late November 1976), McLaren decided that it should buck the new record industry trend of releasing 7-inch vinyl singles in picture sleeves – as opposed to the more traditional record company branded paper sleeves with a hole cut out to reveal the record label. Instead, the Pistols debut would be released (initially, at least) in a plain black sleeve.

McLaren and Jamie Reid – who would produce a memorable graphic of a torn Union Jack flag held together with safety pins and clamps – were at odds with the EMI promotional machine from the outset. They wondered if they could design a cover that said 'Don't Buy Me!':

How are we going to do that, let's fucking do that . . . let's really strip it right fucking down, we're not having any stupid group

London's Notre Dame Hall, off Leicester Square, 15 November 1976. Sid Vicious (far right, with torn white T-shirt) watches from the crowd.

on the cover, no crazy faces, we're just going to run this like a fucking clandestine campaign, it's going to be a record that's gotta disappear . . . in a black bag with no hole in the middle.[74]

McLaren and Reid had the idea that they could make an anti-product. They weren't interested in creating stars as convention-ally understood; becoming famous for being bad was what they were interested in. (And the Pistols, for their part, didn't want to be stars in the old music business sense anyway.) And it was in tune with the fascination that black had held for McLaren since his days as a painter.

*

On 1 December 1976, two days before their first headline tour of UK theatres was due to begin, EMI wangled the Pistols a last-minute appearance on Thames Television's *Today* show, as a replacement for their new EMI label mates Queen. The host – or master of ceremonies, as he was more appropriately described in some later reports – Bill Grundy was an old hand at interviewing guests who were unknown or inconsequential, but no stranger to interviewing prime ministers, either. On this particular day, he thought it was a case of the former: nobodies of minor interest, squeezed in at the end of the show to fill up a few minutes. 'Bill and the Sex Pistols', the last item on his running order read. All he had to do, he thought to himself, was 'introduce yet another quite ghastly pop group' and then he'd be finished for the day.[75]

As the Pistols and the assorted faces of the Bromley Contingent helped themselves, and then helped themselves again, to the free bar in the TV studios hospitality room, Grundy – who had not long returned from a long lunch at his gentlemen's club, where whisky and wine were served – was shuttling around the studio

'You dirty fucker.' Johnny Rotten and Steve Jones on the *Today* show, December 1976.

and going over the running order of the show. In his hands he held a sheaf of papers detailing the hullabaloo surrounding the Sex Pistols and their recent signing to EMI Records, which he was going over as the band and their friends lumbered into the studio to face the cameras. Maybe it was the news from the crew that the Pistols and friends had drunk their way through numerous bottles of wine and beer, but once the band had settled down in their chairs, with the Bromley lot standing behind in their bizarre outfits, with hair looking as if it had been 'spiked in machine oil', Grundy began on the offensive.[76] 'They are punk rockers,' he said, addressing the mothers and fathers and children sitting in the living rooms of Greater London and the Home Counties:

the new craze, they tell me. They are heroes, not the nice clean Rolling Stones. No. You see, they are as drunk as I am; they [The Rolling Stones] are clean by comparison. They are a group called the Sex Pistols. And I'm surrounded now by all of them.

143

The interview passed in a blur for the members of the Pistols, sufficiently lubricated that they weren't even really sure what was going on. McLaren was watching on from behind the cameras and, as Glen Matlock remembered it, seemed to be laughing. Just a few minutes after being introduced as a new group that had already plumbed depths that even those former enemies of good taste, The Rolling Stones, had never reached, the show was over. It drew to a close with Grundy addressing the audience once again: 'We'll be back tomorrow,' he said, trying to look chipper. 'I'll be seeing you soon.' And then turning to the Pistols and their entourage – as the cameras kept rolling – he said, 'I hope I'm not seeing you again.'

The bemused Pistols filed out of Thames TV's studio to a car waiting outside. They headed for rehearsals at The Roxy in Harlesden to continue preparations for the tour, while McLaren – having persuaded EMI to let him use their limousine in return for doing the TV programme – set off for Heathrow Airport to collect Johnny Thunders, ex-New York Doll and current member of The Heartbreakers (who were to join the Pistols on their 'Anarchy in the UK' tour). No one really thought too much about the television interview, and Malcolm was too concerned with giving Thunders a suitable welcome to linger on what he had just witnessed.[77]

At the end of the day, Sophie Richmond, the secretary at McLaren's management company, Glitterbest, recorded, as usual, the important events of the day in her diary: 'Thames TV ring. Want to have Pistols on *Today*. It fucks the rehearsals a bit, but we agree . . . Steve swears at Bill Grundy until they are shut off.'[78]

5 The New Elizabethans

The impact of the *Today* show was almost immediate. Within a day the whole country knew about the Sex Pistols, and the effect on everyone involved with the group was overwhelming. Beyond the predictable shock headlines of the Fleet Street tabloids, broadsheets such as *The Guardian*, while musing that the Pistols were on a free publicity bonanza courtesy of the newspapers, felt obliged to explain what was going on:

> After too many years of drug-taking, peace-loving, long-haired gentlemen, what better news value than drug-hating, hate-loving, short-haired gentlemen who, as Bill Grundy said on *Today*, 'make the Rolling Stones seem clean'?[1]

If old assumptions and expectations had been in some way inverted or shaken up, it was all regarded by the daily papers as the unwelcome arrival of something new. 'TV FURY OVER ROCK CULT FILTH' and 'THE FILTH AND THE FURY!' ran the headlines on the front pages of two editions of the *Daily Mirror* the day after the broadcast. It was a sign that the press were hungry for anything that would foment outrage and sell newspapers. It obviously hadn't been part of the plan that the group would jeopardize the EMI relationship before it had even really started, but the label soon took fright at the reaction to the *Today* show when it became clear that rather than the furore dying down, the Sex Pistols' 'Anarchy' tour was merely providing more headline fodder.

History would record that the principal villain of the teatime debacle, aside from Grundy himself – who encouraged the members of the band to 'say something outrageous' as the clock wound down on his teatime Thames TV show on 1 December 1976 – was the inebriated, no-nonsense Pistols guitarist Steve Jones. But he had just been acting naturally, being himself, as McLaren would later try to explain to the outraged EMI hierarchy.

While it was Jones who unloaded the most sustained and memorable torrent of profanity that had, up to that point in time, ever been broadcast in Britain, the more visible and easily identified punk-styled figure of Rotten became the quick and easy focus of most media attention. If there was one way that the whole punk ethos could be packaged and presented to the masses, it was in the form of Rotten's scrawny visage and ramshackle appearance. Coupled with that name, Johnny Rotten, he would – for the time being – become the living embodiment of the entire phenomenon.

The 'Anarchy in the UK' tour, which was due to start with a show at the University of East Anglia in Norwich on 3 December, met its first cancellation; the university authorities feared that the appearance of the Pistols would be an incitement to the kind of violence that had been reported at their London appearances earlier in the year. Most of the venues on the tour were theatres that were licensed by local government authorities. They had the power to decide who and what could be performed in their towns and cities, which meant that shutting out the Pistols could be achieved without much difficulty.

When the next date, this time in Derby, fell to the council censors as well – after the Pistols refused to perform in a judge's chambers before members of council to determine whether the group's act was fit for public consumption – the tour bus rolled on through the dark winter nights bearing the fitting destination

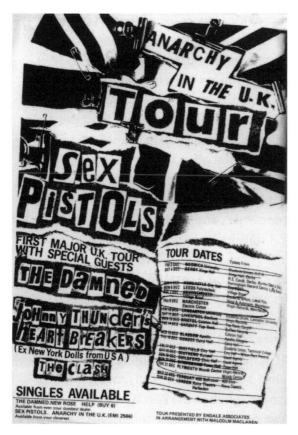

'Anarchy in the UK' tour poster. The 'Anarchy' tour was scheduled to run through the UK for most of December. In the end, only five shows were played following cancellations by local authorities across the country.

sign 'Nowhere', followed all the while by packs of Fleet Street reporters and photographers whose aim seemed to be to goad the members of the band into further self-destructive outbursts. In Leeds the press pack caught Rotten as he was leaving the band's hotel; he gave them a two-fingered salute and shouted in their direction, 'You fucking cunts.' 'These kids', McLaren told one of the music press, 'really don't give a fuck who hates them.'[2]

The pattern was repeated across the country. Other towns and cities on the tour schedule began to follow suit, with councils either cancelling shows outright or requesting that the bands on the tour played auditions before local licensing committees who would then decide whether the performance could go ahead. What was strange, as Buzzcocks' Pete Shelley later recalled, was that this all started like a bad rumour. The story only spread beyond London via the 'shock-horror' headlines, which simply inflated the appeal of the Pistols. Most people in the country, including those sitting on council licensing committees, had not seen the offending TV appearance (and nor was it repeated). The effect was to greatly fuel the Pistols' perceived threat to public decency, as far as the guardians of morality were concerned, and to enhance their already substantial mythical status among young people across the country.[3]

The media furore had ensured that the prospect of a visit from the Pistols was now seen by local authorities, *Rolling Stone* magazine reported, as an event 'on a par with an invasion by Genghis Khan's hordes'.[4] In Glasgow, Scotland, where the Pistols were due to appear at the Apollo Theatre on 15 December, the local council figurehead, known as the Lord Provost (a mayor-type figure), went so far as to ban the Pistols from entering the city. If they were even picked up passing through Glasgow, they ran the risk of being thrown in jail. The city, said the Provost, 'had enough hooligans' as it was, 'without importing them from across the border'.[5] In the end, the Sex Pistols played only seven out of 24 dates, and even the ones that did go ahead were attended by scenes of hysteria and panic outside venues, with local emergency services in attendance to prevent trouble. Various do-gooders were inspired by the example of Mary Whitehouse – then an ever-present campaigner against what she saw as lax moral standards in the British media – to uphold public decency by blockading streets and bringing along young children to sing hymns in the hope that the horrible Johnny Rotten would, like

Johnny Rotten during the 'Anarchy' tour, December 1976.

the Wicked Witch of the East, be reduced to dust and scattered by the wind.

In fact, so quickly had the Pistols, and Rotten in particular, come to represent something utterly profane and violently transgressive, that they became one more element to add to any portrait of Britain's woes – yet another advance warning of the decline of a great nation. Whenever a cultural commentator now needed a handy label to describe something uncouth, disturbing or disorderly, those terms 'punk' and 'Sex Pistol' came readily to hand as the very thing that would dredge up a visual image of impending doom in the minds of readers. A review of a January 1977 London performance of Shakespeare's *Troilus and Cressida* provided one of countless excellent examples of how Rotten's appearance could be read as a warning sign. The character of Thersites, one of the lower rabble of the invading Greek battalions who would crush the more honourable and civilized citizens of ancient Troy, seemed to be best thought of – in the words of this reviewer – as 'a snarling Sex Pistol', appearing like a prototype Johnny Rotten, whose hunched appearance and spiky DIY hair strangely echoed the description of this ancient punk.[6]

As well as the bans and the arrival of the Pistols as an object of fascination, the factory workers who were supposed to be packing the 'Anarchy in the UK' single refused to handle the records, effectively halting its production and prematurely stalling the band's rise up the charts. As the world outside eased towards the seasonal festivities, the Sex Pistols and the other bands on the 'Anarchy in the UK' tour (The Damned, The Clash and Johnny Thunders's Heartbreakers) found themselves trapped in hotels, besieged by reporters and relentlessly demonized; in the apt words of the *New Musical Express*, they had gone from being nobodies to 'scumsurfers of the apocalypse' in one day.[7]

Nevertheless they were compelled to continue the carnival until it ran into the ground, as promoters insisted that despite the council bans, the band should turn up at venues in cities that had already declared they would not be allowed to play, simply to honour their contracts and avoid incurring financial penalties.

Since the Grundy fiasco, the growing public irritation at the mere existence of the Sex Pistols had spread to the House of Commons, prompting one MP to write to the head of EMI to suggest that in simply giving a home to the Pistols, the record company – a well-respected institution whose parent company was the beneficiary of government defence contracts – was doing no more than 'providing funds for a bunch of ill-mannered louts who seem to cause offence wherever they go'. 'Surely', the Honourable Member added, EMI could 'forego the doubtful privilege of sponsoring trash like the Sex Pistols'.[8]

The first sign that EMI were wobbling under pressure came when they noticed that the story had gone global, with all the potential ramifications the adverse publicity might have for their numerous other business interests. Every time the Sex Pistols' name was mentioned it was in a negative light, and always accompanied by a reference to EMI as the company that seemed to be bankrolling their exploits. This was the first and main concern for Sir John Read, the head of EMI. On Christmas Eve 1976 he met with Leslie Hill, then head of EMI's music division, to figure out what could be done about the problems that the Sex Pistols were causing for the company. Their concern at that time, Hill later said, had a particular immediate focus: namely that bad reports in the US news media would damage their 'ability to sell the EMI-Scan', a revolutionary device that had been designed to allow surgeons to 'x-ray inside peoples' heads instead of cutting them open'.[9] This was a major product that had been in development for years, and which they hoped would be sold in every corner of the world. But its commercial viability was being jeopardized by the fact that in the days following those 100 seconds in which the Pistols swore their way to infamy, EMI were being repeatedly linked with the group.

On 6 December 1976, under the headline 'Punk Rock Becomes Latest Outrage to British Public', the *Los Angeles Times* reported that the Sex Pistols represented a new 'alleged' form of music that had already been marked down by its detractors as something irredeemably 'obscene, anarchic and insolent', which – courtesy of the Grundy incident – had TV 'viewers screaming in protest' and advertisers threatening to boycott the TV network that had given the band a platform.[10] The prominence of the *Los Angeles Times* report, in particular, concerned Sir John Read, because he could foresee circumstances in which the negative publicity would be simply uncontrollable. American interest in EMI's new medical scanner was essential – the US was the biggest potential market for such technologies – and the feeling was that some grotesque pop group could not be allowed to undermine the company's dominance in such a market through persistent bad headlines.

If the Pistols' reported behaviour wasn't bad enough in itself, the attention given in the report to this new 'punk rock' also implicitly called into question the artistic judgement of the record company in becoming involved with the group in the first place. Readers who picked up the newspaper that day would have read that punk rock music consisted of 'generally rubbishy performances on the conventional guitars and drums', yet because of its overriding themes of 'anti-love, anti-peace, contempt, [and] defiance of everything', it had been a potent enough force to compel 'young listeners into violent pandemonium'.[11]

Some weeks later it became clear that EMI were intending to reach an agreement with McLaren to terminate the Pistols' contract – which, indeed, they eventually did on 6 January. It was obvious, however, that while adverse headlines and stories may have scared off EMI, with its links to the establishment and its extensive non-entertainment activities, there were others who were intrigued by the Pistols. Mo Ostin, the president of Warner Bros. Records in Los Angeles, took note of the storm that was brewing around the Sex Pistols, and wondered why he had nothing as exciting shaking things up at his label. For the time being, he left it up to the head of the company's UK office to consider signing the band.

Because of the payoff that the Pistols had received from EMI, they were able to continue to record at their own expense – something that in the coming months would give McLaren considerable freedom to sign record deals for specific territories and accumulate cash through a number of deals. In early January the Pistols played a handful of shows in the Netherlands, at which time the news that they had been dropped by EMI first began to filter through to members of the band via phone calls to and from the UK, where the tabloid press had once again erupted in a fit of outrage over the Pistols' behaviour at Heathrow Airport as they were waiting to board their flight to Amsterdam. After sitting around swigging from bottles of wine in the departure lounge, members of the band were accused by KLM airline staff of overstepping the bounds of decency. 'They are the most revolting people I have ever seen,' one staff member told a newspaper:

> They called us filthy names and insulted everyone in sight. One of them was sick in a corridor leading to the aircraft. While this was going on the three others were spitting on the floor and at one another.[12]

The presence of reporters from Fleet Street ensured that the incident was blown out of proportion. 'They may have spat at each other and been a little drunk,' McLaren told *The Guardian*, 'but they weren't flying the plane.'[13] After playing a first show in Rotterdam, the Pistols returned to Amsterdam to perform at the well-known Paradiso, a converted church that had provided a space for live music since the end of the 1960s, when it was at the centre of the city's underground and hippy culture. Following the trip to the Netherlands for *The Guardian*, Robin Deneslow sensed the incongruity of the avowedly anti-hippy Sex Pistols playing the Paradiso, where the old culture still held sway. There were still 'old-fashioned hippies, openly selling drugs' outside the venue, as the gathering crowd passed the time waiting for the show by reading of the Pistols' exploits courtesy of the British tabloid press, whose shock headlines had been stuck to the doors of the Paradiso. Inside, Deneslow reported, the smell of pot hung in the

The Paradiso, Amsterdam, November 1976.

air as Rotten arrived on-stage, telling the murmuring Amsterdam audience, in his inimitable style, to 'shut up'.[14] The acoustics of the old building, with its high vaulted ceiling and large stained glass windows all around, drowned Rotten's voice much of the time in a cacophonous reverb; yet this also lent itself very well to the dynamics of some of the Pistols' best tunes. 'Satellite' – whose repeated vocal chorus allowed Matlock and Jones to join Rotten in the yobbish, ironic chant 'I love you' – made the band sound like it was caught inside a wind tunnel. This sensation was entirely in sync with the swaying, crunching sound of Steve Jones's marvellously warped riff, which sounded like it was constantly changing speed – an effect also captured in the studio recordings – as he moved through its descending chords.[15] At the end of an electrifying rendition of the song, Rotten clearly had the band's offstage woes in mind when instead of thanking the audience he sarcastically said, 'Once again, a big thank you to EMI . . . our record label. Nice people.'

As the set progressed, *The Guardian* reported, the audience in front of the stage started throwing beer at the band – a gesture that was returned with interest when Cook rose up from his drum stool to throw beer back at them, and Glen Matlock angrily kicked his microphone stand into the crowd. 'The musical accompaniment to all this', Robin Deneslow reported, was 'a grinding, crashing ditty with the repeated line *the problem is you*'.[16] And the problem was everyone who stood outside the Pistols' inner circle, but at this specific moment, it was EMI in particular. Leslie Hill, the managing director of EMI Records, had flown to Amsterdam to get McLaren to sign a mutual termination agreement, which had already been written up and presented to the Pistols as a fait accompli. In the early hours of the morning after the Paradiso show, a despondent McLaren was found standing outside in the freezing cold by the canal,

The Pistols at the Paradiso, 6 January 1977.

smoking cigarettes, staring into the distance and talking like a maniac. He might have had other worries on his mind: back home the windows of his flat had been smashed in by Clapham skinheads; Vivienne felt she was living in a bunker and 'faced with a daily assault course' to walk to the local Tube station.[17] Deneslow noted that amid the ranting, McLaren's concerns seemed to be that of a conventional manager of a rock band. He seemed far from the anarchistic purveyor of kinky leisure wear that had been portrayed in the media:

> He claimed that his boys 'were goaded' into their notorious TV utterances, and 'what they did was quite genuine – being working-class kids and boys being boys, they said what they felt was OK. They don't regret it.'[18]

McLaren was genuinely worried that this was the end – that no other record company would now touch the Pistols and, even worse, that they would be forced to pay back what they had already received – half of the £40,000 advance – which had already been largely spent mounting the 'Anarchy' tour and the trip to the Netherlands. In fact, it was only in the days after returning from the Netherlands that McLaren overcame his dismay at the breakdown with EMI. He began to see the situation as offering a potential opportunity to do something else with the Sex Pistols, something that also might further his own ambitions. When they returned to London, McLaren asked the band's sound engineer, Dave Goodman, to take the band into the studio to record the new material they had been working on in the hope that it would keep their spirits up.[19] They entered Gooseberry Studios, located in a basement in Soho's Chinatown, and over a handful of days they recorded versions of 'God Save the Queen', 'Problems', 'Pretty Vacant', 'Liar', 'New York' and a newly minted song titled 'EMI', in which Rotten vented his displeasure at the band's treatment by the 'Sirs' of their previous record label.[20]

During January McLaren was courting a number of record companies, with Warners, CBS and A&M Records all interested. While Warner Bros. in Los Angeles wanted the Pistols, the problem was that the recently installed head of WEA (Warner Bros. Records' umbrella group in the UK), John Fruin, hated them. His deputy, on the other hand – the former Beatles PR Derek Taylor – thought that the company should sign them. Unable to reach a decision, they put it to the company employees in England, only to find that there was 'not so much as one vote in favour of the Pistols', as McLaren told the New Musical Express.[21] After finally accepting that EMI would not reverse their decision to sack the band, McLaren began to eye the future with a renewed sense of optimism – the situation had to be taken as another chance to begin again. He was beginning to think that if they could find the right company, they could 'make a really big deal, [and] get into movies'.[22]

Somewhere in the fallout of the Grundy incident, McLaren had begun to see how the situation might be turned to their advantage, and perhaps even advance the barmy ideas that he and Jamie Reid had only jokingly entertained a year or two earlier: that they could use the pop world as the target for some kind of quasi-Situationist ruse. The record industry, at least, and the gullible public whipped up into a frenzy by Fleet Street, thought that the Pistols were dangerous. Well, it was an interesting idea to play with; it was surely better than being professional or competent or, god forbid, good musicians, he thought. 'The Sex Pistols', McLaren said as he looked into the ever-present camera of Julien Temple at the turn of 1977, 'are an idea':

> The idea is to threaten. The idea is not to allow conformity; and to not allow boredom to take place within your act. The idea is to say something that will change kids' actual outlook on their lives. As soon as the Sex Pistols stop being threatening, they ain't any longer the Sex Pistols.[23]

The role he advocated for the Sex Pistols he was now applying to himself, as the media spectacle that had resulted from the Grundy affair awakened larger possibilities in his mind. 'I think the rock 'n' roll world is a fucking waste of time – I have no interest in it,' he said. 'The industry took over a long time ago. I dunno who they are speaking for.'[24]

In early February Glen Matlock quit the band, although no official announcement was made about the event until the end of the month. He had come to find it impossible to work with

Rotten, and the frenzy that followed the Grundy TV show had only intensified his desire to escape the situation. The first that the press knew about Matlock's resignation was when McLaren confirmed the rumours to the *New Musical Express* in a telegram dated 28 February, which declared that Matlock had been sacked because he liked The Beatles, and 'went on too much about Paul McCartney'. It was the first of many interventions by McLaren that

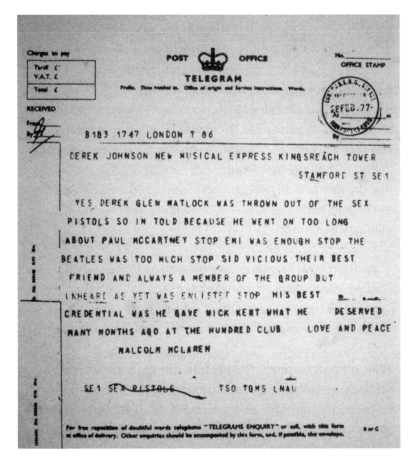

A telegram from McLaren to the *New Musical Express* announcing Matlock's departure from the Sex Pistols.

seemed designed to turn the situation into a game that suited his tendency to provoke disorder. In Matlock's place, McLaren's telegram continued, would be Sid Vicious – Rotten's friend from before his Sex Pistols days.

During the first week of March, as Vicious busied himself learning how to play bass guitar and play the Pistols set, the rest of the band continued recording. The main aim of these sessions was to nail 'God Save the Queen', which was due to be rush-released as their first A&M single, but other songs – 'Did You No Wrong' and 'No Feelings' – were also recorded, with Steve Jones playing both bass and guitar. The following week, the Pistols signed with A&M at the offices of their music publishing arm, Rondor Music, so as not to send shockwaves through the regular A&M Records staff, who were located elsewhere in London.[25] Derek Green, the head of A&M Records in the UK, told the *New Musical Express* that his impression was that the Pistols didn't like him very much. 'McLaren himself says the feeling is mutual,' the *NME* continued, quoting the Pistols manager as saying:

We don't have a fantastic rapport with A&M. I would say that a lot of people there probably don't like us. A&M are a very middle of the road company and I think they probably thought we could change their image.[26]

In an attempt to generate early publicity for their forthcoming single, 'God Save the Queen', the signing was restaged the following day outside Buckingham Palace. The following week's *Sounds*, dated 19 March, carried a cover story on the signing in which Derek Green stated his conviction that the Pistols would 'effect some major changes in rock music', which A&M were excited to be involved with.[27] Unfortunately for all involved, by the time the magazine had hit the streets, the Pistols had once again been sacked by their record label.

The day after the restaged signing, Rotten, Vicious and their friend Jah Wobble had appeared drunk and disorderly at The Speakeasy, the London club where music industry figures and musicians went to relax. Wobble and Vicious had confronted the *Old Grey Whistle Test* presenter Bob Harris and one of his studio crew, George Nicholson, about the absence of the Sex Pistols on their show. According to subsequent reports, Rotten stayed out of the ensuing violence, but Vicious and Wobble landed Harris and Nicholson in hospital, where they had to be treated for minor cuts and bruises. As soon as word of this latest spectacle reached Derek Green at A&M he quickly decided he was wrong to think that he could manage the chaos that seemed to follow the Pistols everywhere, and dropped the band immediately. The company

Rotten, charged with possessing drugs, leaves court with McLaren, 11 March 1977.

then destroyed as many copies of 'God Save the Queen' as it could find (only a few hundred copies had been circulated prior to its official release).

And so it was that in mid-March 1977 a 'stunned and shattered' McLaren called the press into his offices, and with a look of bemusement on his face, declared his frustration at the recent A&M sacking. Inside Glitterbest's offices the members of the band greeted the press with 'belches and swearwords' as they lounged

> listlessly in a corner, in specially designed ill-fitting clothes mutter-
> ing amongst themselves, pausing only to vent their aggression
> on the news that a lot of the £75,000 might go to the taxmen.[28]

'I keep walking out of record company offices with cheques,' McLaren said, 'The boys just want to get their music out.'[29] It was no wonder that to some outsiders it looked like the Pistols were awash in cash. As Mrs Lydon, Johnny Rotten's mother, told Fred and Judy Vermorel for their 1977 book *Sex Pistols: The Inside Story*, her friends assumed that her son, now nationally famous – or notorious – due to his regular appearance in the tabloids, would be able to splash out on a new house for her in the countryside, perhaps even with a swimming pool.[30]

The Pistols did manage to play one show at a church in central London, Notre Dame Hall, which had been specially set up for a visiting television crew from NBC America. They were shooting a documentary on the Sex Pistols and punk, which was to be broadcast across the US later in the summer to coincide with news of the Jubilee, under the title *The New Elizabethans*. This, they wanted to say, was what was really going on in Britain, beneath the obfuscation of the pomp and pageantry that TV viewers around the world would be seeing that summer.

'It is the newest music from the country where Handel composed the Messiah,' the broadcast began:

> This is punk rock and its purpose, one observer said, is to promote violence, sex and destruction in that order ... it is a rare punk performance that doesn't end up with somebody hurt or something destroyed, usually for no discernible reason.

On this occasion the hall was lent to the Pistols – banned almost everywhere else – on the strict condition that only fifty people were allowed in to watch the performance. Inside the newly decorated hall, its ceiling 'decorated with shimmering stars', an expectant *Record Mirror* reporter, Barry Cain, felt as if he was waiting for a 'school nativity play to begin'. The audience was muted and Rotten felt the need to berate them, instructing them to get up and move, but the momentum of a normal show – with the audience feeding off the aggression coming from the stage – was repeatedly broken by the appearance on-stage of a production assistant with a clapper board after every song.[31] The Pistols must have been desperate to get out and perform after two months in and out of the studio, and with the A&M fiasco threatening their existence; in the footage that NBC shot they were on blistering form.

*

By May 1977, around eighteen months after their first appearance, the Sex Pistols had cut two singles, one of which, 'God Save the Queen' for A&M, had been withdrawn before reaching the public; the other, 'Anarchy in the UK', made a target of the public and media backlash that had stalled its rise up the nation's charts, before it too was withdrawn in January. But now, after exhausting all other options, McLaren signed the Pistols to a new label, Richard Branson's Virgin Records, a hippy holdout that was desperate to get its hands on the hottest band associated with the exploding punk scene.

Perhaps it was all part of some scheme devised by McLaren, who at one point in his early involvement with the band had envisaged a teenage phenomenon on the scale of the Bay City Rollers – the UK's last major teen phenomenon – which, in his ideal, they would have achieved without ever having actually released any records. If this really had been McLaren's original intention, as he later claimed, then it was a scam that he had already been unable to pull off. There was always likely to be some little corner of the record industry where the band would be welcomed. The involvement of Virgin Records marked the real beginning of Rotten being made the focal point of the Pistols – the star of the band that was supposedly against such redundant notions. Virgin's first press release after signing the band was not composed by McLaren – he was too preoccupied with developing a script for a film about the Pistols – but rather by Caroline Coon, the *Melody Maker* journalist, whose text not only gave Rotten the star treatment but tried to neutralize McLaren's position that the power of the Pistols lay in the fact that they couldn't play, that they were just bad boys who played badly. 'Johnny Rotten, the angelically malevolent Scaramouche,' it began:

is a third-generation son of rock 'n' roll – the galvanic lead singer of the Sex Pistols. His band play at a hard heart-attacking, frantic pace … Johnny is much more than the lead singer of another rock 'n' roll band. He is already a cult hero with a mass following. He has been elected the style-setting, opinion-forming generalissimo of the new sub-cultural movement, which, since January 1976, has been scything through youth's grass roots disenchantment with society and the state of mainstream rock.[32]

After six months of demonization in the tabloid press, Virgin Records were determined that the Pistols should be taken more seriously, and seen as more-or-less normal human beings, not any more unusual than most of the teenagers up and down the country who would be buying their records. The most interesting engagement to date between the press and the Pistols camp – if it could be called that – was when a local newspaper, the *Islington Gazette*, sent an observant reporter named Robert Addison to meet the Lydon family at home to find out more about Johnny. 'The Sex Pistols have no stauncher ally than Johnny Rotten's mum,' the article stated. Mrs Lydon, it turned out, was not at all happy about how her boy had been treated in the press. As Addison helped himself to tea and biscuits, Rotten's mum was having her say. 'My boy is doing his own thing. He's not going around murdering people,' she argued:

> Groups like Johnny's help society by bringing kids off the streets. A friend of ours thinks the Sex Pistols are doing more for the country than [Prime Minister] Jim Callaghan.

Just then, Addison noted, 'a budgie flew past and landed on the teapot.' It was surely a sign, he reasoned, that 'the Lydon family believes in freedom.'[33]

In the process of being moved along by EMI and then A&M, and passed over by others, such as CBS and Polydor – once keen on signing the Pistols, now scared off by the adverse press they had received – McLaren had collected large amounts of cash in the early months of 1977 to add to the advances the Pistols had already received from EMI and Barclay Records (who released the band's records in France and Switzerland). Indeed, to an uninformed outsider, they probably seemed to be better paid than some members of the Royal Family. When Princess Margaret, fifth in line to the throne, split from her husband Lord Snowdon in 1976, it was reported that she would continue to receive £35,000 a year from the public purse – less than these punk upstarts had so far received from McLaren's record company dealings.

The mainstream press continued to be bemused by the events surrounding the Pistols, and the seeming ease with which they were accumulating new recording contracts. For the broadsheet – or serious newspapers – their success was assured because of the seemingly endless publicity dedicated to their misadventures in the tabloids, 'undertaken', *The Guardian* reported, without irony, 'free of charge by newspapers and television companies'.[34] But the fact that these newspapers and television companies were covering the band's every move, and the sensationalist responses in the scandal sheets, was just one more indication that within a matter of months the Pistols had become established in the public imagination like no other group since the days of The Beatles and The Rolling Stones.

Despite their high public profile and the hullabaloo that surrounded everything they did, there were still attempts to render the Pistols silent and invisible. Anyone walking through London as Jubilee Day approached would have seen buses plastered with a neutered version of Jamie Reid's portrait of the Queen – the safety pin though her lip, and the song title and band name removed. It was the only way the record could be advertised. Major high-street chains such as Woolworths, WHSmith and Boots refused to stock the single, and in some places during Jubilee week, displays of the Top 20 in shops had a blank space in the number-two spot where the Pistols single should have been. A television advert produced by Virgin to celebrate the signing of the Pistols and their first single for the label had been refused airtime by Thames TV. Virgin Records' Al Clark told a trade paper that the situation had resulted in a 'unanimity of bans'. Aside from Virgin's own records stores, and other small and independent shops, the label was facing a shut-out on all fronts. Adverts plastered across the capital and elsewhere, Clark claimed, were being defaced or torn down by royalists.[35]

Even *Sounds*, one of the main weekly music newspapers, ran redesigned – which is to say, censored – adverts for 'God Save the Queen' in the week of the single's release, because their printers refused to handle the advert with Jamie Reid's original illustration included. In both versions of the advert – one with the illustration, the other with just a blank white background – was included a straight announcement, produced to resemble a typewritten note, that read:

> Sex Pistols' God Save the Queen.
> It won't be on the new album and it may not be
> out at all for very long.
> So get it while you can.
> Sex Pistols' God Save the Queen.
> Available only as a single, from Saturday May 28th
> at shops with the sign.

To the horror of many, it was racing towards the top of the nation's pop charts – Virgin's UK distributors had been shipping our 25,000 copies a day to those stores that had not banned it, an 'unprecedented' number for Virgin Records.[36] It was threatening to be the soundtrack to the week for the nation's youth, as well as the inspiration for what the *New Musical Express* would refer to as the 'Jubilee vigilantes' who set out to confront the punks on their own terms, ramping up the violence throughout the summer as clashes raged along the King's Road every Saturday afternoon.[37]

Under different circumstances, London during the Queen's Silver Jubilee might have been an environment in which a self-declared 'slag' like Steve Jones, founder of the Sex Pistols and former burglar, could have prospered. When it all came down to it, that's what musicians were anyway: a bunch of chancers – slags and crims, as he was fond of saying. As the population of London was set to double in size during the week of the Jubilee festivities in the summer of 1977, the Metropolitan Police were warning anyone who would listen that among the number of this swelling mass of humanity would be thousands of additional slags and crims: expert pickpockets – men and women Jones might have, at another time, felt some kinship with – who were apparently making their way to the city from as far away as Australia and South America. It would be a long way to come if the work wasn't so easy and profitable.

The pickings for those involved in the legal fleecing of tourists and well-wishers were no less obvious; a fortune might be made in renting out a modestly sized home for a week, it was reported, even in some of London's less fashionable boroughs. And there was a killing to be made selling tat and bric-a-brac of every variety to the masses: cheap mugs stamped with the obligatory Jubilee crest, T-shirts, satin bomber jackets and anything else prominently displaying the Queen's head that could be fashioned in time for the arrival of the great influx of – they hoped – free-spending visitors.[38]

Those who were not out to make a quick bob or two – most ordinary people – were preoccupied with the opportunities for fun promised by the street parties being planned up and down the country, including over 4,000 in London alone.[39] Even among residents of the countless tower blocks that actually had no streets, but which had sprouted like the advance sign of a bad future to come in the years since the Queen had taken up the throne in 1952, were finding ways of adapting the idea of the street party. These people comprised a surprising proportion of the population, since three-quarters of all new housing built in the country over the previous ten years or so was in the form of tower blocks.[40] But while the narrow walkways and confined balconies of such places were unsuitable to accommodate the long trestle tables that were to be laid out with refreshments in the country's more traditional streets – a prize of £1,000 was to be awarded to the best decorated street – the residents made do by splitting themselves into small groups, led by enterprising mothers who wanted to see that their children didn't miss out.[41]

In fact there was every chance that no one in this country, which had changed so much in the previous 25 years, would fail to notice the occasion; even the 'girlie' magazines, or as *The Guardian* newspaper put it, 'Her Majesty's loyal publishers of sex magazines', had special Jubilee editions.[42] There were, however, some surprising latecomers to the party. Representatives of the far-left republican tendency in the kingdom had remained mostly muted and, indeed, determinedly apathetic, intent on ignoring the entire thing rather than giving it the recognition that protest and opposition would provide. That is, at least, until almost the arrival of the festivities, when they realized there might be a way to take advantage of unfolding events. Yes, by all means do celebrate, advised a London group known as the Movement Against the Monarchy, just days before Jubilee week, but just make sure that what you are celebrating is the Jubilee of the death of George VI, and not the accession of his daughter.[43]

As the day that was marked out as the centrepiece of celebrations approached – 7 June had been declared 'Jubilee Day' – some of the country's most beloved entertainers at the

time, Rolf Harris and Max Bygraves among them, swung
into action and were preparing for a tour that would alight
on almost every London borough, making merry from the
procession of decorated floats that were to carry them around
on their highly publicized itinerary.[44] But the crowning event
on the run-up to Jubilee Day was the lighting of a network of
bonfires, acting as beacons to convey the news of the start of
the celebrations. The lighting began in Windsor Great Park,
with the Queen herself igniting the first torch, 'a dramatic sight',
seen on TV by millions the following evening, of 'huge flames
and great surging crowds of people'.[45] Thereafter, the fires spread
from one location to the next at the sight of a firework shot into
the sky, until the network had spread to all corners of the country,
ending the following day with the lighting of the final beacon on
the Orkney Islands.[46]

As the Queen returned to Windsor Castle that night, the other
Queen, featuring Freddie Mercury and his bandmates – whose
'Bohemian Rhapsody' had been the best-selling single of the
previous year – were performing for a crowd of 19,000 fans under
a new lighting rig that was shaped like a crown, in the first of
two Jubilee benefit concerts. Far from such celebrations, in the
streets around the capital, it wasn't unusual to find angry young
monarchists – perhaps more anti-punk than pro-monarchy –
who could be heard railing against these alien punks now in
their midst. 'They called the bloody Queen a bloody moron,'
screamed a handful of young men encountered by a *Guardian*
reporter (who wanted to tell them that they were the morons
the song referred to), as they ripped down posters for the Sex
Pistols' newest record.[47] It was a record described by Malcolm
McLaren as 'the boys' own personal tribute to the Queen'.[48] But
as tributes go, it was anything but reverential. It was a leering
howl of defiance, presented in a cover that had caused uproar

– with Queen Elizabeth's portrait modified with a safety pin, punk style, through her upper lip.

It may have seemed to be a perfect storm of bad publicity, precisely in line with what one might have expected from the Pistols, but in fact the release of 'God Save the Queen' was an accident of timing. Johnny Rotten, author of the words that had been seemingly misheard by everyone – it was not the Queen he referred to as a moron, but rather her subjects – later said that at the time he wrote the song (then titled 'No Future') in 1976, he had no idea that the Jubilee was even on the horizon.[49]

Republicans may, in retrospect, have considered it a suitable tribute for any monarch. And if it was not something that the Sex Pistols had planned, well at least it was more likely to be remembered than the ill-fated gift proposed to mark this anniversary by the leading republican figure in the British Labour government. Tony Benn, the former Viscount Stansgate who had given up his hereditary title as a matter of principle, had suggested at a Cabinet meeting that the Queen might like to receive a gift that had some meaning attached to it, instead of the usual symbolic baubles that are presented to heads of state. After all, what, he wondered, do you give the woman who has everything she wants? Speaking to a meeting of the Cabinet, he argued that the government should simply re-gift a vase that he already had in his possession – chiefly for its symbolic value. It was an item that was undeniably a product of the workers, and therefore, he thought, the perfect gift from a Labour government that represented the idea of labour. It had been fashioned from coal, a highly symbolic material in the Labour movement, and it had been given to Benn by the Polish Minister of Mines. Alas, the Cabinet balked at the idea of giving the monarch a lump of coal on this, her twenty-fifth anniversary, being afraid that it would offend the Queen. In the end, they opted to gift her a simple coffee pot.[50]

As a senior member of the government, Benn – despite his republicanism – was a member of the Privy Council, the Queen's coterie of advisers, and was expected to attend official functions. As he was driving through a cleaned-up London on the morning of Jubilee Day to the service at St Paul's Cathedral, Benn noted the scene on the streets along a route that took in the Strand, where the gathering crowds 'packed behind crash barriers' were positioning themselves to watch the royal procession. They were faced, Benn recalled, by 'soldiers and Gurkhas, airmen and sailors, some with fixed bayonets'. It was an endless sight of 'crowds and crowds, all waving Union Jacks and cheering', which in spite of his misgivings about the role of the monarchy in British society, nonetheless made the day 'rather fun'.[51] Such was the effect of the Jubilee in overcoming what many had feared would be apathy in the country; and it was in this atmosphere that the Sex Pistols would become prey for those who saw them, and what they represented, as an attack on the very fabric of British life.

On the day of the Jubilee the Pistols and more than 150 guests sailed up and down the River Thames past the Palace of Westminster on an early evening jaunt organized jointly by Virgin Records and Glitterbest. The plan was to have the group launch into song under the half-dozen or so bridges they would stop under as the party got into full swing. Guests on the trip recalled that it started out as a great shebang, but for some the atmosphere on the small boat was claustrophobic, with Rotten caught on camera muttering, 'Did you ever get the feeling you've been trapped?' There was a feeling that this was the beginning of the point of no return, beyond which – for Rotten at least – the music would always be of secondary importance to the spectacle of the Pistols perpetrating endless outrages. The evening ended with McLaren, Westwood and

Jubilee day, on board the *Queen Elizabeth*: Rotten mutters
to the camera, 'ever get the feeling you've been trapped?'
Steve Jones and Sid Vicious during the band's performance,
and McLaren being hauled away by the police.

many others being arrested, with Westwood charged with
kicking and punching police officers as they dragged McLaren
into a waiting van.

Before the river police had directed the boat back to shore,
a fight had already broken out. With the booze flowing and
various occupants on the boat already flying on speed, and
press people jostling for space with photographers and people
carrying sound recording equipment, it didn't take much to upset
Jah Wobble, Rotten's notoriously combustible friend. Someone
barged into him, a press photographer who wasn't looking
at where he was going, and – as in the barroom brawls of
old Hollywood westerns – Wobble's seemingly innocuous

gesture of pushing back at the photographer set in motion a wave of scuffles that swept through the boat.[52]

The arrival of the police brought an end to the truculent Pistols' performance, with Jones dropping in to cover the lead vocals for Rotten, who didn't want to be there and initially didn't want to sing. But the shutdown was not an unwelcome outcome; it guaranteed yet more headlines and outrage.[53] McLaren was aware of Wobble's reputation for reckless acts of tomfoolery, and had been scheming a way to goad him into hijacking the vessel and running it into a bridge or a police patrol boat. As he was dragged away by the police, he even pointed out Rotten to them in desperation, giving them a chance to apprehend public enemy number one: 'There's Johnny Rotten! Arrest him!' But the singer managed to slink away into the night.

*

Whatever the mood in London during that Jubilee week, and despite the fact that it seemed that the country was – against expectations – embracing the numerous celebratory events, it was still far from the kind of euphoria that had pervaded the air at the height of sixties optimism and which, in particular, had given birth to Swinging London. The enthusiasm for the Jubilee was more like a forlorn attempt to make some kind of stand against the general air of deterioration that had hung over what had been, so far, a strange decade of discord and failure. Even London's main tourist streets and prominent buildings, washed down and spruced up, could not for long deflect the air of gloom.

That the mood in the country that summer was still riven with tension was illustrated in the weeks following the Jubilee cele-brations, when members of the Sex Pistols, as well as some of their friends and associates, had been roughed-up in a number of street attacks.[54] Pretty soon there were ritual battles between Teds and Punks on the King's Road every Saturday afternoon. McLaren and Westwood's shop was an easy focal point, and people who tried to get to the shop had to run a gauntlet of Teds who seemed to want to kill them.[55] Nancy Spungen, girlfriend of Sid Vicious, was arrested and charged with carrying an offensive weapon – a truncheon – which she kept handy to fend off Teds.[56] But the chaos spread more widely, encouraged by the mood around the time of the Jubilee, with Teddy boys hunting down their new enemy and

> leaving a trail of destruction from Trafalgar Square through Chinatown and Soho into Oxford Street. They rampaged through the streets, throwing bottles at shop windows and forcing shopkeepers to close their doors.[57]

With their now famous faces and clearly identifiable look – Rotten in particular was frequently recognized – some of the Pistols were now easy targets for anyone who fancied taking a pop at them. Sections of the tabloid press, in fact, were quite keen to make the Pistols (and punk generally) targets in the minds of readers offended by their 'attack' on the Queen. 'Punish the Punks', ran an editorial in the Sunday Mirror soon after Jubilee week. On the front page of the same issue of the newspaper, under the headline 'Punk Rock Jubilee Shocker', the Pistols were accused of an assault on the Queen – in the form of their single 'God Save the Queen', which was incorrectly interpreted as labelling the monarch a 'moron'. Something had to be done, urged the press, to quell this 'spitting, swearing, savage pop music of rebellious youth' that was 'sweeping teenage Britain'.[58]

And punished the punks were. Looking back on the period two years later, the music paper Melody Maker noted that while

'Jubilee Week was a triumph for Glitterbest and their intention of spreading havoc', it was also a 'physically painful success for some of them':

> Jamie Reid, wearing a 'God Save The Queen' tee-shirt with a safety-pin through Her Majesty's nose, was beaten up by patriotic Teddy Boys, his leg and nose broken. Johnny Rotten was twice assaulted within three days. And Paul Cook had 15 stitches in a head wound.[59]

Rotten was not alone at the time of his first assault, on 18 June 1977. He had been enjoying a post-work drink with the other band members and Chris Thomas and Bill Price, the band's producer and studio engineer, after working on 'Holidays in the Sun' at Wessex Sound Studios in North London.[60] Sometime early in the evening Jones and Cook disappeared to go their own way for the night. As Chris Thomas later recalled, the three who remained ventured outside to the car park after drawing the attention of some menacing-looking older men inside the pub, where they were confronted with what looked like a 'football team – eleven blokes':

> they dragged me off . . . I got kicked to the ground, but apparently Bill dragged somebody off me who was lunging at me with a knife. So they took him round the corner and gave him a good kicking. There was like three guys and one knife, they were passing the knife . . . that happened on the Saturday, it was front page on the Tuesday. I went to work [at a McCartney session] and everybody had been scouring the hospitals. I just walked in, they showed me the paper, 'Oh that was Saturday night.'[61]

But even in 1977, in the middle of the storm of publicity that looked like just another passing fad, Jones and the Sex Pistols, and their entourage, seemed destined to be remembered. The day after *The Times* had reported on two (possibly three) attacks on band members in a single day, it noted in its 'Diary' section that a ceremony organized by the London pop music station Capital Radio was due to take place. In celebration of the Jubilee, the radio station had decided to dedicate a time capsule to posterity, to be buried in 1977 and opened on the Queen's Golden Jubilee in 2002. Its contents, which had been voted for by listeners, were selected to provide a snapshot of Britain at that moment in time, and included such items as a pint of North Sea oil, Jubilee coins and stamps, a menu from the Hilton and one from a transport café, a birth control pill, some low-tar cigarettes and 'a tape of that monstrous group, the Sex Pistols, singing their appalling song about the Queen.'[62]

During the year so far, the Sex Pistols had slowly but surely expanded in the public imagination as the most hideous example of a strange new phenomenon that seemed to be gripping the youth of the nation. Punk had exploded in the wake of the Pistols much more quickly and to more devastating effect than anyone could have imagined, and the rash of new bands appearing every week seemed to hark back to the golden era of the previous decade, when pop music went from being a product aimed at teenagers caught in a passing phase of their lives to a new culture and way of life that was far more durable. 'This Definitely Ain't the Summer of Love', ran the front page of the *New Musical Express* a few weeks after the Jubilee. There was a heavy hint in the headline, signalling that there would be no repeat of that summer of 1967, the summer of peace and love. In a fit of disbelief at what was going on across the country, the *NME* ran multiple stories that aimed to provide a snapshot of the recent events that seemed to indicate that various authorities were making every attempt to close down, shut out or expel those parts of the newly blooming music scene deemed undesirable. 'Deportation and death threats loom over Johnny Thunders' Heartbreakers and the Sex Pistols', the paper's lead story explained:

> On Monday the Home Office ordered Thunders and Co out of the UK – and the Pistols plan to go into hiding after the beatings handed out to Johnny Rotten and Paul Cook . . . a GLC boss says he will use any means within the law to stop the Pistols playing London again. He also thinks the [Bay City] Rollers would be improved by sudden death.[63]

This was the view of the forthright member of the Conservative-controlled Greater London Council and former army officer Bernard Brook-Partridge, who claimed to have 'felt unclean for 48 hours' after he was exposed to the Pistols. 'I think the Sex Pistols are absolutely bloody revolting,' he said:

> I think their whole attitude is calculated to incite people to misbehaviour . . . whether their act is also blasphemous and seditious is another matter. Parts that I heard were certainly blasphemous. I was not elected to support blasphemy, which, by the way, is a crime.[64]

At the same time as all this was going on, and in an attempt to seek an escape from the chaos surrounding the Pistols' daily existence in the often-hostile post-Jubilee London, the band were sent to Scandinavia for two weeks in early July, after Vicious and Rotten pleaded with McLaren to get them out of the country.[65]

*

Russ Meyer on the set of *Who Killed Bambi?* on the one and only day of shooting, September 1977.

Just as the atmosphere around the Pistols became almost intolerable and the group were shuffled off to Sweden, Russ Meyer arrived in London to begin pre-production work on McLaren's Sex Pistols film. Meyer was the director of classic Hollywood trash movies such as *Beyond the Valley of the Dolls* and the fabulously named *Faster, Pussycat . . . Kill! Kill!*, 'a tale of desert lust, murder, and *double entendres*, with the gorgeously menacing Tura Satana leading a pack of karate-chopping strippers'. He flew into London to meet with everyone involved in the Sex Pistols film that he had recently been contracted to direct.[66] Making a film based around a musical or music biz theme was not necessarily alien to Meyer (*Beyond the Valley of the Dolls*, his most successful movie to date, concerned the misadventures of a fictitious female rock band named The Carrie Nations, who graduate from high school proms to stardom, with sex and violence ensuing), and nor, like for McLaren and the Pistols, was running the gauntlet of mainstream censorship.[67] Indeed, critics suggested that Meyer's obsession with Amazonian female dominatrix types indicated that he was 'perhaps the unhappy victim of a neurosis which could be more successfully treated by psychiatry than by filmmaking'.[68] In the days when *Beyond the Valley of the Dolls* was made, studios were keen to avoid their movies being rated X for sexual content, and Meyer represented the limit of Hollywood's testing of the public appetite for soft porn.

Meyer was fond of casting his films with quintessentially all-American specimens: men with granite jaws alongside women who sported industrial-strength bras. His female leads were often – as in *Beyond the Valley of the Dolls* – former *Playboy* magazine models, and usually the story and the creation of characters would follow the casting. With the Sex Pistols, however, he had a readymade core cast of band members who did not match up to the typical Meyer heroes and villains, built for sex and violence. Where, in a Sex Pistols film, would he find space for the leading ladies his own fans demanded, those with 'outrageous balconies'?[69] On first meeting Johnny Rotten he was unimpressed with the star of his film's dole-queue physique. 'You wouldn't last a day in the army,' he said, looking at Rotten's stovepipe arms. 'What the fuck do I need the army for,' replied Rotten.[70] This was perhaps a sign that the two camps would find it hard to meet on terms that they could both comprehend. They ploughed on regardless, however, with the disciplinarian ex-GI in Meyer coming out in his suggestion that to deal with the work-shy Pistols during shooting, it might be advisable to have them all staying in a trailer with him, 'so they couldn't get away'.[71]

Despite this apparent clash of values – if not worlds – as represented by Meyer, the brash and buccaneering maverick, and Rotten, the sneering juvenile nihilist, the director had already got a whiff of the cash, and that was all that mattered. Anything that could fund the next Russ Meyer project was fair game to him, something to be turned to his advantage. McLaren saw Meyer as the best person to further his ends, and also to avoid the Pistols being pulled into the simplified political narrative that the press were beginning to latch onto to make sense of this phenomenon: punk rock as dole queue rock.[72] The Pistols came out of SEX, not out of the dole-queue (not one of them came from the dole queues), and Meyer came on the back of the fantastical *Beyond the Valley of the Dolls*, which, in the words of the McLaren biographer Craig Bromberg, was 'a curiously kinetic combination of experimental camera work, sexploitation antics, and rock 'n' roll chaos'.[73] Hiring Meyer promised to project a bizarre world, perhaps one that had one foot in the future and was far enough removed from the mundane aspects of life in England to separate the Pistols – in telling the story of their origins and rise – from the phenomenon of punk that they had created. Anything but 'a grainy, black and white, Polish, socialist, realist movie', thought McLaren.[74]

The story of how Meyer ended up being brought on board for McLaren's pet project, a film about the Sex Pistols that was conceived mere months after their first public outrage, is probably not as odd as it at first seems, although it does illustrate something of the unusual nature of those times. McLaren's explanation to the band was that the film would be the perfect vehicle to stand in lieu of the Pistols themselves in the face of all the bans that seemed to be preventing them from playing all over the country;

his pitch to the Hollywood moguls that he pursued for funding was that the movie was necessary because the Sex Pistols were not simply a music group, as he told the *Los Angeles Times*:

> They play music and they write songs, but they are more of a social event. With a film, we can demonstrate very clearly the whole social condition that the band came out of and deliver that in its most pure and undiluted form to everyone outside of the UK.[75]

McLaren had managed to convince Meyer that his charges were big fans of *Beyond the Valley of the Dolls* – which was a staple of late-night weekend cinema in London in those days. For the director, finding out that the Pistols' two most notorious members went by the names Sid Vicious and Johnny Rotten had him reaching for the phone to bring on board the screenwriter Roger Ebert (later better known as one of the most respected film critics in America), who had worked with Meyer on *Beyond the Valley of the Dolls* and other films, such as *Supervixens*. 'We can go wild on this,' Meyer told Ebert, adding that the wheels had already been set in motion: 'I've got a couple of big-titted London girls already in mind.'[76] It also helped that Meyer and Ebert were being offered luxurious living quarters for their spell in England, as well as 1 per cent of the film's profits. It might, he thought, offer a way out of 'the straight bosoms-and-brawn' genre that had earned him the title of King of the Nudies.[77]

The next step was for the main parties to convene in Hollywood to try and hash out the details of the working arrangement, and see what could be rescued from McLaren's existing script, which was the product of the efforts of a number of temporary collaborators; in addition to McLaren, there had been input from Johnny Speight, creator of Alf Garnett, and Don Boyd, a young British film director, before he found his way to Russ Meyer and his people.[78]

So, in early July McLaren flew to Los Angeles to meet with Meyer, Rene Daalder, a young scriptwriter Meyer had arranged to work with McLaren on the screenplay, and Roger Ebert, who had written the screenplay for *Beyond the Valley of the Dolls*. For Meyer, *Who Killed Bambi?*, the name of the future Sex Pistols movie, was to be the follow-up to his great success. But Rene Daalder, who quickly became friends with McLaren, was caught between two apparently irreconcilable ambitions: the anarchic art school slant brought by Malcolm, and Russ Meyer's camp sensibilities:

> Russ wanted the movie to be the follow-up to his outrageously campy masterpiece *Beyond the Valley of the Dolls*, written by Ebert. Roger was, of course, totally into Meyer's thing. Malcolm had no idea what he had gotten himself into, since the Sex Pistols came from an entirely different world than Russ.[79]

It fell to Ebert to put 'his twisted stamp' on the script.[80] He was soon holed-up at the Sunset Marquis, a West Hollywood hotel hidden down a tree-lined cul-de-sac off Sunset Strip, favoured by visiting rock stars and actors waiting for appointments with Hollywood industry people. There he worked on infusing the McLaren–Daalder script with the quintessential elements of a Russ Meyer production – most notably, Sid Vicious raping his junkie mother – to ensure that 'the disparate worlds of McLaren and Meyer had intersected at last.'[81]

Ebert quickly knocked out a draft treatment based on McLaren's existing script and the discussions that had taken place since his arrival in Los Angeles. Known as the 'fastest typewriter in the West', Ebert was egged on by the hectoring of Meyer, one of whose common refrains when they were working at close quarters was 'What's wrong?! I can't hear you typing!' as the screenwriter tried to work on character development and

plotting.[82] The film was to be titled *Anarchy in the UK*. It had
initially been conceived of as an updated reworking of The
Beatles' film *A Hard Day's Night*, with the Pistols cast as a kind
of inverted Fab Four: the most hated band in the land.

But, following McLaren's desire to take aim at not only the
British establishment but the rock establishment, figures such
as Mick Jagger and Rod Stewart – now living a life that was
vastly removed from those of the kids in the street – were
made a target. A character with Jagger's initials, 'M.J.', is
portrayed as a defiler of beauty and innocence, appearing
in the opening scene of the newly named *Who Killed Bambi?*,
as Ebert recounted later:

> A millionaire rock star leaps from his Rolls and kills a deer with a
> bow and arrow. He is witnessed committing this act by a young
> girl who reappears at the end of the film to assassinate the star
> and shout the immortal line, 'That's for Bambi!' . . . The action
> included such passages as Vicious fighting a dog named Ringo
> and Johnny Rotten demolishing a street-corner Scientology-style
> testing centre.[83]

Given the film's allusion to the successful animated movie of
the Bambi story, which had recently been playing at the King's
Road cinema within eyeshot of McLaren's shop, *Who Killed Bambi?*
was conceived as a dark perversion of a Disney film set in 'a very
unreal Dickensian-type London'.[84] The final script showed the
Pistols emerging from this imaginary London where:

> Chimney sweeps, laughing Cockney bobbies, blind beggars
> playing concertinas and a Jack the Ripper necrophile mingle
> with a modern cast of punks, Teds, whores and the Levantine
> doormen of grubby stripclubs.[85]

Recent actual events, such as the attack suffered by Paul Cook in the dark passages of a London Tube tunnel, were also incorporated into the script, with roving gangs of Teddy boys seeking revenge on members of the Pistols for the affront caused by 'God Save the Queen'. At this point in proceedings neither Meyer nor Ebert had met the Sex Pistols, so they had to rely on McLaren's tales of their exploits to draw such characterizations. Meyer began to envision Rotten as Mr Micawber from Dickens's *David Copperfield*. And if these characters, with names like Rotten and Vicious, sounded unbelievable, or too good to be true, McLaren himself was something of an oddity in the Hollywood setting where they hashed out their script. Judging by the way he dressed, Ebert thought, he could have been an excellent subject for a film all on his own.

McLaren arrived in Hollywood outfitted with some of his boutique's most distinctive and popular items of clothing, including the famous 'Destroy' T-shirt and 'leather pants equipped with buckles and straps' – the famous bondage trousers. 'On his feet', Ebert noted, 'he wore what Russ approvingly noted were [called] Brothel Creepers.'[86] For the two B-movie veterans, McLaren, with his London boutique of sex wares and bondage gear, was a curiosity, and represented someone surely within the imaginative orbit of the kind of films they made: sex, trash and exploitation were their preoccupations and, arguably, had also been McLaren's, since the transformation of 430 King's Road into SEX. Just as Meyer had shown himself to be the film director who affirmed the widely held view that 'sex sells, beyond doubt', courtesy of his ability to inhabit a space somewhere between the outskirts of the Hollywood mainstream and the porn industry out on the further fringes, so McLaren had wanted to make sexual liberation and clothing with fetishistic overtones daily wear for the next generation.[87] Yet it was nonetheless strange for Ebert and Meyer to see someone walking around dressed in quasi-bondage gear as if it was normal. (Meyer himself wore practical army khakis or jodhpurs more often than not.) The bondage pants, Ebert thought, were clearly intended to make the wearer ready for action wherever and whenever the moment took hold – capable of 'being rendered immobile at the crack of a whip'.[88]

More often than not, these strange trousers, when transplanted into the milieu of entertainment industry meetings and lunches, represented obstacles to negotiating the most benign activities – activities that were far removed from the boudoir of the typical S&M aficionado (many of whom, of course, were McLaren's customers back in London). It was to prove, in a strange way, a practical test of McLaren and Westwood's stated aim of designing bondage and rubber wear for the street and office. 'The buckles and straps' of the bondage pants, Ebert noted, 'saw action in restaurants, where he'd sometimes get his restraints tangled and overturn his chair'.[89] Following completion of a second draft of *Bambi* in Los Angeles, McLaren, Meyer and Ebert flew to London to meet the ostensible stars of their movie, the four members of the Sex Pistols. On the flight over to England with McLaren, Meyer refused to sit anywhere but the aisle seat. If the plane went down, he reasoned, McLaren would get his bondage trousers tangled in the seat, and perhaps mortally endanger the life of anyone stuck in the inside seats.[90]

Once in London, they soon cast Marianne Faithfull to play the mother of Sid Vicious and the American singer P. J. Proby to play the part of the manager of the decadent rock star M.J. But it was proving more difficult to find the kind of actors Meyer typically used to populate the busy scenes he was known for. What London lacked, it seemed, was women with sufficiently Meyer-esque physical attributes. And so one of McLaren's friends, Gerry

Goldstein, was hired on the then handsome wage of £100 per week to 'scour the clubs and brothels' of Soho and beyond to search out women who possessed busts of 'at least 48 inches', but which were, in Meyer's words, 'cantilevered'.[91]

McLaren, Meyer and Ebert continued with their preparations for *Who Killed Bambi?*, driving around London scouting locations, with the director enthusiastically suggesting that the most grotesque of all the band members, Sid, should make his first appearance in the film by crawling out of a drain in Wapping – a place name that seemed to become imbued with some unknown sexual connotations 'once submitted to his fantastic imagination', McLaren recalled: 'Wahh-ping', he'd intone in his Texan drawl, as if it really meant 'fucking'.[92]

Rolling Stone journalist Charles M. Young, visiting London for a cover story on the Pistols in the weeks following Meyer and Ebert's arrival in the city, managed to capture some indelible images of the clash of cultures that was taking place. The middle-aged Meyer and Ebert were hauled around the capital to the hotspots of the punk scene, including the Vortex, where McLaren took Meyer to see The Slits perform. There were readings of the script where Vicious would turn up with his girlfriend, Nancy Spungen, who according to Meyer 'always wore dirty gabardine raincoats'.[93] Cook and Jones were quite happy to go along with the film, but Rotten and Vicious were more sceptical about the entire purpose of the project, with Rotten saying at the time that while he liked some things about Meyer's films, particularly the amount of visual detail he squeezed into a shot, he had thrown out several versions of the Pistols movie script because he thought they were ridiculous.[94] The key to getting Rotten on board was to produce a script that he could live with, that he might even identify with, which meant they had to try and get inside his head and closer to the way he thought. They needed to understand what – for them – was the strange language and logic Rotten used; it seemed to offer the key to his character. Jon Savage wrote that it was as if Rotten was a laboratory 'slide specimen'.[95]

As the atmosphere between Rotten and Meyer grew tetchier, the former's explanation of the finer points of English verbal abuse became an excuse to disrespect the film director: 'A weed is a pansy,' Rotten said. 'If you don't know that, it's just an indication of how fuckin' stupid you Americans are.' Meyer was unused to being spoken to in such an abusive manner, and tried to put the young punk in his place: 'Just a minute, boy. In '44 we saved your asses,' he said.[96] Rotten's attempt to defuse the situation by taking a toilet break only confirmed for Charles M. Young the comedy of misunderstanding that was blighting the development of a working relationship between director and star:

> 'Where's the bog?'
>
> 'Down the hall to the left,' says Meyer. 'There's ale in the refrigerator and on the counter, if you want it warm.'
>
> 'No, the bog, man,' says Rotten. 'You know, the shithouse, the wankhole.'
>
> 'Oh! The bathroom!' says Meyer. 'Straight down the hall.' Rotten trots off.
>
> 'Hmmm,' Meyer continues, 'what do you think about "Bog" for a movie title? "Bog," with an exclamation point.'[97]

Rotten and Meyer couldn't get along, and the singer regularly sought to insult the director, befuddling him by speaking in local slang that was as impenetrable to Meyer as Nadsat, the language of the yobs in Anthony Burgess's *A Clockwork Orange*. The director tried to console himself with the fact that the animosity was probably never truly personal, and that it wouldn't stop the film – which could be the crowning achievement of his career – from being made. He thought that Rotten just had a bad attitude and hated all Americans. But he was wrong. Rotten, by this time, was bent on disrupting what he now realized was a project more about Malcom McLaren than about the Sex Pistols.

With Meyer and Ebert sending the script through numerous rewrites, McLaren was losing control of his vision and could only look on bewildered as they began 'turning *Bambi* into Beyond the Valley of the Sex Pistols', with Meyer casting himself in a cameo that allowed him to address the audience at the beginning and end of the film.[98] As well as the never-ending verbal spats with McLaren, Meyer continued to be 'emphatically unimpressed by Rotten's aggressive rudeness'.[99] He expected total commitment from his 'actors' and here was his star, Rotten, conforming to all of his ideas of lazy indifference: intimidating waiters and swearing casually and profusely with no qualms about offending anyone within earshot. Meyer may have been King of the Nudies, but there were limits. 'In all the years I knew him,' Ebert later wrote,

> I never heard Russ Meyer say the word 'fucking'. Perhaps he had too much respect for the concept. He preferred such synonyms as 'wail', 'pound', 'pummel', 'belabour' and 'conjoin', always pronounced with enthusiasm.[100]

And it was because of Meyer's obsession with turning the project into a Russ Meyer film, relegating the singer to 'M.J.'s dour punk competition, a sex-starved antistar whose libidinal cravings lead him to various sordid and anonymous sexual encounters in numerous steamed-up London phone booths', that Rotten's ire continued to send him into more profane harangues.[101]

Caught between being seen by the world as either McLaren's puppet for meekly taking part in a project he had no input into, or else even just being associated in the minds of the public with Meyer and Ebert's twisted caricature, Rotten wanted out, and was going to extremes to avoid cooperating. He started going around to jumble sales, collecting the clothes that he intended to turn up in when shooting began. He decided to upset the idea that he was 'punk incarnate' by dressing like a hated hippy, as Julien Temple recalled: outrageous glitter-era platform shoes and 'big, flared, flowery bell-bottoms'.[102]

The plan had been for the Pistols to film their scenes over two months, between October and December, but it all fell through when Meyer walked out, after three days of shooting in early October, ostensibly because the money had already dried up. With Meyer out of the picture, 20th Century Fox shut down the production. McLaren kept up in his attempts to have the film rescued, and within a month he had found a new director, Jonathan Kaplan, along with a new writer, Danny Opatoshu. They produced a new treatment within three weeks but, despite the approval of Rotten and the other members of the band, McLaren absolutely hated it. It departed entirely from the dark fantasy of *Bambi* and instead conceived of the Pistols as emerging from 'high rise blocks and kids of the dole'. Soon enough, Kaplan and Opatoshu were gone too.[103]

Who Killed Bambi? foundered for various reasons, some of them financial and some to do with the inability of key players to maintain sufficiently good working relationships to make it through to the end of the project. But what ultimately divided the project was that for all McLaren's input into the story and the creation of a mad quasi-Dickensian demimonde that might be outlandish enough to further the Sex Pistols myth, the fact was that his star was Johnny Rotten. And Rotten was a real person, who existed now within the star-making mechanisms and aesthetics of popular music, and had just recently staked out his own right to be considered the artistic voice of the Sex Pistols. As Jon Savage says, at some point film and popular music began to work against each other; they became irreconcilable mediums:

> Pop's power relies on an authenticity that, if not social, is existential: 'We know what we *feel*.' McLaren's models for the film were the rupturing of *Blackboard Jungle* and the sleazy, cartoon flash of *The Girl Can't Help It*, but those were products of pop's first innocence, now lost forever. Pop was self-conscious, burdened by its history.[104]

In writing songs and making records, Rotten and the Sex Pistols were unambiguously the artists within the machinery of a music world that revolved around song publishing, and the copyrights that were held in sound recordings – these were the whole basis of the music industry, and they always had their authors and owners. But when it came to the film, the situation was much more complicated. The principal artist was McLaren; he was the one who had conceived the project and who kept on willing it into existence throughout numerous drafts, new scriptwriters and directors, and in the face of opposition from the ostensible subjects of the film, the Sex Pistols. By the summer of 1977 it had become clear that what was primarily contributing to the difficulties surrounding the making of the film was a battle over the artistic control of the Sex Pistols. McLaren, in the words of Virgin Records' Al Clark, 'clearly had absolutely no time for creative artists', especially those who would compete with him:

> I think John was just getting a bit creative, John wanted to exist as a person, and Malcolm thought he was being the real precious little prat, and that he should just enjoy being a Sex Pistol.[105]

6 Bollocks

By the time the Jubilee week came around, and then passed in a blur of controversy for the Sex Pistols, the band had been working on their album for an unduly long while. With their freedom to move around restricted by the animosity that had developed over the previous month or so, Jones and Cook, in particular, busied themselves refining a set of songs that the band had laid down in a number of sessions between summer 1976 and January 1977 (many of them first recorded with Glen Matlock). Jones got into the habit of layering one thundering guitar track on top of another to capture a sound that Chris Thomas described as the sonic equivalent of 'a panzer division' about to roll over you.[1]

The summer of 1977 marked the beginning of Rotten's determination to assert himself against McLaren's various schemes to manipulate his and the band's image. At Richard Branson's prompting, Rotten decided to take up the invitation of Capital Radio to speak about and play his favourite songs. This was part of Branson and Virgin's attempt to stop the juggernaut of bad publicity. The aim was to show the public that these boys were really quite normal, and, moreover, to single out and indulge Rotten, whom Virgin had recognized as the band member with the greatest potential to be a star in a more conventional sense, in line with the way that the music business had always nurtured talented individuals. During the radio interview – conducted by Tommy Vance, an experienced DJ who sounded authoritative and serious – Rotten revealed his

tastes to be defiantly non-punk in character, thus ensuring that
he generated the sort of media response that McLaren thought
was disastrous for the band: the press, for once, saw Rotten as a
human being. The *Sunday Times* even described this young man
who spoke of his passion for the music of performers including
Neil Young, Captain Beefheart and Tim Buckley – all of them old
hippies in McLaren's view – as 'a mild-mannered liberal chap,
with a streets of Islington accent'.[2]

It seemed like the shock of the Pistols might start to wear off,
that they might even be receiving recognition that flew in the
face of McLaren's attempts to uphold the public's idea of them as
a ramshackle, chaotic and amateurish outfit. Robin Denselow, the
music critic for the broadsheet *The Guardian* – not a paper for the
kids – seemed to have been won over by their latest single, 'Pretty
Vacant'. 'Six months ago', he wrote,

> I'd never have believed I'd be praising Mr John Rotten's musical
> abilities, but there's no denying that this is a single almost up
> to early Who standards. As the Pistols aren't allowed to play
> anywhere at the moment, and indeed are in hiding after a series
> of attacks on them, it's impossible to tell if they could repeat
> this on stage, or just how much the experienced producer Chris
> Thomas was responsible for the sound.[3]

If this brush with respectability wasn't unexpected enough, then
an August 1977 story in the *Los Angeles Times* reporting on the
nominees for the third annual Don Kirshner Rock Music Awards
was even more surprising. Despite having had no official releases
to date in the US, Rotten was suddenly elevated into the higher
echelons of music industry notables: 'Sticking out like a sore
thumb in the list of nominees is the Sex Pistols' Johnny Rotten,'
the story reported. He had been nominated along with 'Barry

Manilow, Stevie Wonder, Fleetwood Mac and Bob Seeger in the Rock Personality category'.[4]

In mid-August members of the band – mostly Jones and Cook – were still returning to the studio to record, overdub and add more nuances to some of the tracks that had been laid down earlier in the spring, and to finish work on some more recent songs. Being in the studio was an escape from the streets – streets that were proving particularly hazardous at the time for anyone associated with the Sex Pistols. 'If I was working in the control room, Steve and Paul used to go out and just go through the set,' Chris Thomas remembered. The set the band was rehearsing to perform would, effectively, become the album:

> which lasted about forty minutes . . . then they'd go and watch a bit of telly, and then they'd go downstairs and go through the set again, just simply to stave off boredom. So literally you'd get to the point where backing tracks would be take one. Then put the bass [guitar] on to see if they'd made a mistake anywhere. But it always worked. So, it became very routine . . . The only thing that was distinguishing about the production was the guitar overdubs.[5]

Others who had been inspired by the Sex Pistols to make their own music, such as The Damned, had been able to move quickly towards recording and releasing records, helped by the fact that they had sidestepped the major record companies and opted for the independent label Stiff Records. The Damned's 'New Rose', released on 22 October 1976, was the first record released by a new band that consciously adopted the 'punk' label (although earlier in 1976 the Pistols had made an album's worth of recordings that didn't see the light of day until late 1977, around the same time as their official debut album). 'New Rose' had been

Steve Jones and Paul Cook, 1977.

recorded in a few hours, in a session overseen by Nick Lowe for
Stiff Records that cost – so contemporary reports said – a mere
£46.[6] The Damned had managed this feat just three months after
forming (supposedly with help from Malcolm McLaren) and their
first public performance was opening for the Sex Pistols at the
100 Club in London. In Wessex Studios, the Pistols were probably
paying around £50 per hour just for studio time (and more on
evenings and weekends), which would have included the services
of Bill Price, the studio manager.

But as the months passed and the end of summer 1977 loomed,
Cook and Jones did the only thing they could do: they hammered
away at the Pistols repertoire until it sounded tougher and more
unstinting than anything else around at the time. On newer songs
like 'Bodies' it sounded like something of a bludgeon.

Given the various upheavals and traumas that marked the
short life of the Sex Pistols, it is tempting to think that with
fewer obstacles to face, there might have been more. It seems
that as the band were denied more and more – the opportunity

to perform, or to appear in public in almost any way without harassment – the more their momentum was broken. The regularity with which mishaps or diversions seemed to randomly spring up suggests that fate (or something more sinister) was against them. But the Pistols simply retreated inwards, focusing on the songs they had and tackling them with a renewed precision. The album, after all, was something they knew now that they owned, that they were able to shape and define free from the insanity that was swirling around the band.

*

Because McLaren had only signed with Virgin Records for the UK market, it left him free to work on deals to release the Pistols' records in other territories. As work on the album neared its conclusion, there was still no deal in place for the biggest market of them all, the United States. After the news of Virgin's deal with the Pistols broke in the trade papers, with the Pistols' manager making it clear that he had deliberately selected Virgin in the UK in order to be free to find another label for the US, Warner Bros. Records president Mo Ostin realized that he now had an opportunity to sign the group – something the UK branch of Warners had decided against six months previously. He called up Bob Krasnow, one of his executives in New York, and asked him to go and meet McLaren and the Pistols in London. Krasnow didn't really know anything about them, but was told to fly to London and meet up with Warner Bros. head of artist relations, Bob Regehr, who was more clued-up about the situation. The pair were to go and meet Malcolm McLaren and see the Sex Pistols in action.

The two men, although in their forties, were known for their interest in music that was more on the fringes than in the mainstream (Regehr had helped to break Alice Cooper, Johnny

Rotten's audition act). Upon their arrival in London, their first impressions were very positive. Krasnow took an instant liking to McLaren, and was utterly captivated by his enthusiasm and the way he sold them the idea of the Pistols. Here, Krasnow thought, was 'a brilliant guy', a 'visionary'. They were taken to meet the members of the band who were rehearsing in a secret basement in an attempt to elude the attention of the press, who by now hounded them everywhere they went.[7] The Warners executives and McLaren descended into a dirty, smelly basement, 'down four flights of stairs', Krasnow recalled. It was like the journey to the centre of the earth, he told colleagues later. On the floor lay some mattresses surrounded by rubbish, as if in some post-apocalyptic film, and suddenly there they were, the infamous Sex Pistols, standing around in front of their amps and speaker cabinets. They offered Krasnow and Regehr a slug from a bottle containing a potent mixture of beer and whisky. After the introductions had been made, the Pistols went into their stage show for the benefit of their distinguished visitors. 'It was the worst shit I'd ever heard,' Krasnow later said. 'Horrific. The music was a train wreck. They weren't even playing the same song.'[8]

Bob Regehr's reaction, on the other hand, couldn't have been more different: that of a man who had just seen the future. As soon as they got back to their hotel, he called up Mo Ostin at Warners in Los Angeles and said, 'We've got to sign them, they're going to be huge.'[9] But, as had been the case with other record companies who had considered the Sex Pistols, some soundings would have to be taken among label staff before they made a decision on signing the band. When they returned to Los Angeles, Krasnow and Regehr brought a tape with them, featuring songs recorded by Dave Goodman from an October recording session at Wessex that captured the Pistols running through some of their stage set as they warmed up.

With some of his key executives present, Mo Ostin cued a
tape of the Pistols in which they exuded the raw chaos that had
characterized reports of their arrival on the London music scene.
The recording captured an off-the-cuff attempt to make a fool
of Rotten, instigated by Steve Jones. He wanted them to merge
two songs: Chuck Berry's 'Johnny B. Goode' and The Creation's
'Through My Eyes', a favourite of Rotten's. 'Tell John, tell 'im.
He can't hear us,' Jones says to the producer Dave Goodman,
who then tells Rotten through another channel: 'They wanna
play "Johnny B. Goode" while you sing "Through My Eyes".'[10] An
exasperated sounding Rotten sighs, 'God . . . Alright, then,' and
then after Goodman, with two simple words – 'Ready? Go!' –
sets them off, the band crashing headfirst into a raucous and
uncontrolled assault on 'Johnny B. Goode'.

On cue, Rotten enters right on time, where Chuck Berry's first
line would begin, but he only manages the first four words of
the lyrics to 'Through My Eyes' before he realizes the experiment
is doomed: 'If you could see . . . oh God, fuck off!' The band,
however, are pummelling the beat, the riff, into the floor and
don't seem to notice anything awry, so on they go. Playing
along, Rotten soon falls into the 'Johnny B. Goode' groove, but
is to all intents and purposes lost for words. To anyone who was
encountering this for the first time, he probably sounded like a
complete lunatic:

Ayan Louisiana ya-ya New Orlean
I was a bada baby an' a little key
Ayiinananananananana Johnny B. Goode!
A-gogogogogogo Johnny B. Goode!
A-gogo, go Johnny, gogogogogo
I don't know the words!
Gogogogogogogogogogoyuh

Ayayayaya-strah yaya-strah-uauaua
Ayayayaya-strah-uauaua
Ayayayaya-strah anda banayaya
I wanna wanna bay, yayayaya
Let's gogo, ago Johnny gogogogo
A-gogo, go go go gogogogogogogogogogogogogo
Oh, Johnny, go, go
Go! Johnny B. Goode
Ayayayayayayayayayayayayayag-wuah
Oh, fuck, it's awful!
Hate songs like that!
The pits
Eeeeeeeyayayayay eeeee!

The performance is brought to a halt by the sound of Goodman shouting 'CUT!' The Warners vice-presidents Lenny Waronker and Ted Templeman, invited in for their opinion, absolutely hated what they had just heard. 'They didn't think it was music,' Mo Ostin recalled. 'They didn't get it and had no interest in bringing the band into the company.'[11] But Ostin was determined that Warner Bros. would land the Pistols this time and, trusting Bob Regehr's opinion, made arrangements to meet with Malcolm McLaren.

If the Pistols represented the old order being swept aside, then the death of Elvis Presley on 16 August 1977 might have been taken as symbolic of a generational shift. Yet while many who adhered to punk's willingness to declare the old stars redundant had predictably welcomed the news – Rotten's response was 'good riddance to old rubbish' – McLaren, who had a more personal attachment to the 1950s, was more philosophical. 'Makes you feel sad, doesn't it?' he said. 'Like your grandfather died . . . it's just too bad it couldn't have been Mick Jagger.'[12]

The following day Mo Ostin of Warner Bros. Records and his lawyer arrived in London to meet McLaren. But McLaren, playing hard to get, seemed unwilling to act desperate and, following the practice he'd established with other record company heads he had won contracts from in the past year, made Ostin go beyond what he would normally do in order to sign a band:

> I got to London and looked all over the city for Malcolm McLaren. I finally found him and we agreed to meet, but every time we'd set a date, he'd break it. It was incredibly frustrating. Finally, we sat down and I offered him a deal. Malcolm said yes, but only if Warner Bros. agreed to finance a film he wanted to do.[13]

Mixing of the album continued during August, when time allowed, and later in September. A few days after McLaren had opened discussions with Warner Bros., the Pistols set off on a short tour of UK clubs, which would come to be known as the SPOTS tour – the 'Sex Pistols On Tour Secretly' tour – during which they played under a number of assumed names in an effort to elude any attempts to ban them. They were billed, variously, as 'The Tax Exiles' (Doncaster), 'Special Guest' (Scarborough), 'Acne Rabble' (Middlesbrough), 'The Hamsters' (Plymouth) and 'A Mystery Band of International Repute' (Penzance). It was only on the first date of the tour, at the Lafayette Club in Wolverhampton, that they would be billed as 'S.P.O.T.S.', but the secret was out, as Charles Young reported for his American readers from the packed-out club. Inside the venue things were heating up during the DJ set before the Pistols took to the stage, as pogoing punks bashed into each other and the crowd seemed to form one big scuffle in front of the stage. Young's only point of comparison for this kind of audience interaction was the Vortex show with The Slits that he had witnessed a few days before. But here the crowd was more intense and up for whatever was going to take shape:

> The fights are both more frequent and more violent. One battle seems to swirl around the entire floor, bodies tripping like a line of dominoes until it stops at the foot of the stairs in back, directly below Malcolm McLaren. A half-smile on his lips, he is an island of serenity, magically untouched by the chaos . . . At midnight the Sex Pistols finally emerge from the dressing room. The crush around the foot-high stage is literally unbelievable and skirmishes with the security men immediately erupt. The ten foot stacks of PA speakers are rocking back and forth and are dangerously close to toppling over.[14]

The chaos amid which the Pistols played to these audiences was in direct contrast to the atmosphere in which the work in the studio continued again in September. With each visit to the studio for a new round of sessions working on the same material once again – some of which the band had been playing for eighteen months – there would be subtle refinements; a result of the growing awareness that what constituted a performance on-stage should not impose limitations on how the material, the songs, were handled as studio artefacts. In the studio they were the object of careful deliberation, and the determined application of newfound skills and stylistic flourishes that had been absent six months before, all of which contributed to the precision and power of the recordings that emerged. In the repeated absence of the wayward Sid Vicious, Jones was left to record all the guitar parts, including bass. With Paul Cook he began to develop a 'wall of sound' that would make their records stand apart from the looser and more spontaneous efforts of other punk bands.[15] The two built up the guitar tracks, adding little details here and there that on their own might have seemed unremarkable – a two-note lick here, submerged feedback there – 'little bits that don't jump out at you', Cook told one interviewer, but rather layers, 'layers upon layers'.[16]

It was fortunate that the scandals that had seen the Pistols unceremoniously dumped by two record companies had left them with enough cash to fund these prolonged studio sessions during which Jones and Cook honed their craft, overcoming the jibes about their musical incompetence. But the notion that the Pistols could not play was, at this stage, still a perception that could be manipulated to sustain their notoriety. McLaren's view was that the Sex Pistols were an idea, and that key to this idea was the perception that they couldn't play. As soon as they could, there would be no point in their existence.

When *Never Mind the Bollocks, Here's the Sex Pistols* was completed and had been mixed, the sound of the record was no surprise – close to half of the album had already been released by then on single A- or B-sides. The fact that it sounded refined and professional was, to all but those who had witnessed the early Pistols in person, just how they sounded. No matter how it was judged by the standards of the then punk ethos, *Never Mind the Bollocks* was an album that in one way or another would break apart things in the world around it, as it transformed the chaos and energy of early Sex Pistols performances into a sound that was at once violent and carefully calibrated. It negated the insipid and throwaway pop music that had come to dominate the charts – records that were aimed, it seemed, at mums and dads or children – and it offered an alternative sound to the increasingly indulgent, self-important and often flaccid 'rock' that had taken hold in the 1970s, indulged by a record industry that seemed to have struck gold in the post-'60s era. In the voice of Rotten, *Never Mind the Bollocks* delivered a rawness and immediacy the like of which had rarely been heard in the last twenty years. It wasn't long before Rotten was being described as the most charismatic rock figure since David Bowie, blessed with 'a rage so rabid that you can feel the spittle hitting the microphone' as he snarled his way through the relentless sonic assault of an album that did not let up.[17]

McLaren, who had left the band to get on with it and taken no interest in the music, thought that what he heard was too good. In an unwelcome reversal of his own guiding maxim, they had produced something that was so good that it was bad; the band sounded too accomplished. It was not so much that he had no idea they had it in them, but rather that by being so good, it would now be easier than ever for them to be assimilated into the mainstream. Virgin's Richard Branson was dragging his heels over the release, however, and dithering over the running order and which previously released songs should be included. This created space for even more confusion, which was exploited by those behind other, non-Virgin releases.

Because the Pistols and Glitterbest were in the unusual position of owning the masters of their recordings and had signed separate distribution deals with record companies in foreign territories, the Pistols' French label, Barclay Records, hatched plans to flood the British market with imported copies of the new album before Branson's Virgin could get theirs out. On top of this, and because he disliked the over-refined sound that Jones and Cook had brought to the album, McLaren allegedly allowed a bootleg of what amounted to an alternative debut album – compiled from disparate 1976 and early '77 sessions recorded when Glen Matlock was still in the band – to be covertly slipped to a pressing plant, and which would then find its way into independent record shops. That release, later made available under the title *Spunk*, would for a brief period sow confusion and further enrage Richard Branson, who seemed to be spending a great deal of time doing battle with McLaren on one front or another. Today this collection of demos and B-sides, produced by Dave Goodman, stands as an important document of how the band sounded in its earliest days and, in the eyes of many, is considered to be a more authentic document of what the Pistols were really like in the summer of 1976.

Despite the potential confusions of the Barclays version – which had one song less than the UK version – and the bootleg alternative 'debut' album, Virgin's release of *Never Mind the Bollocks, Here's the Sex Pistols* arrived in late October and went straight to number one in the charts. This was despite the fact that the high-street chains Boots, Woolworths and WHSmith were cornered into refusing to stock the album because it included 'God Save the Queen' – the song they had earlier banned when it was released as a single. 'Denied the face-saving formula of an album with that track removed,' which it is likely they would have stocked, 'they had been pushed by their own pre-stated hard line' on the offending song into banning the album.[18]

The album sleeve, created by Jamie Reid, represented the pinnacle of a new DIY style that had been the hallmark of the Pistols' releases to date, and would help to usher in a new approach to record sleeve graphics. The designs of the Pistols' record sleeves came both as a warning and a slap in the face to the high conceptualism and (often) movie-like set-ups of their old Denmark Street neighbours Hipgnosis. Those had been album cover concepts that were realized – in a time before computer trickery – only as a result of very high budgets. Where Hipgnosis covers often featured actors or stuntmen in far-flung locations, and elaborate concepts to play with in order to conjure up that all-important image that would define a record, it was all seemingly working towards the end of remaining as inscrutable as possible. The cover of Pink Floyd's 1975 album *Wish You Were Here*, for example, shows two men – one with a good portion of his body in flames – shaking hands over a business transaction of some kind. The cover for Led Zeppelin's 1976 album *Presence* depicts a family sitting at a dining table looking at an enigmatic black ornament. The Pistols' sleeves, in contrast, inaugurated a new mood of blunt directness. The cover of *Never Mind the Bollocks, Here's the Sex Pistols* also looked as if it had cost nothing to produce.

The effect of the luminous colouring and ransom-note lettering of the record sleeve, and its success, left establishment sleeve designers aghast at suddenly plummeting budgets, as record companies realized that DIY- or amateur-style covers didn't prevent people from buying records. The reaction of Hipgnosis design guru Aubrey Powell was one of 'shock, horror, and outrage'.[19] The Sex Pistols, those noisy louts who had a year before made their presence felt in the very place where the slick design gurus held sway, had now, with this one release, made them look out of step with the new realities.

Starting with the first graphic for 'Anarchy in the UK' in October 1976, this new kind of visual approach – 'homologous with punk's subterranean and anarchic style', in the words of the academic Dick Hebdige – attained an increasing visibility that seemed to be in tune with the apocalyptic fervour swirling around punk and, in particular, the Sex Pistols.[20] As another witness to their impact noted, it was all there in the 'grafted-on Situationist slogans, the Dada-defaced images, [and] the faded xerox textures gifted to punk by Jamie Reid and Sex Pistols manager Malcolm McLaren', which 'no sooner satirized the cityscapes of Britain than they became part of it'.[21]

No sooner was the record in the shops and selling faster than any other album around than the police took an interest.

Poster for the album *Never Mind the Bollocks, Here's the Sex Pistols*. Artwork by Cooke Key Associates from a concept by Jamie Reid.

In yet another example of 'the routine legal mischief and retail bans a Sex Pistols record seemed to bring in its wake', Craig Bromberg wrote:

> No less than three London record shops were charged with offenses under the 1889 Indecent Advertisement Act and the 1824 Vagrancy Act for displaying the album cover with its prominent kidnap letter logo of the terrifying word 'Bollocks'.[22]

It all began on 7 November when a Nottingham policewoman had informed Christopher Seale, the manager of the city's Virgin store, that his display of the album contravened the antiquated Indecent Advertisements Act 1899. When he later refused to hand over all copies of the record at the time of a subsequent police visit, he was arrested and charged. Richard Branson was in turn charged with causing obscene material to be delivered to the store. If the police were right in their apparent assumption that 'bollocks' could only refer here to testicles, and had further understood the meaning of the name Sex Pistols correctly – or not, as the case may be – then to their minds it could only mean one thing: *never mind our balls, look at the cocks*. Minor tremors were sent through the retail sector, as record shop managers began to feel that they could be prosecuted for displaying the album cover. The Gramophone Record Retailers' Committee advised its members to display the album at their own risk, with Harry Tipple, the body's secretary, opining that no matter what the demand for the album, he would like to see retailers drop it 'like a hot cake', leaving the Pistols and Virgin high and dry.[23]

Following the complaint made in Nottingham, there was no telling how the police in one town or city might respond to displays of the album. The charges against the Nottingham shop manager and Branson had been followed by charges against shop managers in Notting Hill and Marble Arch for displaying the album – these were both brought under the 1824 Vagrancy Act – and the subsequent confiscation of copies of the record from Guy Norris Ltd, a hardware shop that also carried records, in Station Parade, Barking. This was all happening in the run-up to a test case on the issue, which would be fought in the magistrate's court in Nottingham on 24 November.

In court, the renowned QC John Mortimer defended Mr Seale and Virgin Records (although, implicitly, it was also a defence of the Sex Pistols for having the nerve to use the word in the first place), delving into lengthy arguments about the etymology and meaning of the offending word 'bollocks' within the context of the album title. The title of the Pistols album had come from Steve Jones, the Pistols' master of offensive verbal barbs, who was merely reusing the kind of language he had heard all around him when growing up. In this case he had been inspired by the patter of two characters he used to hear on the street, saying to each other, 'Never mind the bollocks' – that is, something like 'cut to the quick', 'forget the crap', 'get to the point', 'say what you mean', 'stop talking nonsense', 'forget all that rubbish' and so on. The chief witness for the defence was Professor James Kingsley, a former Anglican priest and then head of the English department at the University of Nottingham. He explained that his background gave him a unique insight into the meaning of the term. The word 'bollocks', he said, was originally a term used to describe clergymen: 'Clergymen are well known to talk a good deal of rubbish and so the word later developed the meaning of nonsense,' and in this particular usage he understood it to mean, 'never mind the nonsense, here's the Sex Pistols.'[24]

In the end, it was accepted that it was a 'legitimate' slang term with a long history in the English language. The album title, the defence successfully argued, simply meant 'never mind all the rubbish – listen to this.' The judgement of the magistrates – 'two of whom were women', reported *The Times*, as if surprised that two representatives of the fairer sex could reach such a ruling – represents a classic example of the comedic value of the British establishment when faced with something it doesn't like. It upheld fairness, but through gritted teeth, and with just a hint of exaggerated outrage at the threat posed to general moral well-being:

> Much as my colleagues and I wholeheartedly deplore the vulgar exploitation of the worst instincts of human nature by both you and your company we reluctantly find you not guilty.[25]

McLaren, though, wasn't happy about the grudging approval of the establishment; he would have preferred the band to be perceived still as an irritant to respectability. He thought the whole court case was 'boring' and declared that he would have preferred it if Branson had been jailed for obscenity: 'then I could have went and visited the old hippie in prison'.[26] McLaren, in fact, was half a decade older than Branson, but though Branson may have had youth on his side, he was clearly not as filled with the spirit of obscene adolescence as the Pistols' manager.

While it took judges, legal representatives and a professor of English who was also a man of the cloth to come to a conclusion that was probably apparent to everyone all along – that bollocks meant nonsense or rubbish – the Americans, to whom this was a foreign word, seemed able to work it out from the context alone. 'Do they mean never mind all the shit you've heard about this group, the hype, the filthy reports and hateful innuendos, here's the music?' asked a reviewer in California's *Slash* magazine. If the meaning of the title was ever in doubt, the redoubtable Kickboy suggested, the music couldn't have been less unambiguous:

The music is scary in its precision and power, with the drums and guitars burning their way through your head as napalm through the jungle, but it is Rotten's voice and stance that make any comparison useless. The shady little character has to be the most mesmerizing visionary ever produced by the underworld of rock 'n' roll, an unholy prophet of unavoidable instant nihilism, the common voice of everyone's darker side. It's not often one can *taste* honesty seeping through one's latest album, and it's not often one can feel grateful for such a load of so-called nasty immature and self-destructive emotions.[27]

By the time of the Nottingham court case, the album had, within the space of three weeks, sold 200,000 copies in the UK. And before Warner Bros. had released the album in the United States it had already been the hottest seller in memory as an import for some of New York's main importers, with copies flooding in from the UK and France. As the year drew to an end the band – internally fractious and seemingly intent on self-destruction, even without McLaren's machinations – might have had no idea that the end was closer than some of them, Rotten in particular, might have wished. The year-end issue of *Investors Chronicle* seemed to seal the success confirmed by *Never Mind the Bollocks* surviving the censors and hitting number one on the album charts; it featured the Sex Pistols on the cover, under the heading 'Young Businessmen of the Year'.

At the start of 1978 the Pistols began their first and last tour of the US. It was to be a short series of dates mainly intended to raise the band's American profile and generate some publicity for the album. Arriving in New York on 3 January they were, as Jon Savage notes, 'like the men who fell to earth'.[28] As the home of the New York Dolls, Richard Hell and the Ramones – and a place McLaren knew very well – the city might have seemed like a

The Sex Pistols: Young Businessmen of the Year, *Investors Chronicle*, 1977.

perfect setting for the Sex Pistols to make their formal entrance into the American music world. But New York would not be seeing anything of the Pistols on this tour. McLaren didn't like the idea of playing to easy-to-please audiences in New York and the West Coast, who were likely to be incapable of being shocked, so he made sure to confine the band's appearances to dates in places where they were more likely to be seen as alien invaders. Besides, it was important to keep Vicious away from easy access to heroin, now that he seemed fully in the grip of addiction to the drug.

The shows would be in cities in the South and across the Bible Belt: Atlanta, Memphis, San Antonio, Baton Rouge, Dallas, Tulsa. The tour was to end with a final show in California, but not in Los Angeles, which had for the last eighteen months been the site of the most explosive punk scene in the United States. Instead the Pistols would play San Francisco, the 1960s hippy citadel of the West Coast peace and love generation, and thus the embodiment of much that McLaren had hated since that decade.

In Atlanta, Georgia, where the Pistols were booked to play at the Great Southeast Music Hall – 'beer in buckets, better pinball than CBGB, and an official capacity of 523' – the audience was comprised mostly of 'gawkers who heard the freak show was in town'.[29] Before the Pistols had even set foot on American soil, their exploits back in England had been aired and 'exaggerated to an absurd degree', thanks to reports that had appeared in US print and broadcast media since early 1977:

> Authorities in the South had heard rumors of onstage rapes and of band members urinating on the audience; consequently, vice-squad officers from Memphis, Baton Rouge, San Antonio, and Tulsa all flew into Atlanta to find out what to expect at the upcoming shows in their respective cities.[30]

They weren't the only ones interested in finding out more about this strange phenomenon, whose legend was already established in advance of the actual proof of their existence. Local sheriff officers were joined by film crews from five TV channels, another uninvited documentary crew whose footage would emerge in a documentary and 'a team of sociologists led by Dr Richard Dixon of the University of North Carolina and Dr Richard Levinson of Emory', who were distributing questionnaires as they mingled with the crowd.[31] The Pistols started well, and despite an inadequate sound system and the evident hostility of a crowd that seemed to be waiting for something bad to unfold before their own eyes (to validate the experience of seeing the most notorious rock band on the planet), their performance was described by one witness as 'utterly electrifying'.[32] But trouble began immediately after the show, with Vicious disappearing in search of drugs and the American road manager manhandling the late-arriving McLaren backstage for plotting a tour through some of the most dangerous places they could possibly have ended up and not even having the good manners to show up for the show.[33] When Vicious was found the next day – he had tagged along with the documentary film crew who were following the tour – it resulted in a series of scuffles with hotel security and the Warner Bros. minders, who had to knock him unconscious to get him back to the band's hotel and ready for the show. Rotten, Jones and Cook were not happy with 'Mr Drug', as Rotten referred to him on his return. Later as they gathered to leave for the venue, Vicious addressed the others:

> 'Hello sidemen', he says. 'How does it feel to be part of the backing band?' Rotten, Jones and Cook avoid all contact with Vicious. They walk to the bus in silence. No one in the band answers Sid when he speaks to them.[34]

The Memphis show was oversold, with five hundred more angry ticketholders gathering outside than it was permissible for the venue to accommodate. Adding to the sense of chaos that was already enveloping the tour, the city sent a SWAT team to deal with the situation.[35] In the audience, Jim Dickinson – a noted local musician and producer steeped in the blues-country-rock traditions of the South who, at almost forty years old, was a teenager when rock 'n' roll first hit – watched as the Pistols made their entrance, walking up to the stage through the audience and having to push aside people to make their way through. Vicious was brandishing a bottle of vodka:

> he had what I guess you could call a suit on: a tie, a jacket, a white dress shirt. When they stood onstage, all the lights went off, and then when they came back up, he'd ripped off all of his clothes except for his pants and his tie, and you could see I NEED A FIX or something like that, looking like he'd gashed it into his chest with a needle. He was absolutely brilliant, what he was doing to the instrument . . . it was offensive and frontal and aggressive in a way that I thought was gone from rock and roll. Part of the idea of rock and roll in the '50s – it was purely one-generational music; and through the commercialization of rock and roll over the years, all of that was gone, before the punks, and I was glad to see it back. There was something so hostile. It wasn't just in your face, it was up your nose.[36]

At Cain's Ballroom in Tulsa, too, Vicious drew as much attention as Rotten. Like two madmen trapped by the events of 1977 and drawn on-stage by the sheer need to just get to the end of the tour, they were riding a wave of shock and hostility that was pushing them on to their final show in two days' time. Rotten, with a stare that seemed as if it could penetrate solid objects, *Slash* magazine reported, looked likely to 'wrench around and spit venom' at any moment; Vicious, the incompetent non-musician, 'was cooking' – playing as if he was all of a sudden a man connected to some rock 'n' roll source – 'the best fuckin' bass player in the whole world'.[37]

By the time of the last date in San Francisco, Rotten was fed up with the situation: 'I shared the cover of *Rolling Stone* with Willie Nelson, and here I am broke, hungry, stuck on a bus, dehydrated – with a junkie.'[38] After the second show in Memphis, his separation from the others was as clear as day. McLaren, Jones and Cook started flying between shows, leaving Rotten on the bus with Vicious and the heavy-duty Warners bodyguards, as well as a few others, like the photographer Bob Gruen. Often they would be stuck on the bus for extended periods as the tour manager Noel Monk tried to elude the reach of the press who were following them around, and to avoid confrontations with locals in roadside diners. It resulted in them deviating from their travel itinerary and ending up in the middle of nowhere, instead of in their reserved and presumably comfortable hotel rooms, as Gruen recalled:

> Monk would pull into town, check out the venue, and then divert us to these dumpy motels. He'd hide the bus behind the motel

Johnny Rotten and Sid Vicious on tour in America, January 1978.

and book the band into it, the result being that nobody knew where the band was. That way he was doing his job. It got to be very boring because we were alone a lot of the time.[39]

The San Francisco show at Bill Graham's famous Winterland Ballroom had sold out its 5,400 tickets in two days. The local punks were coming to see them from all over California and this would be the biggest audience the Pistols had ever played to. Graham was used to dealing with peaceful hippies and wasn't sure what this crowd was going to be like. 'People with nuts and bolts and chains and purple hair', he later wrote, who looked like they were 'auditioning for *Ben Hur*'.[40] Two local bands, The Nuns and the Avengers, had been billed as the opening acts for the Sex Pistols. To McLaren, the night looked too much as if it was all under Graham's control.

'We're turning into a rock band,' McLaren told Howie Klein, a local DJ. 'I hate rock bands. I want to make it all exciting again. I want a great band to come up there and wipe us into oblivion and make us start all over again.'[41] McLaren demanded to know the name of the worst, most likely to offend, band in San Francisco. Klein told him they were called Negative Trend, and McLaren set out to track them down. With the show already under way and the Avengers on-stage, McLaren turned up backstage with Negative Trend, who were armed with their instruments. He wanted them on-stage before the Pistols. After some heated conversations, Graham agreed to let Negative Trend appear, but only after the Pistols. Still looking for a way to rile up the audience and upset its expectations, McLaren got hold of the emcee for the night – the renowned rock writer Richard Meltzer, who at that time was fronting a punk band in Los Angeles called Vom – and asked him to go out and be as rude and insulting to the audience as he possibly could. 'It all seemed too placid, too pat – like a Grateful Dead show,' was how it was put to him.[42] Unfortunately for posterity, Meltzer's brief performance was not captured in the film of the show that Bob Regehr of Warner Bros. had made that night, but various partial recollections of his inflammatory tirade survive:

> Skinheads suck! You all suck dick! . . . Hey you with the mirror shades and orange frames – think you're cool, dontcha? Screw you, you're an asshole . . . You stupid bastards in San Francisco are paying $10 to see this show. It would have cost $5 in L.A. What a stupid fucking town. You people are all fucking idiots.[43]

Meltzer later wrote that he dispensed all the invective he could muster. 'I was one uncouth lout – until Bill Graham physically picked me up and threw me out of the building – "You can't insult my city!"'[44] After dusting himself down and turning his jacket inside out, Meltzer found a way back in. By the time the Pistols finally arrived on-stage, the audience had abandoned any of the suspected 'Grateful Dead' vibe that McLaren had probably mistakenly sensed, and welcomed their antiheroes with – what else – a shower of trash:

> Rotten hangs on the mike stand, dodging the missiles . . . and paces the stage, pocketing the most useful debris, asking 'Cameras? Anyone got any cameras?' and sure enough, what looks like a camera flies through the air and lands at his feet.[45]

The Pistols went on to play the worst set of the tour, a show that was 'dull beyond belief' when compared to the earlier sets in the South.[46] For Bill Graham, writing in 1994, the Pistols 'were an expression of an attitude I abhor to this day. But as a piece of theatre, it was extraordinary.'[47]

After the show Rotten found out about a previously unmentioned trip to Brazil to hang out with Ronnie Biggs, the exiled Great Train Robber, which was planned to begin immediately after the Pistols were due to leave the United States on the expiration of their visas. It proved to be the last of Malcolm's stunts that Rotten was prepared to put up with. It was him or McLaren; one or the other of them had to go. Vicious had, predictably, vanished again, and wouldn't turn up until the next day, when he was found strung out on heroin. Jones and Cook were with Malcolm and they wanted to go to Brazil; they didn't want to go back to London or to Europe to do any more shows. Rotten stormed over to the hotel where McLaren was staying to make it clear that he was not going to Brazil. But all Jones and Cook wanted was a break and they didn't see what Rotten's problem was. As Paul Cook recounted later, it was Jones who made the first move:

Final show at the Winterland Ballroom, San Francisco, January 1978.

Steve said to John, 'It's getting too much. We can't see it going on much longer. It's falling apart.' I said I agreed. To give John his due, he tried to hold it together. He told us we were stupid and we should get rid of Malcolm and carry on. Steve and I told him we didn't think that was the answer.[48]

McLaren, Jones and Cook flew to Brazil to meet the exiled train robber Biggs. Rotten, left stranded and broke, eventually found his way first to New York and then on to the Caribbean, where Richard Branson arranged for him to stay. Sid Vicious was flown on a stretcher from San Francisco to New York and taken to a hospital to recover from his heroin overdose. Little over two years since their first public performance, the Sex Pistols were no more. The week following the Winterland concert, news about the split made it back it to the UK, where a statement – described as a 'Punk-Dadaist manifesto' by The Guardian and 'un-cooperative' by Virgin Records – was released by McLaren and Glitterbest:

The management is bored with managing the successful rock and roll band. The group is bored with being a successful rock and roll band. Burning venues and destroying record companies is more creative than making it.[49]

Rotten and McLaren: the lookalikes who ended up hating the
sight of each other.

Afterword: Fables of the Sex Pistols

In one of the Sex Pistols' final appearances in England, shortly before they set off on their doomed American adventure, Johnny Rotten ended the show with the kind of gesture that had become characteristic of this greatest anti-hero of punk. 'Ladies and gentlemen that was the end of a wonderful evening,' he announced to the crowd crammed into Wolverhampton's Club Lafayette. 'Thank you very much and drop dead.'[1]

He may have had some inkling that the end was near, or it may just have been another way of refusing to act like the star he had become, but the one who would 'drop dead' in this scenario would – within less than a month – be Johnny Rotten. His transformation into John Lydon was a reinvention that seemed to recognize that as Johnny Rotten he would remain forever trapped in the schemes cooked up by Malcolm McLaren. Rotten was smart enough to know that the 'kill your heroes' attitude that he had so often voiced himself was about to upend him.

One Julien Temple-directed curio, a short film from 1979 called *Punk Can Take It*, which he made for the popular punk band the UK Subs, provides an interesting dramatization of this attitude. The film shows the UK Subs and their fans as punk's only hope after the failure of the Sex Pistols to remain intact. As a narrator declares that punk faces extermination, the camera pans onto a statue of its former figurehead, Johnny Rotten, clad in Roman robes and sited on the banks of the Thames opposite the Houses of Parliament. The plinth on which his statue stands reads 'Johnny Rotten, 1956–1977'. Around it dozens of punks are jostling to get close to the figure as the voiceover intones:

> Careless talk costs lives. The enemy is always listening: autograph-hunters and rumour-mongerers with their slack minds and silly blathering mouths – through their interviews – caused stars to be born. Punk has had its share of traitors [the camera zooms in on the Rotten statue]: ordinary kids, even idiots, elevated to the rank of idols. But each time a collaborator is exposed, a hundred punks spring up to take his place [the camera zooms in on kids pogoing around Rotten's statue and pulling it over], adamant in their belief that musicians are no different and no more talented than their audience.[2]

And with that, the punk kids smash up the statue of Rotten. He had gone over to the other side, stepped out of the permanent wreckage of the Sex Pistols, probably in search of his own sanity. As Johnny Rotten, Lydon may not have been directly manipulated by McLaren, but McLaren did manipulate the Sex Pistols' media image, fuelled by his determination to cut the ground from under any attempts of the mainstream media to turn the Pistols, including Rotten, into something acceptable. It was this that drove Rotten and McLaren in different directions.

The demise of the Sex Pistols was a curious affair that in the end would be resolved in the law courts, as John Lydon battled it out with McLaren and his Glitterbest company for the rights to the band name and all associated copyrights. Following the revelation of Rotten's broad musical tastes during the July 1977 Capital Radio interview – and in virtue of the singer's fondness for dub and reggae – Richard Branson and Virgin's A&R department were convinced that if the band folded, they should at least try to hold on to Rotten, whom they saw now as the main creative force of the group. Early in the aftermath of the US tour, Branson flew Lydon to Jamaica with an A&R brief to scout some new reggae and dub acts for Virgin's Front Line imprint. At the same time McLaren, Jones and Cook were in Brazil filming with the on-the-run Ronnie Biggs, who in 1980 would be cast in the film *The Great Rock 'n' roll Swindle* as a kind of replacement for Rotten, a ruse intended to put the exiled criminal into the Top Ten among the nation's most-loved pop stars. The film, though, would end up being seen as a vehicle for McLaren's final performance as himself, the Sex Pistol-in-chief – although, as the director Julien Temple said at the time of the film's release, 'Malcolm originally didn't want to be the rock and roll manager' acting out ten 'lessons' in how to swindle the music business, 'but he certainly got into it and developed it a lot'.[3]

'My name is Malcolm McLaren,' is how the character known as 'the Embezzler' is introduced: 'I have brought you many things in my time . . . but the most successful of all was an invention of mine they called the punk rock.'[4] It was a deliberate distortion and amplification of the reality, but in the court case over the assets of the Sex Pistols that followed the demise of the group, McLaren's role in the film would be taken as an autobiographical statement.

*

Over the course of 1978 and 1979, Lydon and McLaren projected their own competing public views of who or what the Sex Pistols were, and where the ideas and creativity came from. The truth was that there were two Sex Pistols: McLaren's Pistols and Rotten/Lydon's Pistols. Lydon's new band, Public Image Ltd (or PiL), gradually became more removed from the rock 'n' roll thrash of 1976/7 Sex Pistols, to explore, in albums such as *Metal*

Box (1979), the outer reaches of dub as it might be imagined by
a four-piece rock band of guitar, bass, drums and vocals. This was
Lydon's idea of punk: it was the unwillingness to have anything to
do with the stereotypes that, by 1978/9, were manifested in bands
that seemed to take the Sex Pistols and 1976 punk as their sole
influence, and which were totally oblivious to the diverse
influences that had led Lydon to forge something new in the
first place.

As far as his involvement with the Sex Pistols went, Malcolm
McLaren was an opportunist who had seized on the chance that
a group of bored teenagers with vague aspirations of being in a
band had presented him with. Through his role in conceptualizing,
marketing and selling the Sex Pistols and what we know as punk,
he played a crucial role in derailing the musical entity that was
the Sex Pistols. But for McLaren, failure – the bigger the better –
always seemed nobler and more true to his guiding spirit than
success. As he said to Melvyn Bragg in a 1980s *South Bank Show*
profile, he wound up not paying that much attention to the group
or how his antics impacted on them, because:

> great art, or any real art, has never ever worried about running
> people over – because the idea is more important. That's why we
> [Westwood and McLaren] have been accused of evil cunning, of
> being manipulating Svengalis – it's all absolutely true. Yes, we did
> do some very dastardly things. I don't regret it for one minute,
> otherwise it would have been a hell of a boring job.[5]

Despite McLaren's initial post-Sex Pistols persona resting on
the deliberately exaggerated and provocative tale of corporate
subversion that was played out in *The Great Rock 'n' roll Swindle*,
the most curious development in the aftermath of the band was
McLaren's own musical emergence as a producer/recording artist

himself. Throughout the 1980s, as Lydon's band PiL continued to follow the progress of a conventional rock band, touring and releasing albums in the age-old way, it was McLaren, in the eyes of some observers, who seemed to be doing something different, attempting to pioneer a kind of popular music that gave form to his belief that the best art was always a hodgepodge of elements stolen from somewhere else, fused into a form that might develop a new understanding of what popular culture could do. He saw it as a continuation of what he had always sought to do, from the Let It Rock and SEX days through to managing the Sex Pistols, in 'always dealing with something old, with a root' – certain clothing styles, rock 'n' roll music – 'and then turning it upside down and making it new again'.[6]

His first single and album, 'Buffalo Gals' (1982) and *Duck Rock* (1983), were substantial hits, and combined (several years before Paul Simon and other artists did) South African rhythms with other musical forms – in this case, American hip hop and hillbilly music. The records were seen as the first manifestations of a new kind of postmodern 'world music'. They were followed a few years later by the album *Fans* (1985), in which McLaren set arias from *Madam Butterfly* and *Carmen* within a rhythm and blues context. He thought that opera and its characters seemed to embody badness in a mythical way that rock 'n' roll figures could only dream of. Instead of 'sculpting characters out of the street' like the Sex Pistols, he decided to

> make a rock 'n' roll record just by taking those characters out of those librettos. That for me was another way of being bad, and another way of trying to retain whatever passion I must have felt when I pulled the plug on the Sex Pistols when they were beginning to play too good.[7]

London Olympics 2012 opening ceremony with pogo dancers
(top) and the ghost of Johnny Rotten singing 'Pretty
Vacant'.

At the time of his death in 2010 McLaren had released eight albums – precisely the same number as Lydon had with Public Image Ltd. Between these stabs at being a strange kind of pop conceptualist and producer, McLaren worked in Hollywood as production head at the short-lived CBS Pictures. His final involvement in the movie business was as co-producer of the Richard Linklater-directed *Fast Food Nation* (2006). McLaren's last artwork was also a film, completed just before he died, entitled *Paris, Capital of the XXIst Century*. It was a collage of movements and sounds that – harking back to the epigram at the front of this book, that what was important was to jump out of the twentieth century – was described as 'a terrific symphony that catapults Walter Benjamin's "Paris, Capital of the 19th Century" into the future'.[8]

*

Outside of the Beatles, there may be no rock or pop band or performer who has inspired as many words as the Sex Pistols have. Even as early as 1978 their story was so familiar and had been put to work so often that the *New Musical Express* writer who played his own part in their development, Nick Kent, felt able to say, 'it almost groans when set to print.'[9]

And if the spectacular opening ceremony of the London 2012 Olympic Games – an event orchestrated by the Oscar-winning film director Danny Boyle – is anything to go by, the Sex Pistols are part of a shared British history. There they were, alongside re-enacted key moments from modern British history, beamed out to the globe in all their audiovisual splendour from gigantic screens inside the Olympic Stadium. At the same time, dozens of performers – in exaggeration of the odd phenomenon of pogo dancing that sprung up at punk gigs in 1976 – bounced around on huge springs like the advance sign of some invading alien race, looking as futuristic as some witnesses thought the first punks were, while 'Pretty Vacant' momentarily blared loudly and the Queen looked on.

References

Introduction: Tales from the Near Future

1 Peter Ackroyd, *London: The Concise Biography* (London, 2012), p. 161.
2 J. G. Ballard, *J. G. Ballard: Quotes*, ed. V. Vale and Mike Ryan (San Francisco, CA, 2004), pp. 16–17.
3 Martin Amis, *The War Against Cliché: Essays and Reviews, 1971–2000* (London, 2002), p. 116.
4 Jon Savage, 'Punk: An Aesthetic', in *Punk: An Aesthetic*, ed. Johan Kugelberg and Jon Savage (New York, 2012), p. 346.
5 Steve Severin of Siouxsie and the Banshees, then one of the so-called 'Bromley Contingent' who stood behind the Sex Pistols during the TV show, quoted in Mark Paytress, *Siouxsie and the Banshees: The Authorised Biography* (London, 2003), p. 46.
6 The words of Bertie Marshall, in *Punk and the Pistols*, film, dir. Paul Tickell (BBC Arena, 1995).

1 I Will Be So Bad

1 'Match held under Stars and Stripes', *The Times* (26 July 1966), p. 1. On Henry Adler's influence, see Fred Vermorel, 'Blowing Up Bridges So There Is No Way Back', in *Eyes for Blowing Up Bridges: Joining the Dots from the Situationist International to Malcolm McLaren*, ed. Paul Gorman et al., exh. cat., John Hansard Gallery, Southampton (Southampton, 2015), p. 20.
2 McLaren quoted in Tom Templeton and Kate Kellaway, 'These were the Days that Shook the World', *The Observer*, www.theguardian.com, 20 January 2008.
3 Vivienne Westwood and Ian Kelly, *Vivienne Westwood* (London, 2014), pp. 194–5.
4 Malcolm McLaren, 'Antihero', *Spin*, IV/9 (December 1988), p. 79.
5 Ibid.
6 Westwood and Kelly, *Vivienne Westwood*, p. 116.
7 Ibid., pp. 194–5.
8 In Jon Savage, *The England's Dreaming Tapes* (London, 2009), p. 8.

9 Michael Löwy and Robert Sayre, *Romanticism Against the Tide of Modernity* (Durham, NC, 2001), p. 222.

10 Vermorel, 'Blowing Up Bridges So There is No Way Back', p. 25.

11 See Katherine Levy, 'Malcolm McLaren's Long-lost Paintings', *Daily Telegraph*, www.telegraph.co.uk, 18 May 2010. None of these paintings exist today, apart from in the few photographs of them that were uncovered and discussed in this article.

12 The quotation is from an advert for the new gallery: 'Calling All Artists', in the classifieds of *The Observer*, 13 September 1964, p. 22. The opening on 7 October 1964 was featured in George Seddon, 'Briefing: Who and When', *The Observer* (20 September 1964), p. 23.

13 Fred Vermorel, *Fashion and Perversity: A Life of Vivienne Westwood and the Sixties Laid Bare* (London, 1996), p. 147.

14 Ibid., p. 148.

15 McLaren, 'Antihero', p. 79.

16 See, for example, Michel Pastoureau, *Black: The History of a Color* (Princeton, NJ, 2008), pp. 184–6.

17 Marco Pirroni, in John Robb, *Punk Rock: An Oral History* (London, 2006), p. 83.

18 Malcolm McLaren, 'Foreword', in Paul Gorman, *The Look: Adventures in Pop and Rock Fashion* (London, 2001), p. 10.

19 Westwood and Kelly, *Vivienne Westwood*, p. 216.

20 '5-Day Arts Freak Plan', *International Times* (4 July 1969), p. 21. See a more extended account of the plans for the event in Craig Bromberg, *The Wicked Ways of Malcolm McLaren* (New York, 1989), pp. 35–7.

21 Quoted in Bromberg, *The Wicked Ways of Malcolm McLaren*, p. 36.

22 Quoted ibid.

23 More details about the nature of the film can be found in Vermorel, *Fashion and Perversity*, pp. 56–7, and the interview with Helen Wallington-Lloyd in Savage, *The England's Dreaming Tapes*, pp. 29–30.

24 Alistair O'Neill, *London: After a Fashion* (London, 2007), p. 171.

25 Vermorel, *Fashion and Perversity*, p. 57.

26 Levy, 'Malcolm McLaren's Long-lost Paintings', www.telegraph.co.uk.

27 Ibid.

28 This culture of preservation, or heritage, is examined at length in Raphael Samuel, 'Retrochic', in *Theatres of Memory*, vol. I: *Past and Present in Contemporary Culture* (London, 1994), pp. 83–118.

29 Simon Reynolds, *Retromania: Pop Culture's Addiction to its Own Past* (London, 2011), pp. 186–7.

30 Vermorel, *Fashion and Perversity*, p. 183.

31 See Neil Spencer, 'Malcolm and Bernard: Rock 'n' Roll Scoundrels', *New Musical Express* (9 August 1980), p. 27.

32 See Spencer, 'Malcolm and Bernard: Rock 'n' Roll Scoundrels', p. 27.

33 Westwood and Kelly, *Vivienne Westwood*, p. 143.

34 This version of events is taken from the account given by McLaren himself in Paul Taylor, 'The Impresario of Do-It-Yourself', in *Impresario: Malcolm McLaren and the British New Wave*, exh. cat., New Museum of Contemporary Art, New York (New York and Cambridge, MA, 1988), p. 20; Bromberg suggests that the stolen camera equipment story about the origins of Let It Rock is a myth – see *The Wicked Ways of Malcolm McLaren*, p. 38.

35 Various artists, *Rock Archive*, sleeve notes (Windmill Records, 1972).

36 Max Décharné, *King's Road: The Rise and Fall of the Hippest Street in the World* (London, 2005), p. 262.

37 Westwood and Kelly, *Vivienne Westwood*, p. 143.

38 McLaren, 'Antihero', p. 79.

39 Colin MacInnes, 'Smart Schmutter', quoted in Christopher Breward, *Fashioning London: Clothing and the Modern Metropolis* (London, 2004), p. 131.

40 George Melly, *Revolt into Style: The Pop Arts* (London, 2008), p. 32.

41 Levy, 'Malcolm McLaren's Long-lost Paintings'.

42 Joanna Bourke, *Working Class Cultures in Britain, 1890–1960: Gender, Class and Ethnicity* (London and New York, 1994), p. 38.

43 Melly, *Revolt into Style*, p. 34.

44 See Paul Rambali, 'How the West Was Won: An Epic Trek Across the Myth of Malcolm McLaren', *The Face*, 38 (June 1983), p. 43.

45 David May, 'Sado Sex for the Seventies', *Gallery International*, I/4 (November 1975), p. 61.

46 John F. Lyons, *America in the British Imagination: 1945 to the Present* (Basingstoke, 2013), p. 25.

47 Stanley Cohen, *Folk Devils and Moral Panics* (London and New York, 2011), p. 204.

48 Michael Macilwee, *The Teddy Boy Wars: The Youth Cult that Shocked Britain* (London, 2015), p. 11.

49 Jerry Hopkins, 'Beatle Loafers Return: Britain's Teddy Boys', *Rolling Stone*, 103 (2 March 1972), p. 14.

50 Décharné, *King's Road*, p. 263.

51 Quoted in Hopkins, 'Beatle Loafers Return', p. 16.

52 May, 'Sado Sex for the Seventies', p. 61.

53 Westwood and Kelly, *Vivienne Westwood*, p. 143.

2 Dolls, Crims and Rock 'n' Roll

1 Miles, 'They Simper at Times: New York Dolls, Wayne County: The Mercer Arts Center, New York City', www.rocksbackpages.com, accessed 1 December 2015.
2 Nina Antonia, *Too Much Too Soon: The New York Dolls* (London, 2005), p. 41.
3 Binky Philips, 'December 19th, 1972: Me, Opening for the New York Dolls 40 (!) Years Ago', www.huffingtonpost.com, 21 December 2012.
4 Antonia, *Too Much Too Soon*, p. 44.
5 The best account is in Legs McNeil and Gillian McCain, *Please Kill Me: The Uncensored Oral History of Punk* (London, 1996), pp. 143–58.
6 Arthur Kane, *I Doll: Life and Death with the New York Dolls* (Chicago, IL, 2009), p. 131.
7 Ibid., p. 161.
8 In Antonia, *Too Much Too Soon*, p. 57.
9 Malcolm McLaren, 'Dirty Pretty Things', www.theguardian.com, 28 May 2004.
10 McLaren, quoted in McNeil and McCain, *Please Kill Me*, p. 235.
11 Quoted in David May, 'Sado Sex for the Seventies', *Gallery International*, I/4 (November 1975), p. 61.
12 Fred and Judy Vermorel, *Sex Pistols: The Inside Story* (London, 1987), pp. 180–81.
13 Julien Temple, quoted in Pat Gilbert, *1977: The Bollocks Diaries*, book included with *Never Mind the Bollocks, Here's the Sex Pistols*, Special 35th Anniversary Edition (Universal Music Group, 2012), p. 9.
14 Vermorel, *Sex Pistols*, p. 167.
15 Quoted ibid., p. 12.
16 Ibid., p. 14.
17 Nick Kent, 'The Life and Crimes of Two Simpleton Workin' Class Tossers', *New Musical Express* (19 August 1978), p. 26.
18 Chrissie Hynde, *Reckless* (London, 2015), p. 158.
19 Matlock quoted in Vermorel, *Sex Pistols*, p. 12.
20 Kent, 'The Life and Crimes of Two Simpleton Workin' Class Tossers', p. 26.
21 Vermorel, *Sex Pistols*, p. 176.
22 Ibid.
23 David Buckley, *Strange Fascination: David Bowie: The Definitive Story* (London, 2005), p. 165.
24 Ibid.
25 Ibid.
26 Kent, 'The Life and Crimes of Two Simpleton Workin' Class Tossers', p. 26.

27 Ibid.

28 Ibid.

29 On the cymbals story, see Glen Matlock, *I Was a Teenage Sex Pistol* (London, 2012), p. 46.

30 Ibid., p. 128.

31 Hynde, *Reckless*, p. 157.

32 This memorable description comes from Steven Van Zandt, 'Little Steven's Underground Garage', *Billboard* (11 November 2006), p. 16.

33 Recounted in Ben Edmonds, 'New York Dolls, Greatest Hits Volume 1', *Creem* (October 1973), reprinted in Robert Matheu and Brian J. Bowe, *Creem: America's Only Rock 'n' Roll Magazine* (New York, 2007), p. 99.

34 Ibid.

35 Bromberg, *The Wicked Ways of Malcolm McLaren* (New York, 1989), p. 59.

36 Vivienne Westwood and Ian Kelly, *Vivienne Westwood* (London, 2014), p. 158.

37 Antonia, *Too Much Too Soon*, p. 88.

38 Quoted ibid., p. 105.

39 Nick Kent, 'Welcome to the Faabulous Seventies', *New Musical Express* (25 August 1973), p. 36.

40 McLaren, quoted in McNeil and McCain, *Please Kill Me*, p. 157.

41 Nick Kent, 'Malcolm McLaren: Meet the Colonel Tom Parker of the Blank Generation', *New Musical Express* (27 November 1976), p. 26.

42 Quoted in Vermorel, *Sex Pistols*, p. 15.

43 Nick Kent, 'The Politics of Flash', *New Musical Express* (6 April 1974), p. 21.

44 McLaren, quoted ibid.

45 Ibid.

46 Price, quoted ibid., p. 39.

47 Ibid., p. 21.

48 Jon Savage, *England's Dreaming: Sex Pistols and Punk Rock* (London, 1991), p. 83.

49 Ibid.

50 McLaren quoted in Kent, 'The Politics of Flash', p. 21.

51 Nick Kent, *Apathy for the Devil: A 1970s Memoir* (London, 2010), p. 186.

52 Ibid.

53 Matlock, *I Was A Teenage Sex Pistol*, p. 44. In his autobiography, *Life*, Keith Richards recounts staying at the house during the recording of Wood's album, although he makes no mention of the enigmatic notes supposedly left by Steve Jones; *Life* (London, 2010), p. 366.

54 Matlock, *I Was a Teenage Sex Pistol*, p. 46.

55 McLaren, in an interview with Momus (3 August 2002), www.imomus.com, accessed 5 June 2015. One of McLaren's final projects was to be a film about

Led Zeppelin's notorious manager Peter Grant, which McLaren was set
to produce. Grant had enough knowledge about the old music business
gangsterism from his early days looking after Chuck Berry and Little
Richard, and had even cast himself as a gangster in Led Zeppelin's 1976
movie *The Song Remains the Same*. The two men worked on the project
for some time, with McLaren hiring the scriptwriter of the famous British
gangster film *The Long Good Friday* to work on the film. In the end Grant
pulled out of the project, fearing that McLaren was only interested in
portraying him as a gangster.

56 See Savage, *England's Dreaming*, pp. 84–5.
57 Kent, *Apathy for the Devil*, p. 246.
58 Ibid., p. 237.
59 Ibid., p. 186.

3 London and New York

 1 Harry Doherty, 'Robin Scott: Now Pop for Pure People', *Melody Maker*
    (5 May 1979), www.rocksbackpages.com, accessed 15 July 2015.
 2 On the origins of these T-shirts, see Paul Gorman, *The Look: Adventures in
    Pop and Rock Fashion* (London, 2001), pp. 121–3.
 3 Neil Spencer, 'Malcolm and Bernard: Rock 'n' Roll Scoundrels', *New Musical
    Express* (9 August 1980), p. 29.
 4 Don Letts, quoted in John Robb, *Punk Rock: An Oral History* (London, 2006),
    p. 101.
 5 Pat Gilbert, *Passion is a Fashion: The Real Story of The Clash* (London, 2009),
    p. 82.
 6 McLaren quoted in Spencer, 'Malcolm and Bernard: Rock 'n' Roll Scoundrels',
    p. 29.
 7 Jon Savage, *The England's Dreaming Tapes* (London, 2009), p. 83.
 8 Chrissie Hynde, *Reckless* (London, 2015), p. 157.
 9 See Clinton Heylin, *From the Velvets to the Voidoids: A Pre-punk History for a
    Post-punk World* (London, 1993), p. 84.
10 Nina Antonia, *Too Much Too Soon: The New York Dolls* (London, 2005), p. 160.
11 Ibid., p. 161.
12 Ibid., p. 163.
13 Quoted in Heylin, *From the Velvets to the Voidoids*, p. 88.
14 Richard Hell, *I Dreamed I Was a Very Clean Tramp: An Autobiography*
    (New York, 2013), p. 147.
15 Heylin, *From the Velvets to the Voidoids*, p. 89.
16 Hell, quoted in David Dalton, 'What Fresh Hell is This?', *Gadfly* (2002),

www.rocksbackpages.com, accessed 7 January 2016.

17 McLaren, in an interview with Momus (3 August 2002), www.imomus.com, accessed 5 June 2015.

18 Hell, *I Dreamed I Was a Very Clean Tramp*, p. 147.

19 Richard Hell's own words, ibid., p. 147.

20 Quoted in Momus, 'Interview with Malcolm McLaren', 2002.

21 Quoted in Heylin, *From the Velvets to the Voidoids*, pp. 117–18.

22 McLaren, quoted in Spencer, 'Malcolm and Bernard', p. 49.

23 Simon Napier-Bell, *Black Vinyl White Powder* (London, 2002), p. 197.

24 John Rockwell, 'Disbanding the Dolls Tells a Tale of One City', *New York Times* (25 April 1975), p. 28.

25 Quoted in Legs McNeil and Gillian McCain, *Please Kill Me: The Uncensored Oral History of Punk* (London, 1996), p. 235.

26 Antonia, *Too Much Too Soon*, pp. 176–7.

27 Some stories from those days were recounted when Steve Jones interviewed Malcolm McLaren on his Los Angeles radio show, 'Jonesy's Jukebox' (on Indie 103.1 FM), in 2005. The precise broadcast date is unknown. Audio of the show is available as 'Steve Jones interviews Malcom McLaren on Jonesy's Jukebox' (in three parts) at www.youtube.com, accessed 15 August 2015.

28 Antonia, *Too Much Too Soon*, p. 176.

29 See Viv Albertine, *Clothes, Clothes, Clothes. Music, Music, Music. Boys, Boys, Boys.* (London, 2014), p. 131.

30 Jon Savage, *England's Dreaming: Sex Pistols and Punk Rock* (London, 1991), p. 53.

31 Neil Spencer, 'Malcolm and Bernard', p. 29. On Laing's views, which were influenced by Reich and Marcuse (as discussed below), see Daniel Burston, *The Wing of Madness: The Life and Work of R. D. Laing* (Cambridge, MA, 1998), p. 100.

32 Paul Connerton, *How Societies Remember* (Cambridge, 1989), p. 13.

33 'Sex', profile in *Curious: The Sex Education Magazine for Men and Women* (1975), p. 14, available at www.worldsendshop.co.uk, accessed 10 January 2016.

34 Vivienne Westwood and Ian Kelly, *Vivienne Westwood* (London, 2014), p. 158.

35 The photo was taken by a film student, William English, in 1975, to form part of a portfolio he put together to apply to film school. It can be seen in Jane Mulvagh, *Vivienne Westwood: An Unfashionable Life*, revd edn (London, 2003), photo inserts after p. 178.

36 Albertine, *Clothes, Music, Boys*, p. 127.

37 Westwood and Kelly, *Vivienne Westwood*, pp. 185–6.

38 Hynde, *Reckless*, p. 155.

39 Ibid.

40 Midge Ure, *If I Was . . .: The Autobiography* (London, 2004), p. 29.

41 Fred and Judy Vermorel, *Sex Pistols: The Inside Story* (London, 1987), pp. 15–16.

42 Glen Matlock, *I Was a Teenage Sex Pistol* (London, 2012), pp. 80–81.

43 John Lydon, *Rotten: No Irish, No Blacks, No Dogs* (London, 1994), p. 74.

44 Temple quoted in David Fear, 'Julien Temple on "Lost" Pistols Film, Punk Docs and Joe Strummer's Socks', www.rollingstone.com, 30 July 2015.

45 Patrick McDonald, 'Interview: BADASSS Winner Julien Temple at 2015 Chicago CIMMfest', www.hollywoodchicago.com, 19 April 2015.

46 See Nick Kent, *Apathy for the Devil: A 1970s Memoir* (London, 2010), p. 247.

47 Albertine, *Clothes, Music, Boys*, p. 126.

48 Westwood quoted in Len Richmond, 'Buy Sexual', *Forum* (June 1976), p. 21.

49 David May, 'Sado Sex for the Seventies', *Gallery International*, I/4 (November 1975), p. 99.

50 Ibid., p. 61.

51 Richmond, 'Buy Sexual', p. 21.

52 Mulvagh, *Vivienne Westwood*, p. 79.

53 For an account of Reich's influence and the opposition it faced, see Sebastian Normandin, 'Wilhelm Reich: Vitalism and its Discontents', in *Vitalism and the Scientific Image in Post-Enlightenment Life Science, 1800–2010*, ed. S. Normandin and C. T. Wolfe (Dordrecht, 2013), pp. 179–204.

54 See Harvie Ferguson, *The Lure of Dreams: Sigmund Freud and the Construction of Modernity* (London and New York, 1996), pp. 206–14.

55 The quote is by Erik Davis, *TechGnosis: Myth, Magic and Mysticism in the Age of Information* (London, 1999), p. 67.

56 Charles M. Young, 'Rock is Sick and Living in London: A Report on the Sex Pistols', *Rolling Stone* (20 October 1977), p. 72.

57 Normandin, 'Wilhelm Reich', p. 198.

58 In relation to London in the 1970s, see Gordon Carr, *The Angry Brigade: A History of Britain's First Urban Guerrilla Group* (Oakland, CA, 2010), p. 37.

59 According to Ferguson, Reich's influence is revived in the 1950s and '60s via Herbert Marcuse (*Eros and Civilization*) – see *The Lure of Dreams*, pp. 206–7.

60 William S. Burroughs, 'My Experiences with Wilhelm Reich's Orgone Box', in *The Adding Machine: Selected Essays* (New York, 1986), pp. 164–6. Burroughs and a friend 'decided to make an orgone accumulator', which consisted of 'a plywood box big enough to put a chair inside, with a layer of cork and a galvanized steel lining. On the outside he draped half a dozen ratty old rabbit-fur coats, to beef up the orgone charge. The rabbit coats give the

box a surrealist look, very organic, like a fur-lined bathtub. I spent fifteen to twenty minutes a day in the box meditating, with the comfortable feeling that I was at least cutting down the odds of contracting cancer' (p. 166).

61 Raoul Vaneigem, *The Revolution of Everyday Life*, trans. Donald Nicholson-Smith (Oakland, CA, 2012), p. 78.

62 See Jim Martin, 'Orgone Addicts: Wilhelm Reich versus the Situationists', in *What is Situationism? A Reader*, ed. Stewart Home (Edinburgh, 1996), pp. 173–91.

63 Vaneigem, *The Revolution of Everyday Life*, p. 242.

64 Stephen A. Diamond, *Anger, Madness, and the Daimonic: The Psychological Genesis of Violence, Evil and Creativity* (Albany, NY, 1996), p. 146.

65 See Raymond Durgnat, *W.R.: Mysteries of the Organism* (London, 1999).

66 May, 'Sado Sex for the Seventies', pp. 63–4.

67 Arabella Melville and Colin Johnson, 'Who's Afraid of Whom?', *International Times*, LXXVI/4 (1976), p. 6.

68 Barry Miles, *London Calling: A Countercultural History of London since 1945* (ebook), n.p.

69 Richmond, 'Buy Sexual', p. 21.

70 Nik Cohn, *The Noise from the Streets: A Musical Journey in Nine Key Dates* (Harpenden, 2014), p. 14.

71 In the DVD extras of Sex Pistols, *There'll Always Be an England*, film, dir. Julien Temple (Freemantle Media, 2008).

72 Nick Kent, 'The Life and Crimes of Two Simpleton Workin' Class Tossers', *New Musical Express* (19 August 1978), p. 26.

73 Ibid.

74 Paul Du Noyer, *In The City: A Celebration of London Music* (London, 2010), p. 71.

75 See Antonia, *Too Much Too Soon*, p. 176.

76 Matlock, *I Was a Teenage Sex Pistol*, p. 84.

77 Ibid., p. 85.

78 Mike Dempsey, 'RDInsights: Ben Kelly', audio interview, Royal Society of Arts, www.thersa.org, 7 December 2015.

79 Aubrey Powell, *Classic Album Covers of the 1970s* (London, 2012), p. 188.

80 Ibid.

4 The Bizarro Cabaret Begins

1 Glen Matlock, *I Was a Teenage Sex Pistol* (London, 2012), p. 86.

2 Paul Cook, quoted in Fred and Judy Vermorel, *Sex Pistols: The Inside Story* (London, 1987), p. 17. Adam Ant remembers himself as more Roxy Music:

'fake leopard-skin jacket, black T-shirt, jeans rolled up, black lurex socks and crepes, which was basically a Roxy thing' – see Jon Savage, *The England's Dreaming Tapes* (London, 2009), p. 272.

3 John Robb, *Punk Rock: An Oral History* (London, 2006), p. 115.
4 Ibid., p. 119.
5 Quoted in Savage, *The England's Dreaming Tapes*, p. 158.
6 Adam Ant, ibid., p. 273.
7 A. A. Gill, *Pour Me: A Life* (London, 2015), p. 54.
8 Quoted in Savage, *The England's Dreaming Tapes*, p. 273.
9 Ibid., pp. 273–4.
10 John Lydon, *Anger is an Energy: My Life Uncensored* (London, 2014), p. 98.
11 Jonh Ingham, quoted in Savage, *The England's Dreaming Tapes*, p. 490.
12 Viv Albertine, *Clothes, Clothes, Clothes. Music, Music, Music. Boys, Boys, Boys.* (London, 2014), pp. 84–5.
13 Ibid., p. 84.
14 Ibid., p. 85.
15 Ibid., p. 86.
16 Jon Savage, *England's Dreaming: Sex Pistols and Punk Rock* (London, 1991), p. 145.
17 Bertie Marshall, *Berlin Bromley* (London, 2006), pp. 33–4.
18 See, for example, Caroline Coon, 'Parade of Punks', *Melody Maker* (2 October 1976), available at www.rocksbackpages.com, accessed September 2105.
19 Savage, *The England's Dreaming Tapes*, p. 322.
20 Pete Shelley, interview ibid., p. 539.
21 See Jarman's account in Savage, *The England's Dreaming Tapes*, pp. 661–3.
22 Nick Kent, 'Malcolm McLaren: Meet the Colonel Tom Parker of the Blank Generation', *New Musical Express* (27 November 1976), p. 26.
23 Jane Mulvagh, *Vivienne Westwood: An Unfashionable Life,* revd edn (London, 2003), p. 95.
24 Logan, quoted ibid.
25 Vivienne Westwood and Ian Kelly, *Vivienne Westwood* (London, 2014), pp. 188–9.
26 Kent, 'Malcolm McLaren', p. 26.
27 Steve Severin, in John Lydon, *Rotten: No Irish, No Blacks, No Dogs* (London, 1994), p. 177.
28 Neil Spencer, 'Don't Look Over Your Shoulder, but the Sex Pistols are Coming', *New Musical Express* (21 February 1976), p. 31.
29 Spencer discusses the audience taunts at the show in Savage, *The England's Dreaming Tapes*, pp. 463–5.

30 Quoted in Dave Thompson, *London's Burning: True Adventures in the Frontline of Punk, 1976–1977* (Chicago, IL, 2009), p. 145.
31 Vermorel, *Sex Pistols*, p. 19.
32 There's an account of McLaren and the early 1960s London R&B scene in Craig Bromberg, *The Wicked Ways of Malcolm McLaren* (London, 1989), p. 22.
33 Simon Wright, 'That's Me in the Picture', www.theguardian.com, 14 November 2014.
34 See Savage, *The England's Dreaming Tapes*, p. 349.
35 Billy Idol, *Dancing with Myself* (London, 2014), p. 50.
36 Savage, *England's Dreaming*, p. 155.
37 Chrissie Hynde, *Reckless* (London, 2015), p. 196. She discussed this show with Steve Jones on his radio show, 'Jonesy's Jukebox', 22 March 2006; a transcript is archived at www.cookandjones.co.uk.
38 Matlock, *I Was a Teenage Sex Pistol*, p. 136.
39 Hynde, *Reckless*, p. 196.
40 Ibid.
41 Matlock, *I Was a Teenage Sex Pistol*, p. 137.
42 Pat Gilbert, *Passion is a Fashion: The Real Story of the Clash* (London, 2009), pp. 59–60.
43 Savage, *The England's Dreaming Tapes*, p. 256.
44 Ibid.
45 Ibid.
46 Ibid.
47 In Caroline Coon, 'The Summer of Hate', *The Independent* (5 August 1995), www.independent.co.uk.
48 Savage, *The England's Dreaming Tapes*, p. 491.
49 Westwood and Kelly, *Vivienne Westwood*, p. 188.
50 See Jonh Ingham interview in Savage, *The England's Dreaming Tapes*, p. 492.
51 Gilbert, *Passion is a Fashion*, p. 75.
52 Hynde, *Reckless*, p. 196.
53 Jason Gross, 'Alternative TV: Mark Perry Interview', *Perfect Sound Forever* (February 2001), www.furious.com/perfect.
54 Aubrey Powell, *Classic Album Covers of the 1970s* (London, 2012), p. 188.
55 Savage, *The England's Dreaming Tapes*, p. 422.
56 Clinton Heylin, *Never Mind the Bollocks, Here's the Sex Pistols* (New York, 1998), p. 24.
57 Footage can be found on the Sex Pistols DVD *There'll Always Be an England*, film, dir. Julien Temple (Freemantle Media, 2008).
58 Idol, *Dancing with Myself*, p. 56.

59 Neil Spencer, 'Malcolm and Bernard: Rock 'n' Roll Scoundrels', *New Musical Express* (9 August 1980), p. 27.
60 See Bromberg, *The Wicked Ways of Malcolm McLaren*, p. 21.
61 Ibid., p. 89.
62 Nils Stevenson, in Savage, *The England's Dreaming Tapes*, pp. 401–2.
63 Charles Shaar Murray, 'Sex Pistols, Screen on the Green', *New Musical Express* (11 September 1976), p. 41.
64 Ibid.
65 Ibid.
66 Nik Cohn, *The Noise from the Streets: A Musical Journey in Nine Key Dates* (Harpenden, 2014), p. 14.
67 Hynde, *Reckless*, p. 150.
68 Clark quoted in Savage, *The England's Dreaming Tapes*, p. 641.
69 Chris Welch, 'Eddie and the Hot Rods: "Punk? We Just Do It"', *Melody Maker* (26 September 1976), available at www.rocksbackpages.com, accessed September 2015.
70 Vermorel, *Sex Pistols*, p. 24.
71 Brian Southall, *Sex Pistols: 90 Days at EMI* (London, 2007), p. 15.
72 'Fast Draw by EMI on Pistols', *Billboard* (6 November 1976), p. 62.
73 Southall, *Sex Pistols: 90 Days at EMI*, p. 31.
74 McLaren, in an interview with Momus (3 August 2002), www.imomus.com, accessed 5 June 2015.
75 Grundy quoted in Bromberg, *The Wicked Ways of Malcolm McLaren*, p. 115.
76 Ibid.
77 The best account, including an interview with Bill Grundy conducted many years later, is in Bromberg, *The Wicked Ways of Malcolm McLaren*, pp. 114–16.
78 In Vermorel, *Sex Pistols*, p. 30.

5 The New Elizabethans

1 Steve Turner, 'The Anarchic Rock of the Young and Doleful', *The Guardian* (3 December 1976), p. 13.
2 Mick Brown, 'UK Report: Sex Pistols and Beyond', *Rolling Stone* (27 January 1977), available at www.rocksbackpages.com, accessed 15 October 2015.
3 Pete Shelley, in Jon Savage, *The England's Dreaming Tapes* (London, 2009), p. 503.
4 Brown, 'UK Report: Sex Pistols and Beyond'.
5 Mick O'Shea, *The Anarchy Tour* (London, 2012), p. 8.
6 'Troilus and Cressida at the Roundhouse', *The Times* (20 January 1977), p. 13.

7 Phil McNeil, 'Spitting into the Eye of the Hurricane', *New Musical Express* (15 January 1977), p. 16.

8 Quoted in Pat Gilbert, *1977: The Bollocks Diaries*, book included with *Never Mind the Bollocks, Here's the Sex Pistols*, special 35th anniversary edition (Universal Music Group, 2012), p. 9.

9 Craig Bromberg, *The Wicked Ways of Malcolm McLaren* (New York, 1989), p. 119.

10 Tom Lambert, '"Punk Rock" Becomes Latest Outrage to British Public', *Los Angeles Times* (6 December 1976), p. B19.

11 Ibid.

12 KLM employee, quoted in Gilbert, *1977: The Bollocks Diaries*, p. 9.

13 Quoted in Robin Deneslow, 'Something Rotten', *The Guardian* (10 January 1977), p. 8.

14 Ibid.

15 There is a bootleg recording from the Paradiso, which is labelled/dated 5 January 1977, but the Pistols only played two shows at the Paradiso, on Thursday 6 January and Friday 7 January 1977. The bootleg that is in circulation comes from one of these shows.

16 The quotation is from Deneslow, 'Something Rotten', p. 8; but my account of the audience throwing beer and the band's response also draws on the reporting in McNeil, 'Spitting into the Eye of the Hurricane', pp. 17–18. Deneslow and McNeil attended the show together, and also interviewed McLaren together (as reported in the *NME* article).

17 Vivienne Westwood and Ian Kelly, *Vivienne Westwood* (London, 2014), p. 200.

18 Deneslow, 'Something Rotten', p. 8.

19 See Clinton Heylin, *Never Mind the Bollocks, Here's the Sex Pistols* (New York, 1998), p. 59.

20 These songs appear on the 35th anniversary deluxe box set of *Never Mind the Bollocks, Here's the Sex Pistols* (Universal Music, 2012). See the Discography for further details.

21 See the report on the Pistols' signing to A&M, 'Sex Pistols Sign for £150,000', *New Musical Express* (19 March 1977), reproduced in Gilbert, *1977: The Bollocks Diaries*, p. 18.

22 Fred and Judy Vermorel, *Sex Pistols: The Inside Story* (London, 1987), p. 56.

23 In Julien Temple, dir., *The Clash: New Year's Day '77* (BBC Four, 2015), *c.* 26 mins.

24 Temple, *The Clash*.

25 'Sex Pistols Sign for £150,000'.

26 Ibid.

27 *Sounds* (19 March 1977), p. 1.
28 Peter Hillmore, 'Guardian Diary: Pistol Packing', *The Guardian* (18 March 1977), p. 13.
29 There is footage of McLaren meeting the press, as described here, in Julien Temple, dir., *The Filth and the Fury* (Film Four, 2000), beginning at 54:40 mins.
30 Vermorel, *Sex Pistols*, p. 160.
31 Barry Cain, *'77 Sulphate Strip: An Eyewitness Account of the Year that Changed Everything* (London, 2007), p. 57.
32 Caroline Coon, Virgin Records press release; reproduced in Gilbert, *1977: The Bollocks Diaries*, p. 33.
33 Robert Addison, 'Johnny's Top of the Pops with Me Says Mrs Rotten', *Islington Gazette* (27 May 1977); original clipping reproduced in Gilbert, *1977: The Bollocks Diaries*, p. 35.
34 'Pistols Sign Two Deals', *The Guardian* (18 May 1977), p. 2.
35 'Pistols' 45 Hits Target Despite Bans', *Billboard* (25 June 1977), p. 65.
36 Ibid.
37 Phil McNeill, 'Pistols, Thunders Jubilee Elbow', *New Musical Express* (9 July 1977), p. 3.
38 Philip Jordan, 'The Darker Side of the Great Jubilee Jamboree', *The Guardian* (31 May 1977), p. 2.
39 Martin Wainwright, 'Tower Blocks Rise to Jubilee', *The Guardian* (23 May 1977), p. 4.
40 Dominic Sandbrook, *State of Emergency: The Way We Were: Britain, 1970–1974* (London, 2010), p. 188.
41 Wainwright, 'Tower Blocks Rise to Jubilee', p. 4.
42 Martin Wainwright, 'Jubilee Strips from the Girlie Mags', *The Guardian* (3 June 1977), p. 4.
43 Peter Chippindale, 'Anti-Jubilee Brigade on the March', *The Guardian* (2 June 1977), p. 2.
44 'Holiday Guide to Jubilee Celebrations', *The Observer* (5 June 1977), p. 4.
45 Michael Palin, *The Python Years, 1969–1979: Volume One* (London, 2007), p. 443.
46 'Holiday Guide to Jubilee Celebrations', p. 4.
47 Stanley Reynolds, 'Three Bloody Sundays in a Row!', *The Guardian* (11 June 1977), p. 10.
48 McLaren quoted in Michael Watts, 'The Rise and Fall of Malcolm McLaren, Part Two: The Four Horsemen of the Apocalypse go Riding', *Melody Maker* (23 June 1979), p. 40.
49 'Pistols Sign Two Deals', p. 2.
50 Tony Benn, *The Benn Diaries, 1940–90* (London, 2013), p. 396.

51 Tony Benn, *Conflicts of Interest: Diaries, 1977–80* (London, 1990), p. 160.

52 Accounts of the fight are given in Jah Wobble's interview, in Savage, *The England's Dreaming Tapes*, p. 313; and Sophie Richmond's diary, in Vermorel, *Sex Pistols*, pp. 79–80.

53 See Jordan's account in Savage, *The England's Dreaming Tapes*, p. 50.

54 'Attacks on Punk Rock Group outside Public House', *The Times* (22 June 1977), p. 13.

55 As recounted by Viv Albertine, *Clothes, Clothes, Clothes. Music, Music, Music. Boys, Boys, Boys.* (London, 2014), p. 126.

56 'Rock Star to Rescue', *The Guardian* (8 July 1977), p. 5.

57 Michael Macilwee, *The Teddy Boy Wars: The Youth Cult that Shocked Britain* (Preston, 2015), pp. 308–9.

58 'Punish the Punks', *Sunday Mirror* (12 June 1977); 'Punk Rock Jubilee Shocker', *Sunday Mirror* (12 June 1977), p. 1.

59 Watts, 'The Rise and Fall of Malcolm McLaren, Part 2', p. 41.

60 See Heylin, *Never Mind the Bollocks, Here's the Sex Pistols*, pp. 81–2. Thomas was working on the Wings album *London Town*, which was released in early 1978.

61 Thomas quoted in Heylin, *Never Mind the Bollocks, Here's the Sex Pistols*, pp. 81–2.

62 'Diary', *The Times* (23 June 1977), p. 16.

63 'This Definitely Ain't the Summer of Love', *New Musical Express* (9 July 1977), p. 1.

64 Brooke-Partridge quoted in 'Move Over Sid Vicious: GLC Tory Jumps on "Good Kickin'" Bandwagon', *New Musical Express* (9 July 1977), p. 10.

65 See Vermorel, *Sex Pistols*, p. 90.

66 The quotation is from Michael Musto, 'Moving Images: Russ Meyer', *Spin*, IV/10 (January 1989), p. 56.

67 For a summary, see Gary Mulholland, *Popcorn: Fifty Years of Rock 'n' Roll Movies* (London, 2010), pp. 94–7.

68 David K. Frasier, *Russ Meyer: The Life and Films* (Jefferson, NC, 1990), p. 133.

69 Musto, 'Moving Images: Russ Meyer', p. 56.

70 Quoted in Roger Ebert, 'McLaren & Meyer & Rotten & Vicious & Me', www.rogerebert.com, 11 April 2010.

71 Interview with Russ Meyer, in John Waters, *Shock Value: A Tasteful Book about Bad Taste* (New York, 2005 [1981]), p. 121.

72 See Steve Turner, 'The Anarchic Rock of the Young and Doleful', *The Guardian* (3 December 1976), p. 13.

73 Bromberg, *The Wicked Ways of Malcolm McLaren*, p. 146.

74 Charles M. Young, 'Rock is Sick and Living in London: A Report on the Sex Pistols', *Rolling Stone*, 250 (20 October 1977), p. 73.

75 McLaren quoted in Richard Cromelin, 'Sex Pistols Trigger Punk Rock Invasion', *Los Angeles Times* (31 July 1977), p. O84.
76 Ebert, 'McLaren and Meyer and Rotten and Vicious and Me'.
77 See Young, 'Rock is Sick and Living in London', p. 75.
78 See Bromberg, *The Wicked Ways of Malcolm McLaren*, pp. 142–5.
79 Quoted in Mark Spitz and Brendan Mullen, *We Got the Neutron Bomb: The Untold Story of L.A. Punk* (New York, 2001), p. 153.
80 Bromberg, *The Wicked Ways of Malcolm McLaren*, p. 149.
81 Ibid.
82 Ebert, 'McLaren and Meyer and Rotten and Vicious and Me'.
83 Roger Ebert, *Life Itself: A Memoir* (New York, 2011), p. 212.
84 John May, 'The Stalls Are Alive with the Sound of Chaos' (interview with Julien Temple), *New Musical Express* (27 October 1979), p. 39.
85 Michael Watts, 'The Rise and Fall of Malcolm McLaren, Part One: Tin Pan Alley Meets an Idea whose Time has Come', *Melody Maker* (16 June 1979), p. 36.
86 Ebert, 'McLaren and Meyer and Rotten and Vicious and Me'.
87 Carmine Sarracino and Kevin M. Scott, *The Porning of America: The Rise of Porn Culture, What It Means, and Where We Go from Here* (Boston, MA, 2008), p. 84.
88 Ebert, *Life Itself*, p. 213.
89 Ibid.
90 Ebert, 'McLaren and Meyer and Rotten and Vicious and Me'.
91 Watts, 'The Rise And Fall of Malcolm McLaren, Part One', p. 37.
92 McLaren's recollection, in *The Incredibly Strange Film Show: Russ Meyer*, television broadcast, Channel 4 (9 September 1988).
93 Russ Meyer in Waters, *Shock Value*, p. 200.
94 Vermorel, *Sex Pistols*, p. 101.
95 Jon Savage, *England's Dreaming: Sex Pistols and Punk Rock* (London, 1991), p. 389.
96 Quoted in Young, 'Rock is Sick and Living in London', pp. 73–4.
97 Ibid.
98 Bromberg, *The Wicked Ways of Malcolm McLaren*, p. 154.
99 Ebert, *Life Itself*, p. 214.
100 Ebert, 'McLaren and Meyer and Rotten and Vicious and Me'.
101 Bromberg, *The Wicked Ways of Malcolm McLaren*, p. 154.
102 Quoted in May, 'The Stalls are Alive with the Sound of Chaos', p. 39.
103 The quotation is from Julien Temple in May, 'The Stalls are Alive with the Sound of Chaos', p. 39; see also the account of the change of directors in Savage, *England's Dreaming*, pp. 425–46.

104   Savage, *England's Dreaming*, p. 388.
105   Al Clark, in Savage, *The England's Dreaming Tapes*, p. 646.

6 Bollocks

1   Chris Thomas, in *Classic Albums: Never Mind the Bollocks, Here's the Sex Pistols*, dir. Matthew Longfellow, DVD (Eagle Rock Entertainment, 2002).
2   In Jon Savage, *England's Dreaming: Sex Pistols and Punk Rock* (London, 1991), p. 381.
3   Robin Denselow, 'Punk Up', *The Guardian* (12 July 1977), p. 10.
4   Richard Cromelin, 'Rock 'n' Roll's Generation Gap', *Los Angeles Times* (27 August 1977), p. B11.
5   Thomas quoted in Clinton Heylin, *Never Mind the Bollocks, Here's the Sex Pistols* (New York, 1998), pp. 74–5.
6   Jonh Ingham, 'The (?) Rock Special #5: Other Bands', *Sounds* (9 October 1976), available at www.rocksbackpages.com, accessed 26 September 2015.
7   This event is recounted from two sources: Warren Zanes, *Revolutions in Sound: Warner Bros. Records: The First Fifty Years* (San Francisco, CA, 2009), p. 133; and 'Stay Tuned by Stan Cornyn: Warners Courts the Sex Pistols', www.rhino.com, 21 May 2013.
8   Zanes, *Revolutions in Sound*, p. 133.
9   Ibid.
10 This recording is used in Julien Temple's film *The Great Rock 'n' Roll Swindle* over Derek Jarman's footage from the Pistols' Valentine's Day 1976 performance at Andrew Logan's party (discussed in Chapter Four).
11 Quoted in Zanes, *Revolutions in Sound*, p. 133.
12 Quoted in Young, 'Rock is Sick and Living in London: A Report on the Sex Pistols', *Rolling Stone* (20 October 1977), p. 73.
13 Ostin, in Zanes, *Revolutions in Sound*, p. 133.
14 Young, 'Rock is Sick and Living in London', p. 75.
15 Steve Jones's description of the sound, in Nick Kent, 'The Life and Crimes of Two Simpleton Workin' Class Tossers', *New Musical Express* (19 August 1978), p. 28.
16   In Kent, 'The Life and Crimes of Two Simpleton Workin' Class Tossers', p. 28.
17 James Wolcott, 'Kiss Me, You Fool: Sex Pistols '77', *Village Voice* (21 November 1977), p. 53.
18 Terri Anderson, 'Virgin Deaf to Pleas to Alter Pistols Album', *Billboard* (5 November 1977), p. 88.
19 Aubrey Powell, *Classic Album Covers of the 1970s* (London, 2012), pp. 188–9.

20 Dick Hebdige, *Subculture: The Meaning of Style* (London and New York, 1979), p. 112.

21 Richard Evans, 'Foreword', in Powell, *Classic Album Covers of the 1970s*, p. 9.

22 Craig Bromberg, *The Wicked Ways of Malcolm McLaren* (New York, 1989), p. 159.

23 'GRRC Advises Shops on Sex Pistols Album', *Music Week* (19 November 1977), p. 4.

24 'Shop Man Cleared on Pistols Charge', *The Guardian* (25 November 1977), p. 1.

25 Ibid.; 'Record Sleeve of Punk Rock Album Ruled Not Indecent', *The Times* (25 November 1977), p. 2.

26 McLaren, in *Classic Albums: Never Mind the Bollocks*, DVD.

27 Kickboy, 'Never Mind the Bollocks, Here's the Sex Pistols', *Slash*, I/6 (December 1977), p. 25.

28 Jon Savage, *England's Dreaming*, p. 444.

29 Robert Christgau, 'Sex Pistols Winn Dixie', *Village Voice* (16 January 1978), p. 77; Mark Binelli, 'The Sex Pistols in Enemy Territory: Their Southern Tour of '78', in *The Oxford American Book of Great Music Writing*, ed. Marc Smirnoff (Oxford, MS, 1998), p. 253.

30 Binelli, 'The Sex Pistols in Enemy Territory', p. 253.

31 Lech Kowalski's film *D.O.A.: A Rite of Passage* (1980) includes footage of the Pistols alongside other American punk bands; Christgau, 'Sex Pistols Winn Dixie', p. 77.

32 Binelli, 'The Sex Pistols in Enemy Territory', p. 254.

33 Monk and Guterman, *12 Days on the Road: The Sex Pistols and America* (New York, 1990), p. 80.

34 Ibid., p. 109.

35 Ibid., p. 102.

36 Jim Dickinson, quoted in Binelli, 'The Sex Pistols in Enemy Territory', pp. 254–5.

37 Kickboy, 'A Cheap Holiday in Other People's Misery', *Slash*, I/8 (February 1978), p. 18.

38 John Lydon, *Rotten: No Irish, No Blacks, No Dogs* (London, 1994), p. 247.

39 Bob Gruen, quoted ibid., p. 249.

40 Bill Graham and Robert Greenfield, *Bill Graham Presents: My Life Inside Rock and Out* (New York, 2004), p. 419.

41 In Monk and Guterman, *12 Days on the Road*, p. 215.

42 Richard Meltzer, 'Vinyl Reckoning', in *A Whore Just Like the Rest: The Music Writings of Richard Meltzer* (New York, 2000), p. 561.

43 The recollection of Meltzer's tirade comes from, in order: Monk and Guterman, *12 Days on the Road*, p. 219; Jonh Ingham, 'Sex Pistols:

This Could Be the Last Time', *Sounds* (28 January 1978), available at
www.rocksbackpages.com, accessed 3 January 2016; Art Fein, 'Another
Fein Mess: AF Stone's Monthly, May 2007', www.sofein.com, May 2007.

44 Meltzer, 'Vinyl Reckoning', p. 561.

45 Steven Rubio, 'Oh Bondage, Up Yours! Thoughts on the Rhino Punk
Anthology *DiY*', in *Bad Subjects: Political Education for Everyday Life*
(New York, 1998), pp. 183–6.

46 In Monk and Guterman, *12 Days on the Road*, p. 219.

47 Graham and Greenfield, *Bill Graham Presents*, p. 421.

48 Paul Cook, in Lydon, *Rotten*, p. 252.

49 Quoted in Nicholas de Jongh, 'Rotten Day for Punks', *The Guardian*
(20 January 1978), p. 20.

Afterword: Fables of the Sex Pistols

1 In John Ogden, 'The Rotten Treatment', *Express and Star* (22 December 1977),
p. 1.

2 Julien Temple, dir., *Punk Can Take It* (Boyd's Co./GTO/Kendon Films Ltd,
1979), 12:30–13:01 mins.

3 Quoted in John May, 'The Hills are Alive with the Sound of Chaos',
New Musical Express (27 October 1979), p. 40.

4 In Julien Temple, dir., *The Great Rock 'n' Roll Swindle* (Boyd's Co./Kendon
Films Ltd/Matrixbest/Virgin Films, 1979), 01:04–01:26 mins.

5 'Malcolm McLaren', *The South Bank Show*, episode 179 (London Weekend
Television, broadcast 2 December 1984).

6 Jim Sullivan, 'Malcolm McLaren's New Wave', *Boston Globe* (20 February
1985), available at www.rocksbackpages.com, accessed 2 July 2015.

7 Malcolm McLaren, 'Antihero', *Spin,* IV/9 (December 1988), p. 80.

8 'US Premiere: Malcolm McLaren: Paris, Capital of the XXIst Century',
www.swissinstitute.net, accessed 27 July 2016.

9 Nick Kent, 'The Life and Crimes of Two Simpleton Workin' Class Tossers',
New Musical Express (19 August 1978), p. 26.

Select Bibliography

Albertine, Viv, *Clothes, Clothes, Clothes. Music, Music, Music. Boys, Boys, Boys.* (London, 2014)

Antonia, Nina, *Too Much Too Soon: The New York Dolls* (London, 2005)

Binelli, Mark, 'The Sex Pistols in Enemy Territory: Their Southern Tour of '78', in *The Oxford American Book of Great Music Writing*, ed. Marc Smirnoff (Oxford, 1998), pp. 251–6

Bromberg, Craig, *The Wicked Ways of Malcolm McLaren* (New York, 1989)

Cain, Barry, *77 Sulphate Strip: An Eyewitness Account of the Year that Changed Everything* (London, 2007)

Gilbert, Pat, *Passion is a Fashion: The Real Story of the Clash* (London, 2009)

Gorman, Paul, *The Look: Adventures in Pop and Rock Fashion* (London, 2001)

Hell, Richard, *I Dreamed I Was a Very Clean Tramp: An Autobiography* (New York, 2013)

Heylin, Clinton, *From the Velvets to the Voidoids: A Pre-Punk History for a Post-Punk Age* (London, 1993)

——, *Never Mind the Bollocks: Here's the Sex Pistols* (New York, 1998)

Hopkins, Jerry, 'Beatle Loathers Return: Britain's Teddy Boys', *Rolling Stone*, 103 (2 March 1972), pp. 1, 14–16

Hynde, Chrissie, *Reckless: My Life as a Pretender* (London, 2015)

Idol, Billy, *Dancing with Myself* (London, 2014)

Kent, Nick, 'The Politics of Flash', *New Musical Express* (6 April 1974), pp. 20–21, 39

——, 'The Life and Crimes of Two Simpleton Workin' Class Tossers', *New Musical Express* (19 August 1978), pp. 25–8

——, *Apathy for the Devil: A 1970s Memoir* (London, 2010)

Kugelberg, Johan, and Jon Savage, eds, *Punk: An Aesthetic* (New York, 2012)

Lydon, John, *No Irish, No Blacks, No Dogs: The Authorized Autobiography of Johnny Rotten of the Sex Pistols* (London, 1994)

——, *Anger is An Energy: My Life Uncensored* (London, 2014)

McLaren, Malcolm, 'Antihero', *Spin*, IV/9 (December 1988), pp. 79–80

McNeil, Legs, and Gillian McCain, *Please Kill Me: The Uncensored Oral History of Punk* (London, 1996)

Matlock, Glen, *I was a Teenage Sex Pistol* (London, 2012)

May, John, 'The Stalls Are Alive with the Sound of Chaos' [Interview with Julien Temple], *New Musical Express* (27 October 1979), pp. 38–40

Melly, George, *Revolt into Style: The Pop Arts* (London, 2008)

Monk, Noel E., and Jimmy Guterman, *12 Days on the Road: The Sex Pistols and America* (New York, 1990)

Mulvagh, Jane, *Vivienne Westwood: An Unfashionable Life* (London, 2003)

Rambali, Paul, 'How the West Was Won: An Epic Trek across the Myth of Malcolm McLaren', *The Face*, 38 (June 1983), pp. 40–46

Robb, John, *Punk Rock: An Oral History* (London, 2006)

Savage, Jon, *England's Dreaming: Sex Pistols and Punk Rock* (London, 1991)

——, *The England's Dreaming Tapes* (London, 2009)

Spencer, Neil, 'Malcolm and Bernard: Rock 'n' roll Scoundrels', *New Musical Express* (9 August 1980), pp. 25–9

Southall, Brian, *The Sex Pistols: 90 Days at EMI* (London, 2007)

Taylor, Paul, *Impresario: Malcolm McLaren and the British New Wave*, exh. cat., New Museum of Contemporary Art, New York (New York and Cambridge, MA, 1988)

Thompson, Dave, *London's Burning: True Adventures on the Front Lines of Punk, 1976–1977* (Chicago, IL, 2009)

Vermorel, Fred, and Judy Vermorel, *Sex Pistols: The Inside Story* (London, 1987)

——, *Fashion and Perversity: A Life of Vivienne Westwood and the Sixties Laid Bare* (London, 1996)

Walsh, Gavin, *God Save the Sex Pistols: A Collector's Guide to the Priests of Punk* (London, 2003)

Watts, Michael, 'The Rise and Fall of Malcolm McLaren Part One: Tin Pan Alley Meets an Idea Whose Time has Come', *Melody Maker* (16 June 1979), pp. 35–40, 50–51

——, 'The Rise and Fall of Malcolm McLaren Part Two: The Four Horsemen of the Apocalypse Go Riding', *Melody Maker* (23 June 1979), pp. 39–42, 44, 67

——, 'The Rise and Fall of Malcolm McLaren Part Three: Last Tango in Paris – Je ne regrette rien', *Melody Maker* (30 June 1979), pp. 35–9, 50

Westwood, Vivienne, and Ian Kelly, *Vivienne Westwood* (London, 2014)

Young, Charles M., 'Rock is Sick and Living in London: A Report on the Sex Pistols', *Rolling Stone*, 250 (20 October 1977), pp. 68–75

Discography

The material detailed in this discography relates only to the period covered in this book, and includes recordings by the Sex Pistols and others. While the Sex Pistols released only one official album and four singles before John Lydon's departure in January 1978, there is now a great deal of material available from many recording sessions that offers an insight into the development of the Pistols as a musical entity during 1976 and 1977. These recordings are available on numerous official album releases, including compilations and box sets that also contain outtakes and alternative versions of many songs. The album releases are indicated by uppercase letters in the discography and the list of sessions that follows. Note: the apparent discrepancies in some of the song titles listed here reflect the session and label listing of songs.

Sex Pistols albums

A *Never Mind the Bollocks, Here's the Sex Pistols*
(Virgin Records, UK/Warner Bros., US, October 1977)

B *The Great Rock'n'Roll Swindle*
(Virgin Records, UK/Warner Bros., US, February 1979)

C *Flogging a Dead Horse*
(Virgin Records, UK/Warner Bros., US, February 1980)

D *Kiss This* [2-CD limited edition]
(Virgin Records, UK, 1992)

E *Jubilee*
(Virgin Records, UK, 2002)

F *Sex Pistols* [3-CD box set]
(Virgin Records, UK, 2002)

G *Spunk*
(Sanctuary Records, UK, 2006; originally released as a bootleg, October 1977)

H *Never Mind the Bollocks, Here's the Sex Pistols* [super deluxe box set, 3-CD + 1 DVD] (Universal Music Group, 2012)

Other albums

New York Dolls, New York Dolls (Mercury Records, 1973)
SEX: Too Fast to Live, Too Young to Die (Only Lovers Left Alive, 2003)
A compilation of 45s from the jukebox at 430 King's Road, compiled by Marco Pirroni. The track listing is:

'Psychotic Reaction', Count Five (1966)
'Through My Eyes', The Creation (1967)
'Ain't Got No Home', Clarence 'Frogman' Henry (1956)
'Shake Some Action', Flamin' Groovies (1976)
'You're Gonna Miss Me', The Spades (1965)
'Liar Liar', The Castaways (1965)
'In the Nighttime', The Strangeloves (1965)
'Brand New Cadillac', Vince Taylor (1959)
'You Better Move On', Arthur Alexander (1961)
'Eighteen', Alice Cooper (1970)
'Night of the Vampire', The Moontrekkers (1961)
'Monster in Black Tights', Screaming Lord Sutch and the Savages (1963)
'I Can't Control Myself', The Troggs (1966)
'I Put a Spell on You', Screamin' Jay Hawkins (1956)
'Have Love Will Travel', The Sonics (1965)
'Joue Pas le Rock'n'Roll Pour Moi', Johnny Hallyday (1976)
'The Pill', Loretta Lynn (1975)
'We Sell Soul', The Spades (1965)
'Valerie', Jackie and the Starlites (1960)
'Roadrunner', The Modern Lovers (1972)

Chronology of Sex Pistols recordings on official releases

3 April 1976
Live at the Nashville Rooms, London: John Lydon (vocals), Steve Jones (guitar), Glen Matlock (bass), Paul Cook (drums)

'Understanding' (F)

15 May 1976
Chris Spedding sessions, Majestic Studios, London: John Lydon (vocals), Steve Jones (guitar), Glen Matlock (bass), Paul Cook (drums)

'Problems' (F)
'No Feelings' (F)
'Pretty Vacant' (F)

29 June 1976
Live at the 100 Club, London: John Lydon (vocals), Steve Jones (guitar), Glen Matlock (bass), Paul Cook (drums)

'Flowers of Romance' (F)

July 1976
Dave Goodman sessions, Denmark Street and Riverside Studios, London: John Lydon (vocals), Steve Jones (guitar), Glen Matlock (bass), Paul Cook (drums)

'Pretty Vacant' (F, G)
'Seventeen' (F, G)
'Satellite' (F, G)
'No Feeling' (27 July) (F, G, H)
'I Wanna Be Me' (B, C, D, F, G)
'Submission' (F, G)
'Anarchy in the UK' (F, G)

14 August 1976
Live at Barbarella's, Birmingham: John Lydon (vocals), Steve Jones (guitar), Glen Matlock (bass), Paul Cook (drums)

'Flowers of Romance' (F)

29 August 1976
Live at the Screen on the Green, London: John Lydon (vocals), Steve Jones (guitar), Glen Matlock (bass), Paul Cook (drums)

'Anarchy in the UK' (F)
'I Wanna Be Me' (F)
'Seventeen' (F)
'New York' (F)
'(Don't Give Me) No Lip' (F)
'(I'm Not Your) Stepping Stone' (F)
'Satellite' (F)
'Submission' (F)
'Liar' (F)
'No Feelings' (F)
'Substitute' (F)
'Pretty Vacant' (F)
'Problems' (F)
'Did You No Wrong' (F)
'No Fun' (F)

October 1976
Dave Goodman sessions, Lansdowne Road and Wessex Studios, London: John Lydon (vocals), Steve Jones (guitar), Glen Matlock (bass), Paul Cook (drums)

'Anarchy in the UK' (F)
'Substitute' (B, F)
'(Don't Give Me) No Lip' aka 'Don't Give Me No Lip, Child' (B, D, F)
'(I'm Not Your) Stepping Stone' (B, C, D, E, F)
'Johnny B. Goode' (B, F)
'Road Runner' (B, F)
'Watcha Gonna Do About It?' (B, F)
'No Fun' (16 October) (B, F)
'No Fun' [edited] (16 October) (D, F, H)
'Through My Eyes' (F)

Chris Thomas session, Wessex Studios, London: John Lydon (vocals), Steve Jones (guitar), Glen Matlock (bass), Paul Cook (drums)

'Anarchy in the UK' (A, C, D, E, F, H)
'Anarchy in the UK' [rejected version] (B, F)

December 1976
Mike Thorne session, EMI Studio, Manchester Square, London: John Lydon (vocals), Steve Jones (guitar), Glen Matlock (bass), Paul Cook (drums)

'No Feelings' (F)
'No Future' (F)
'Liar' (F)
'Problems' (F)

17–20 January 1977
Dave Goodman sessions, Gooseberry Studios and Eden Studio, London: John Lydon (vocals), Steve Jones (guitar), Glen Matlock (bass), Paul Cook (drums)

'No Future' [demo version of 'God Save the Queen'] (F, G, H)
'Problems' (G, H)
'Pretty Vacant' (G, H)
'Liar' (G, H)
'Unlimited Edition' [Demo Version of 'EMI'] (G, H)
'New York' (G, F, H)

February 1977–September 1977
Chris Thomas/Bill Price sessions, Wessex Studios, London: John Lydon (vocals), Steve Jones (guitar and bass), Paul Cook (drums), Sid Vicious (bass, 'Belsen Was a Gas')

'Did You No Wrong' [alternate vocal] (3 March) (H)
'God Save the Queen' (10 March) (A, C, D, E, F, H)
'Pretty Vacant' (3 March) (A, C, D, F, H)
'Did You No Wrong' (10 March) (C, D, F, H)
'No Feelings' (21 April) (A, D, F, H)
'Liar' (21 April) (A, D, F, H)
'Problems' (21 April) (A, D, F, H)
'Seventeen' (21 April) (A, D, F, H)
'Seventeen' [alternate vocal] (21 April) (H)

'Holidays in the Sun' [rough mix] (11 June) (H)
'Submission' (22 April) (A, D, F, H)
'Submission' [rough mix] (22 April) (H)
'New York' (22 April) (A, D, F, H)
'EMI' aka 'EMI (Unlimited Edition)' (22 April) (A, C, D, E, F, H)
'EMI' [rough mix] (22 April) (H)
'Satellite' (22 April) (D, F, H)
'Satellite' [rough mix] (22 April) (H)
'Seventeen' [rough mix] (16 May) (H)
'Holidays in the Sun' (11 June) (A, C, D, E, F, H)
'Holidays in the Sun' [alternative mix] (11 June) (H)
'Body' [demo version of 'Bodies'] (11 June) (H)
'Bodies' (18 June) (A, D, F, H)
'Submission' [alternative mix] (12 August) (H)
'Belsen Was a Gas' [demo version] (20 September) (H)

May–August 1977
Undated outtakes

'Satellite' (F)
'EMI' (F)
'Seventeen' (F)
'No Feelings' (F)
'Submission (Version #1)' (F)

21 July 1977
Live at Studentersamfundet, Trondheim, Norway: John Lydon (vocals), Steve Jones (guitar), Sid Vicious (bass), Paul Cook (drums)

'Anarchy in the UK' (D, H)
'I Wanna Be Me' (D, H)
'Seventeen' (D, H)
'New York' (D, H)
'EMI' (D, H)
'No Fun' (D, H)
'No Feelings' (D, H)
'Problems' (D, H)
'God Save the Queen' (D, H)

Discography

10 January 1978
Live at the Longhorn Ballroom, Dallas, Texas: John Lydon (vocals), Steve Jones (guitar), Sid Vicious (bass), Paul Cook (drums)

'Belsen Was a Gas' (F)

Filmography

Jubilee (dir. Derek Jarman, 1977)
Punk in London (dir. Wolfgang Büld, 1977)
The Punk Rock Movie (dir. Don Letts, 1978)
D.O.A.: A Rite of Passage (dir. Lech Kowalski, 1980)
The Great Rock 'n' Roll Swindle (dir. Julien Temple, 1980)
Punk and the Pistols (BBC Arena/dir. Paul Tickell, 1992)
The Filth and the Fury: A Sex Pistols Film (dir. Julien Temple, 2000)
London: The Modern Babylon (dir. Julien Temple, 2012)
Never Mind the Baubles: Xmas '77 with the Sex Pistols (dir. Julien Temple, 2013)
Punk '76 (dir. Alyson Byron and Mark Sloper, 2013)
The Clash: New Year's Day '77 (dir. Julien Temple, 2014)

Acknowledgements

I would like to acknowledge the help of Young Kim, who, on behalf of the McLaren Estate, was generous with her time in answering my queries and who also kindly allowed me to reproduce a number of documents created by Malcolm McLaren. I am also grateful to the Estate for the permission to use the photograph of Malcolm Edwards (as he then was) at Croydon Art College in 1968 that appears in Chapter One.

Photo Acknowledgements

The author and the publishers wish to express their thanks to the below sources of illustrative material and/or permission to reproduce it.

Alamy: pp. 6 (Pictorial Press Ltd), 38, 161 (Trinity Mirror/Mirrorpix), 140 (United Archives GmbH); photo Collection Anefo (National Archives, Holland): p. 156 (Suyk Koen); Author's Collection: p. 78; The Financial Times Ltd/Charles Bibby © all rights reserved: pp. 104, 105; Getty Images: pp. 45 (P. Felix), 53 (Steve Wood), 127 (Ian Dickson), 130 (Erica Echenberg/Referns), 147 (GAB Archive/Redferns), 206 (Brian Cooke/Redferns), 218 (George Rose); © Bob Gruen: p. 215; used with permission of the McLaren Estate: pp. 57, 67, 75; Museum of London: p. 30 (Henry Grant); REX Shutterstock: pp. 62 (Sheila Rock), 88, 90, 113, 122, 125, 139, 149 (Ray Stevenson), 141 (Ian Dickson), 220 (Mike Hollist/Daily Mail); Rijksdienst voor het Cultureel Erfgoed/Cultural Heritage Agency of the Netherlands: p. 154.

Index